DANGEROUS BEAUTY

 This Large Print Book carries the
Seal of Approval of N.A.V.H.

DANGEROUS BEAUTY

Life and Death in Africa:
True Stories from a Safari Guide

Mark C. Ross

Thorndike Press • Waterville, Maine

Published in 2001 by arrangement with
Hyperion, an imprint of Buena Vista Books, Inc.

Thorndike Press Large Print Adventure Series.

The tree indicium is a trademark of Thorndike Press.

The text of this Large Print edition is unabridged.
Other aspects of the book may vary from the original edition.

Set in 16 pt. Plantin by Minnie B. Raven.

Printed in the United States on permanent paper.

Library of Congress Cataloging-in-Publication Data

Ross, Mark C.
    Dangerous beauty : life and death in Africa : true stories
from a safari guide / Mark C. Ross.
      p. cm.
    ISBN 0-7862-3764-3 (lg. print : hc : alk. paper)
    1. Wildlife watching — Africa, Eastern.   2. Safaris —
Africa, Eastern.   3. Ross, Mark C.   4. Tourists — Crimes
against — Uganda — Bwindi Impenetrable National Park.
I. Title.
QL337.E25 R67 2001b
  599′.09676—dc21   2001056311

*For Judy and Mike Rainy,
who gave me the keys to
both their car and a continent.
They stand their watch well.*

*And for Susan and Rob,
whose embracing love is
far from forgotten.*

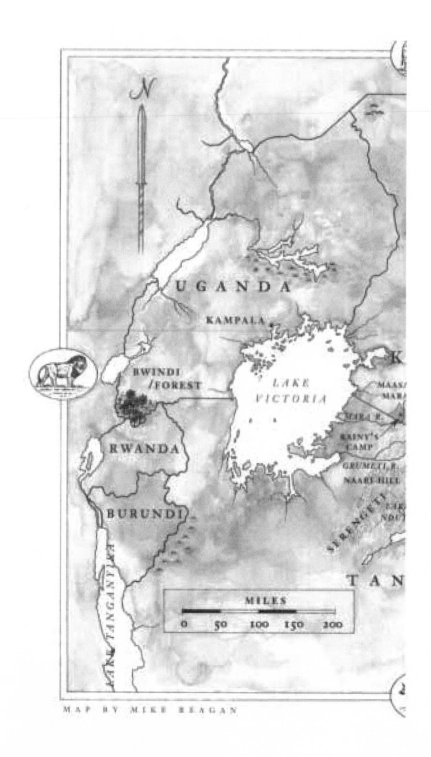

N

UGANDA

KAMPALA

BWINDI
/FOREST

LAKE
VICTORIA

RWANDA

MAASA
MARA

MARA R.

KEINY'S
CAMP

GRUMETI R.
NAABI HILL

BURUNDI

SERENGETI

LAK
NDU

TAN

LAKE TANGANYIKA

K

MILES

0   50   100   150   300

MAP BY MIKE BEAGAN

"People say that we're all seeking a meaning for life. I think that what we're seeking is an experience of being alive, so that our life experiences on the purely physical plane will have resonance within our innermost being and reality, so that we will actually feel the rapture of being alive."

JOSEPH CAMPBELL,
The Power of Myth

"What we get from this adventure is sheer joy. And joy is, after all, the end of life."

GEORGE MALLORY

Contents

1

Life Before Death

February 25, 1999, 5:30 a.m.

I lay on my stomach, slightly chilled, and listened to the scops owl's churring call. His soft staccato was coming from somewhere near my tent, probably the umbrella acacia tree; the other shrubs would be too low for him to feel safe. As the first low morning light reached the Serengeti from Ngorongoro Crater, I pondered where I should lead my safari group this morning. We had already been camped here on the north side of Lake Ndutu for four days, encountering probably more than one hundred lions and fifteen cheetahs. By blind luck, we had stumbled onto a leopardess and her two cubs as they chewed on a young wildebeest, which they had stashed in a low and thick acacia kirkii tree. We "needed" to see nothing else; today was one of those rare days when I felt no pressure to produce something. I knew we would still be given some sighting, as a reward for the four days of dusty driving that had brought us here.

Exactly ninety-seven hours later, it would be machine-gun fire that would roust me, not a five-inch owl. Before that day ended, thirty-one of us would be captured, sixteen kidnapped, and ten murdered in the jungle along the border between Uganda and the Congo. Right now, however, I felt the natural promise Africa has always provided me, as I listened to the owl again, picturing his fluffed body vibrating ferociously with each burst of sound.

It was cold for February, considering we were on the African equator during the hot season. I was worn down from seven weeks of being on safari. I rolled my legs onto the canvas floor, pulled on my clothes, slid into my tire-tread sandals, grabbed my binoculars and bush jacket, and stumbled through the open tent flaps into the darkness, toward the campfire and the smell of coffee. Feeling the remarkable cold wetness on my ankles and feet, I paused a moment in the damp grass to hear the owl call from the acacia.

I sat before the flickering wood, coffee already heating my hands and stomach, and decided to let my clients sleep a little longer. A couple years earlier, I had led two of them, Rob Haubner and Susan Miller, on their honeymoon safari, when they had seemed permanently joined either by arms or legs, and on this trip they appeared no less intimate. Both Rob and Susan and the other couple on this safari, Bob McLaurin and Susan Studd, slept in tents complete with queen-size beds. I envied the way I imagined Rob and Susan intertwined, completely at ease, trusting, and sound asleep. My life was a good one, but it was sometimes lonely to have my prime allegiance lie with Africa.

Our driver, Emanuel, spoke a soft greeting, as is the African custom no matter how urgent the matter. We briefly talked of the plan to pack a breakfast and head north again to the tall rock islands of the Gol Kopjes, so remarkable in their smoothness as they rise out of the gentle plains of the Serengeti, and a favorite haunt for predators because of the cover they offer. Emanuel disappeared back to the kitchen tents and out of habit I tossed the last quarter inch of coffee from my enameled cup and stood. I hate waking people up.

I tapped on the canvas of Bob McLaurin and Susan Studd's tent once, twice, and then spoke. Bob answered with a muffled "All right," and I shuffled off to the other tent, twenty yards away. Rob Haubner and Susan Miller had furled their tent flaps back, as I had, so I stopped short and told them in a strong voice that it was morning, or close enough. An immediate and bright answer came from Rob, with a groan from Susan, and I turned back to the beckoning firelight.

Exactly one year earlier, we had been here as well, all five of us. But the rains of El Niño had chased us away, making it almost impossible to drive, and when we flew out it had taken us three tries to get airborne because of the mud. This safari had more than made up for that: Yesterday alone we had watched a terrific, though horrendous, battle between two hyenas and a wildebeest. Its entrails hanging, the wildebeest had fought off its two attackers for forty-five minutes before it weakened and was killed. Bob McLaurin and Susan Studd, understandably, had not been able to watch the killing, and they had urged us to leave. They finally relented, however, allowing Rob, Susan Miller, and me to document with our cameras this once in a lifetime experience. Maybe Bob and Susan were right not to watch, but the biologist

14

in me had to record it, and the three of us were captivated by the vital and basic life that was this death.

"Morning, Mark," Rob said. He'd crept up on me, and I jumped as he settled into the chair beside me. He already had his coffee as well, and I could just make out the firelight reflecting on his Teva sandals as he hunched toward the fire. His long frame settled deeper into the canvas chair, his boyishness belied only by the three-day stubble that caught the firelight. The flames swayed in a slow belly dance. "Flawless," he said, as he cocked his head toward the ice-clear stars pricking holes in the flat blue-black of the sky.

Susan ran her hand across my shoulders as she passed on her way to Rob. There she leaned forward and collapsed sleepily into him from behind. His coffee spilled as her arms encircled him and her head landed at the back of his neck, against his left shoulder. He did not complain. After a minute, she raised up and moved to the chair beside him and Rob rose to get coffee for her.

Both Rob and Sue were from Portland, Oregon, but they had lived all over the world. Rob had been based in the Philippines and Southeast Asia, traveling throughout the Third World for Intel. Susan organized big multimedia conferences and presentations everywhere, and she had all the "people skills" anyone could want. They had been married at the Portland Zoo and their 1997 honeymoon trip, at the Maasai Mara Reserve, was our first safari together.

Emanuel appeared again, telling me in Kiswahili that both breakfast and lunch were packed in the truck, that we had coffee, tea, and water as well. Everything was set.

Susan Studd, without a hint of meanness, had warned us all not to talk to her in the morning for the first hour or so, whether she had had coffee or not. Bob didn't argue with his wife and I certainly wasn't going to, so when the two of them showed up a few minutes later, festooned with cameras and extra clothing, no one even uttered a hello as they settled into the remaining chairs. Titus, the camp waiter, held out a silver tray with two more blue enamel cups. The steam wove its way toward the star-dotted blue-black sky, holding the orange light of the fire, as it twisted upward and melded with the dark.

We were morgue-quiet, half-awake. I was loath to speak, but did. "We probably should get rolling if we want to be at Naabi Hill as the light breaks."

With Emanuel deft at the wheel of the Land Rover he had driven for some ten years in territory like this, we rode in silence for forty minutes to the ranger's post that guarded the Gol Kopjes. I sat on the roof, as always, steady cold tears in my eyes because of the chilly wind. A year later, as I drove down into the crater of Ngorongoro with a different safari group in tow, I would cry hot tears as I recalled this camp and the softness of this dawn.

We found and followed a cheetah for almost two hours before she killed. It took another thirty minutes for her to finish her breakfast of young Thomson's gazelle, and then we went for our own breakfast of bacon and cheese rolls and fruit salad that Arthur, our camp manager, had made for us. Because it was still early and we were still cold, the six of us sat in the sun on a rib of granite that surfaced like a whale's back as it breached from the grassy ocean. Rob and Susan sat on the ground, their backs propped against the stone, their shoulders touching, as we talked about the photographs we'd hoped we'd captured of the running cheetah as she slapped down the Tommie and strangled it. We actually reveled in the images of the cheetah's bloody face as she rapidly devoured the young gazelle. Not only in location but also in attitude, this place was a world away from Rob's and Susan's lives in Portland, and at Intel. The success we had seen the cheetah achieve in the dawn hours was definitely different in kind from what software competitiveness or even city living required. Here the tasks of life were more elemental and clean, even if, at times, they appeared brutal to human eyes. I think Rob and Susan relished it for those reasons, withdrawing from their own urgent lives to be witnesses to nature's necessary rhythms.

By 11:00 a.m., we were back in the truck and heading farther north. We paused; I scanned the landscape with the binoculars and saw lions almost two miles away. Against the short green grasses, their dark yellow coats stood out boldly, even though they were at the base of another kopje. As we drove closer, more and more cubs grew distinct against the grass, until the pride numbered sixteen in all. We would have lunch with them.

For over ninety minutes we photographed and studied the lions. In spite of the rapidly rising heat the cubs were still full of piss and vinegar, attacking anything that moved, and a lot of things that didn't. Even in the relatively cramped quarters of our Land Rover, time blew by like wind. At 2:30, we drove to a cluster of fig trees on the west side of a distant set of rocks. We could safely rest here because the plains are so open that I could see for ten miles in any direction. After I scouted the rocks for any hidden predators, we all got out, taking the seat cushions from the car, and flopped heavily onto the ground, sighing like lionesses, and slid into sleep. The broad leaves of a ficus sheltered us like a green roof, supported by white rafters.

I lay on my back, knowing I would not doze off in that position. Pleased to see that all four in my group were comfortable enough to sleep right out on the plains, skin touching earth, I watched the ever-present raptors as they moved across the vast blue above the equally vast green. In Africa, some predatory eye is always watching.

Rounding out the day by watching the lion cubs at Simba Kopjes and a sunset over the Moru Mountains that swept us into awed silence, we had come back to camp, showered by lantern light, and now sat tired and hushed by the fire. The night was once again flawless; the few clouds of the hot afternoon had gone westward with the light. Venus dominated the west, while Jupiter ruled brightly overhead.

I had asked the staff to pull the linen-covered dining table out of the long mess tent so we could eat under the stars. The candles, protected from the light breeze by glass globes, sent tiny bolts of light ricocheting off the silver and the stemware.

I do not remember what we had for soup, perhaps groundnut, and I do not recall the main course; maybe it was roast chicken or beef Wellington. I can still clearly see the faces at the table. After nine days in the equatorial sun, everyone glowed various shades of healthy tan and red in the candlelight. Susan Miller, in particular, radiated, but perhaps her aura lay as much in her wide smile and easy gut-laugh as on her skin. This was also apparently a time of day that sat well with Susan Studd. The tension, even the slight scowl, inhabiting her face that morning had long since drifted away with the Serengeti wind. "I'm glad our restaurant table isn't by the kitchen door," she commented wryly. "The view will suffice." The corners of her mouth were barely turned up. Rob just smiled.

After the two couples whispered exhausted good-nights and strolled arm in arm back to their tents, I sat alone at the fire, drowsing, happy about the way I had helped the day acquit itself. The camp crew, a hundred yards away, talked in low tones as they washed the dishes and packed up the kitchen for the night. Hyenas, leopards, and genets had sneaked in every single night since our arrival. The little they had snitched was a small price to pay for their presence. But tomorrow we would leave the Serengeti, so the crew was getting ahead a bit on the massive packing that had to be done. It would take the eight of them all morning to break down the huge, steel-framed canvas tents and their adjoining shower rooms, then pack all the china and glasses, and stow it all securely in the truck. It would take them another two, perhaps three, days to drive the rough road all the way back to Arusha, where the equipment would be checked, washed, repaired if necessary, and stored in a warehouse, awaiting the next safari.

Finally, when my head fell slowly forward and snapped back as if I were in church, I roused and headed for my tent, out of habit checking for shoes left out, snack food forgotten, and clothes and cameras perhaps left exposed to the coming dew. But there was nothing to do. In the tent, my firm mattress and flat pillow were beyond cool and I pumped my legs for a few seconds before settling on my stomach. I listened for lions but all I heard from the west end of the lake were the hyenas, calling to one another as they gathered for another killing foray on the night plains.

February 26, 1999, 5:30 a.m.

It must have been the lions' roaring that woke me. They had obviously moved closer during the night and were just to the northwest of us, probably within the woodland. I fell back heavily, knowing that I did not have to wake anyone early this morning. We had only to eat breakfast, pack, board my plane, and fly northwest, maybe over the now-roaring lions, to Kisumu, Kenya. We would clear immigrations outbound first, then, after Kisumu, head back southwest twenty minutes to Rusinga Island, which lolls in the warm and clear waters of Lake Victoria.

After two cups of coffee, I was still the only white body moving, so I headed for the dirt track that ran behind camp. Ever since I was a boy growing up in southern Illinois, I have loved being outside. My dog, Tumbleweed, and I spent hours and hours in the forest every day. Often we would return home just as darkness descended on us. Now, as then, I love "reading the morning paper," the tracks and signs left by whatever had passed during the dark hours. Composed mostly of fine ash blown from the volcanoes to the east, the soil registers the lightest of tracks as cleanly as an artist etches a tawny lithograph on the ground.

A male leopard had come by, just before a white-tailed mongoose and a ratel. Much later, after the dew had fallen, the lions had purposefully passed our camp. Only three of the lions had used the track, the others preferring the short, wildebeest-trampled grass to the north of the twin tire ruts. The days are busy here, I thought; they are full of life and death and the passing of energy from one creature to another. But the nights are infinitely more crowded, and more lethal.

"Hey, Mark, couldn't you make those

lions shut up?" Susan Miller called out from beside the campfire. She poked Rob, and I just smiled as she teased Emanuel about his driving yesterday. "Emanuel, you must have hit every conceivable aardvark hole between camp and the Gol Mountains. Some of them *twice*." She threw her coffee grounds on my feet when I drew up beside her.

"She's ready to see new country," Rob remarked.

"If this is the way she always gets," I replied, "I don't think I'd ever take her on vacation."

Susan ignored us both and bounded toward the waiting table. "Let's eat," she chirped as she sat down, waiting for no one.

An hour later, the dust hung in the air behind our wheels as we motored slowly to the dirt airstrip where I had left my bright blue-and-green plane. On the way, we circled the lake, stopping one last time at the den of the bat-eared foxes. "Good-bye, little foxes!" Susan Studd called, and they turned their narrow-nosed faces in our direction at the sound of her words. During our days here we had passed this den, morning and evening, and sometimes even at lunch. They had to know our vehicle, our voices, and perhaps our odor by now. They certainly couldn't be bothered to run anymore, which seemed right to me.

An hour into our flight, Lake Victoria stretched like a trapped inland ocean below our plane. Across its dappled, silver palette lay Uganda and the aptly named Impenetrable Forest. The sharp green of Rusinga Island rose low above the scalloped waves. As I dipped the left wing and dived shallowly to the south, I saw a fleet of dhows sailing in from Mfangano Island. Their hulls, black and slim, were pushed northward by their billowing breasts of sails.

We were across the island in seconds and back out over the open water, and I turned again to line us up with the little strip that runs right up to the gate of the small lodge where we would be staying on Rusinga Island. I dropped twenty degrees of flaps as our speed decreased. I could make out a flock of some kind of four-footed beasts grazing on the southern end of the runway, but it's a long strip, so I decided to land beyond the herd instead of going around again for another approach.

"Mark, are you going to land us in the water? I didn't wear my rubber boots!"

Susan Studd called over the intercom from the backseat, where she always volunteered to sit in the plane. All she could see was the water below.

"Don't know yet, Susan," I yelled back. "Give me a couple seconds to decide!"

A shepherd watched my plane swoop down, ignoring his grazing flock. They had to be sheep, I figured, because goats always have enough brains to run to the side, while sheep just cluster and wait to die. Sure enough, the animals rushed into a clump in the center of the runway, and then disappeared under the plane's nose as I shot over them.

We skinned the grass, touching it so lightly that the plane didn't even seem to change its angle. I reached over and toggled the flap lever back up, kept the yoke well into my stomach, and, as we rolled out, opened the window to let out the hot cabin air. This was not the dry ether of the Serengeti. Heavy with moisture and scented with vegetation, the breeze instantly cooled us, teasing us into what looked like an island paradise. We coasted past a grove of papaya trees and passion fruit vines that had wrapped themselves around the orchard's protective wall.

"Welcome," Rob said, "to Hawaii."

"It definitely has that feel, doesn't it?" Susan Miller observed.

I first came to this little oasis in 1987, as a change of pace after a two-week camping trip. Though my camps are anything but hardship, Rusinga is all luxury and ease. The cottages have no windows, just screens and curtains that are drawn at night against insects. Heavily shaded by fig and papaya, immaculate grass lawns run right to the beach.

Richard, our host, two heavy yellow labs trotting beside him, met us before I turned the plane around and shut it down. He strolled forward, helped Susan Studd out of the cramped rear of the aircraft, and introduced himself, first to her and then to the others. Susan shook his hand and knelt down to pet the two obviously happy dogs. I saw Richard rock back just perceptibly as Susan Miller, her face glowing, squeezed out of the middle row of seats, stretching after the long flight. She hoisted her camera bag, looked at Richard, and said, "Which way to the bar?"

Beguiled by her smile, Richard ignored the luggage, the other visitors, and me, and led Susan to the gate. By the time the rest of us had gotten our stuff into the lodge, with its incredible view of the water, Susan was already stretched out on a recliner, a rum and passion fruit juice in her hand. Seated beside her, Richard was pulling on a beer.

"To hell with the rest of the trip," she said. "Let's stay here."

I turned to Rob, who was beaming. "And she hasn't even seen the cottages yet."

"No," Rob answered, "but this is our kind of place."

Lunch was homemade seviche, cold avocado soup, and gingered Nile perch. From our table, we gazed at the three islands to the west, and let the onshore breeze flow through our hair. This was a break for me, too, after working hard to produce for my clients the excitement and wildlife action of the Serengeti. I felt compelled to "make it happen" — to teach, entertain, and ensure the day's enjoyability. Here it would be simple.

After lunch, the couples peeled off to lie on the chaise lounges in front of the cottages. I went to my room, pulled out the book on cheetahs that I was reading, and followed suit, knowing I wouldn't be up for long. When I awoke at 5:30 p.m., the strong light of the early afternoon had bleached to a softer yellow. Richard had offered to take us to Bird Island for sun-downers, and we needed to be there by 6:00 p.m. in order to have time to watch the tens of thousands of birds come in from the mainland to their roosts there.

Susan Miller stood by Richard, whose parents had built this incredible little paradise, as he piloted the twin-hulled speedboat out of the huge bay and turned us southward. Susan Studd and Bob sat quietly in the back of the boat, just hanging on as we bounced along. After twenty-five minutes of flying off the swells, Richard throttled back in the sudden glassiness of the leeward side of Bird Island, actually two islands set closely side by side.

I dropped one of the lures and let the line run out some twenty-five yards before setting the drag and bracing the rod in its stainless steel holder. Richard left the wheel, which Susan promptly took, and unzipped the canvas drinks bag. He opened a bottle of South African red wine, dumped some still-hot roasted cashews into a wooden bowl, held up a fistful of empty wineglasses, and raised his eyebrows questioningly.

"I'll take one," Susan said immediately, stretching out her well-tanned arm. Rob silently extended his as well, still facing west, as if the sun had magnetized his face. Richard talked easily with the foursome, allowing me to stay seated in the back of the boat watching the line. I watched the monofilament as it cut a V in the water behind, like the wake of some fish's fin that was trying, but never able, to catch up with our slow-cruising boat. As we came between the islands, the waves broke hard through the gap, temporarily rocking the boat until we were back in the lee of the island again. I turned to the sound of a giant kingfisher's rattling call, watched it skim low across the surface near the rocks, and pull up sharply to rest on the dead branch of a fig tree.

Occupying ourselves with soft talk, we watched flock after flock of little egrets and sacred ibis come west from the rice fields on the mainland. Silently the white birds found their perches among trees that were already jam-packed with raucous long-tailed cormorants. As the ibis flew low over us, we could easily discern the black hem of feathers on their otherwise flawlessly white wings.

The sun kissed the water just north of Mfangano Island and threw a wide gold lifeline of light all the way to our gunwales. "We should wait until dark," Richard said as we gazed, sunstruck, westward. "That way we can run by the night fishermen on the way back. They'll be setting out their insect-attracting lanterns." He refilled all the glasses as he said this, and the cashews made another round of the boat.

Finally, in complete darkness, and with the birds still flying in to roost, we fired up the twin outboards, stowed the drinks bag, broke free of the glassy surface, and headed north toward a chain of lights strung across the black water. When we reached them, we could see that they were gas-pressure lanterns tied together in a row, and the end of each line was anchored somewhere in the blackness below us. A slim boat filled with shirtless Luo tribesmen were busy completing the set. The lanterns bobbed on the waves, some eighteen inches above the waterline.

Richard explained that the lanterns attracted the lake flies, which, in turn, brought in the fish to feed on them. "Every four hours or so, the men will ring a purse net around the lights and capture the fish as they feed." Tomorrow he would show us where they dried them, simply spread out on sails in the sun. The sardine-sized whiting would later be eaten in soup,

31

mixed with boiled maize meal, or shipped off to Nairobi.

A single brass lantern, its flame encased behind thick glass facets, greeted us when we pulled up to the dock by our cottages. The bar was lit by similar brass lights, which were actually old anchor line lights from Lamu Island, in the Indian Ocean. After showering, we ate a simple but elegant dinner, and had barely enough energy left to make it to the cottages, where the balmy air flowed lightly through the mosquito nets that draped the beds.

February 27, 1999, 7 a.m.

In Africa, you can always get a good idea of your elevation by the species of dove you hear calling in the predawn darkness. Here I heard the descending growls of mourning doves, and knew I was at low elevation again, too low for red-eyed doves, olive pigeons, or even ring-necked doves. The breeze had died during the night but the temperature had fallen as well. Hot coffee still seemed like a good idea, and it was already on my veranda awaiting me. Surprisingly, I had not heard the man bring it. I normally wake at the softest of sounds, but the waves, the balmy breeze, and the long safari days had dropped me into a deeper slumber than normal. I drank my coffee, bare feet propped on the low veranda wall, and pondered the day ahead.

During this nineteen-day safari, Rusinga Island would be our only "one-night stand." I try hard to ensure that my groups stay at least three nights in any one place. It helps to have time to learn the names and faces and feel at ease in a new environment. I knew this group would have preferred at least one more day here, but our gorilla-trekking permits dictated this schedule. Only twelve people on any given day can visit the 320-odd mountain gorillas that live amid the series of extinct and live volcanoes that fall within the Democratic Republic of the Congo (formerly Zaire), Rwanda, and Uganda. I had argued, cajoled, and pleaded with the authorities in the Bwindi Impenetrable Forest to obtain permits for visits two days in a row. My first visit to the region had been in 1986 in Rwanda, where Dian Fossey, who had made these animals famous with her research and her book *Gorillas in the Mist*, had been killed by some of the poachers whose predations had threatened the gorillas for decades, and whose livelihood was threatened by the publicity she had brought to the gorillas.

The previous year, Rob, Susan, and I had tried to visit the gorillas, but the security seemed a bit dodgy at best, due to the warfare in both the Congo and Burundi. I had cancelled that portion of the safari. In April, May, and June of 1994, between eight hundred thousand and one million people were murdered in Rwanda in just one hundred days, with the tribal conflict between the Hutus and the Tutsis ultimately spilling into neighboring Congo and Burundi, where both murderers and refugees fled. I was in Kenya at the time, mostly home in Nairobi, where the international media were based, and I knew some of the reporters covering the massacre. Their stories were heartbreaking, though I could not believe, at first, that over eight hundred thousand people had been murdered *by hand* in one hundred days. We were stunned into silence.

With Rwanda a ruined country and neighboring Congo equally dangerous, only Uganda was left as a destination to see the gorillas. The two camps near there, including the camp managed by Abercrombie & Kent, where we would stay, were completely up to speed. Throughout the season I had e-mailed or visited the A&K office in Nairobi, making certain that things were still fine. No problems.

This season, security was deemed safe, first because Uganda had never had any dangerous incidents that put tourists in peril, and second, because visitors were coming and going regularly, and there were glowing reports from Uganda about their gorilla trips. I had already flown to Bwindi four times this year and had had wonderful experiences each of those times.

Today would be a day of flying, changing countries, and going through immigrations and customs twice — once on our way out of Kenya and again as we entered Uganda. From there, we would fly a couple hundred miles more before landing in the tea fields near Buhoma, less than a mile from the Ugandan border with the Congo. A thirty-minute drive would take us to the edge of the Impenetrable Forest in time for tea.

At a serene breakfast under a fig tree, Rob, Bob, and the two Susans were charged about entering the deep forest on the Congo border. The gorillas really do have a magical pull, and the depth and darkness of the forest holds a vast, romantic mystique. I explained the flying we had to do that day, and about the drive to reach the tent camp stuck on the steep west valley slope, right where the road meets the wall of rainforest. I took the time to explain about the gorillas themselves, their family structure, their species and subspecies, their distribution, and then gave a brief sketch of Dian Fossey's work with other gorillas, far to the south in Rwanda. She may have been a terror of a woman to work for or be around, but without her dedication it is doubtful there would be any mountain gorillas today.

By 9:00 a.m., I was taxiing down to the south end of the airstrip, having checked the engine and electrics, cycled the prop to get warm oil in the governor, cycled the flaps to make sure they were still operating, and set trim and compass. Most of the strips that I use in East Africa are rock, sand, or grass; they can be exceedingly rough, and are always shaking something loose in the instrument panel. Usually it's just the radios that go dead, but twice I've lost the flaps, and once the brakes. As long as I know ahead of time I can plan around it, but takeoff is not a good time for surprises. At the end of the strip, I stepped firmly on the right brake, pivoted the plane, and kept it rolling, slowly feeding in the throttle. As I start my takeoffs, I always pick up rocks that chip my propeller as they are flung backward. If the field is long enough for me to add the power gradually, just at the start, it really saves my propeller blades that damage.

We cleared the trees at the north end with ease, and I climbed straight ahead to gain a margin of air below me, then turned northeast for Kisumu, and glanced backward to view my crowd. All their faces were pressed to the windows, watching the lake and the sailing dhows that dotted it.

Our customs exit at Kisumu proved to have surprisingly few hassles. I had told them the day before that I would be back today on my way through to Uganda. They even remembered to have the fuel truck waiting for me. We had our passports stamped, added one hundred liters of avgas, promised to bring whiskey from Entebbe's duty free on our return, and were soon flying again. After a forty-five-minute flight over sky and water that melded seamlessly together, forcing me to watch my instruments more carefully, we descended gradually past Lake Victoria's rich green islands that marked our path into Entebbe and the Ugandan airport made famous in 1976 when Israeli forces rescued ninety-eight hostages from an airplane that had been hijacked by Palestinian guerillas.

Boeing 747s land at Entebbe's international airport, so, for a change, I didn't have to think about the strip's length. To avoid having to taxi ten minutes to the terminal, I held us just off the runway and skimmed down fully the first half of the pavement before letting my blue bird settle onto the painted centerline. After taxiing up to the terminal, I leaned out the mixture to kill the engine, and a face appeared by my window. I opened the door as the propeller stopped and shook hands with Peter, the representative from the company that ran the gorilla camp. We followed him to the terminal, passports in hand yet again. We took a chance and left all our luggage in the plane, hoping they would not have to search it all.

Peter took the group for lunch upstairs in the airport while I filed a flight plan for the next leg. I was required to check in with the military as well. We shook hands all around, yammered about the lack of rains, how the trip had been so far, and how things were for them. Five minutes later I was joining the two couples for lunch.

Uganda, unlike Kenya and Tanzania, is mostly green and fertile. It was Uganda that both the European colonizers wanted. Britain and Germany were more or less required to "take" Kenya and Tanzania, respectively, just to have port facilities for the bounty that they planned to ship out of Uganda. Since gaining its independence in 1962, the country has suffered from a steady series of brutal dictators: Milton Obote, then the infamous Idi Amin, then Milton Obote again. Finally, in 1985, two rebellions arose, when General Okello started a coup in the eastern and southern half of the country while Yoweri Museveni started a similar war in the west. I had been sent in, working as a photographer and interpreter for both *The New York Times* and *The London Times*, to cover those conflicts.

We were more than an hour out of Entebbe before I could discern the silhouettes of the mountains of Bwindi directly ahead. The moist haze gives no clue as to what it hides behind it until you are startlingly close. The slight turbulence around the low mountains woke up the other four, and they gazed wide-eyed at the mountains, their cloaks of dark green, and the villages hemming their broad bases. I took the little plane up the valley that leads to the Impenetrable Forest, just to show everyone the scale and steepness of the terrain we would traverse. Only from the air can you see how vast and trackless this jungle truly is.

Incredibly thick grass cushioned the runway, bordered on three sides by chartreuse acres of bright tea. As we taxied up to the east end of the strip, a comfortably familiar brown-and-yellow Land Cruiser pulled up onto the grass, reassuring me that even here in the distant rainforest, our arrangements were still working.

Hundreds of children poured out onto the runway. "Listen, everybody," I called out, "help me keep an eye on the kids!" On my trip here three weeks earlier, I had to shut off the engine just after touchdown, for fear of striking a child with the nearly invisible spinning propeller. As fast as I could, I pulled back the mixture and killed the engine. We would manhandle the plane into its parking place. The risk of killing someone was too great.

As we emerged, the children swarmed around out of sheer curiosity. This part of the world virtually never sees airplanes fly over, much less land. The arrival of my bright blue-and-green Cessna was always a major event. My foursome was amazed that an arriving plane would be such a novelty; they loved shaking hands with the all the children, even photographing the scene. I did, however, take the precaution of telling them to help keep an eye on one another's luggage, just in case. We had two hundred hands to carry our five bags and camera gear to the waiting vehicle. After making sure none of it wandered off into the tea fields, I asked an *askari*, or guard, named Mutabe, an old man of the village who had always proved trustworthy, to keep little hands off the plane, and soon our Land Cruiser was bouncing down the burnt orange dirt and rock road toward the forest.

We were certainly outside the normal tourist loop. Bwindi is far too expensive and distant for the average safari-goer. The knowledge that you are "out there" always makes the place feel special. You can see it in the way locals are transfixed by your presence and by the fact that you see no other white faces anywhere. Every hamlet we drove through was lined with little faces and waving arms. In spite of the very rough road, Susan Miller kept her face pressed to the glass, caught between waving at the children who charged to the edge of the road at the sound of our approaching truck and poking Rob to point out something special she had seen. Between the villages, massive horned cattle took over the road, repeatedly forcing us to stop while their keepers beat them with short stout sticks back into the banana plantations that lined both sides of our track.

The road stops where the Impenetrable Forest begins, and the change is instantaneous and stark. Outside the park, virtually all the huge trees have long since been cut, the primal forest replaced by fields of potato and maize, the valley bottom an unending strip of banana palms. No cutting is allowed within the national park. The fields are silent, but the dense, green-black mystery of the rainforest emits constant, strange, and beckoning calls. Some are from birds, some from mammals, and some you just don't know. Even more than dawn on the Serengeti, the rainforest pulls me, excites me. Maybe I am too familiar with those plains and it's the new and the unknown here that is so enticing. Here there are birds I have never seen, butterflies the size of birds, and mammals whose tracks I have yet to see, much less their darkly concealed bodies.

We paused at the park gate, signed in without even leaving the vehicle, and the wooden pole that blocks the road slid aside, and we entered the forest. Two hundred yards farther on, we stopped for the day. I shook hands with the camp staff and introduced their familiar and smiling faces to my group. The crew shouldered the luggage and we ascended the steep stairway behind them that led to the camp. The tents at the camp were built on wooden platforms and featured small beds and flush toilets, but no electricity.

The bush encroached tightly on the stairs of red clay, so it was a sudden surprise when we stepped clear of the vegetation and found ourselves on the camp's lawn. It was so thick that even here in camp we could not see any of the tents that were scheduled to shelter us for the next three nights. Everyone needed a shower, so the camp manager and I arranged for the buckets of hot water to be brought over, the showers filled. I sat alone on the lawn for a few minutes listening to birds familiar to me; great blue turacos, blue-headed coucals, and snowy-headed robin chats were all close and calling. Up the valley rang the echoing call of chimpanzees, as they pant-hooted into the encroaching darkness.

I walked back to my tent, heard the men coming with my hot water, listened as they lowered the canvas shower bucket, and listened to the sudden rush of water as it was filled. I thanked them, stripped, and stepped into the heat. I was clean long before the bucket ran dry, but I stayed under to enjoy the luxury, leaving only when the stream slowed suddenly to drops. My body steamed in the cold moist air.

My foursome were the only ones in the dining tent, except for a single woman, American judging by her accent. We naturally invited her to our table. A heavyset woman in baggy clothes, with an air that kept you a bit at a distance, Linda Adams had traveled, she informed us, all the way from California just to see the mountain gorillas. She was not going to any other game parks in East Africa. Instead, she would have just two visits of one hour each with the primates and then fly back to Entebbe, then to Nairobi, London, and Los Angeles. It struck me as a hell of a long way to come for just two hours. I had come across many single women who had a fascination with Africa, particularly with the primates here. I was disappointed, for her sake, that Linda would be so near to such an amazing array of wildlife, yet see so little of what Africa has to offer.

As we sat by the campfire, the six of us polished off the wine, feeling the immensity of the forest beside us. Except for the crickets and frogs, it was now deathly silent, and so drastically different from the plains, where some animal is always talking about something. We could see nothing, but the massive trees were there, and we knew it. Even in the pitch-blackness that cradled us, I wanted to walk into the forest.

February 28, 1999, 6:30 a.m.

My life was about to drastically and permanently change; but this morning I greeted the lovely man bearing the lovely tray with the lovely coffee. I took it to the deck and listened to the surround-sound symphony of birds. It was beyond belief how crowded the airwaves were. I concentrated on separating the strands of their calls, narrowing the unfamiliar down so that I could at least ascertain their families.

Elephants and buffalo lurked here, along with bushbuck and other antelope. As I pondered the possibilities, a troop of colobus monkeys sounded off in a loud series of rolling, echoing growls, which triggered a response from all the colobus scattered up and down the valley, so that soon the forest was reverberating with their calls. What were the mountain gorillas doing at this early hour? Probably still curled in their night nests.

"We're going to be right on top of the gorillas," I said to the others at breakfast. "You guys should keep the photo equipment minimal — take just what works best." The skies were clear, but with afternoon rains the norm, we would carry our rain jackets. For once, I would spend the day in long pants instead of shorts. With so many scratching vines and trees, wearing shorts wasn't worth the coolness.

Along with Linda and the camp staff, who were carrying our lunches and water, we marched down the stairway to the park headquarters to sign in for our day of gorilla trekking. Because bureaucracies the world over always demand that you hurry up and wait, we sat for thirty minutes. Finally we were assigned four porters, locals who would not only carry our lunches and water, but also push, pull, or drag us if need be, to help us reach the gorillas. The porters offered us all walking sticks to help us negotiate the steep trails. I was glad to see both Bob and Susan Studd accept them, because I was concerned about how they would manage the day. Bob was a big man, and the couple's Portland home lay at sea level. We would be hiking up to perhaps 7,500 feet today, enough for anyone to feel the altitude.

The ranger who would be accompanying us appeared. He was a short, slightly built man with an exceedingly animated and cheerful face and he spoke English well, with a charming habit of accenting the wrong syllable. "If you are sick please do not go, and you will be refunded your gorilla permit and the park entrance fee," he announced. "If I determine later that you have a cold, a cough, or are sick and I turn you back, you will forfeit all you have paid, so know that now." His dictum was fair, considering how easy it would be for the gorillas to catch any disease we might bring into their proximity. Moving closer to the animals than fifteen feet was prohibited, to minimize contagion.

"One hour! We will have only one hour with the gorillas, so take your pictures, though you cannot use flash," he finished firmly. I have learned to time the hour myself. My clients have come from the other side of the world and spent thousands of dollars to see these primates; I was not about to allow their time to be cut short by a ranger or a tracker anxious to beat the rains home. But this was the same ranger I had had three weeks previously, and then I had given him, along with two other rangers, a short ride in my plane. It was their first time airborne, and the whole area knew about their adventure before the day was over. I expected no difficulties from him today.

Finally we boarded our own vehicle for a short drive to the trailhead. There, we lined up behind the ranger as he descended a slippery, hard-packed path of red clay to the valley floor. The stream at the bottom was shallow and wide, and I skipped across the blackened stones to the far side, with Rob Haubner following right behind me. Both Susan Miller and Susan Studd made the wiser and less risky choice of taking off their shoes, rolling up their pants, and wading through. Bob McLarin, carrying a large amount of camera gear, briefly weighed both options before sitting on a log to untie his bootlaces. Voluntarily walking into the water was better than falling into it.

The trail began to climb. We wound through banana fields and passed a number of small mud huts, children wide-eyed in every doorjamb. We greeted them but did not stop. Our trek could take us hours, easily. We knew only where the gorillas had been located the afternoon before, not where they were now. We would climb to the last point where they had been seen and follow their tracks to their night nests. Then the trackers would take over, and slowly, searchingly, follow them to where they were this morning. It sounded simple, but the vegetation would be impossibly thick with vines and tightly packed shrubs and bushes. The sting nettles would slow us to a crawl while the gorillas, even the huge males, just plowed effortlessly through it all. We would work for what we got.

The walking sticks became very useful as the path went straight up along a huge bean field. Neither Ugandans nor gorillas believe in switchbacks. From my position near the rear, I could monitor everyone's progress, and they were all doing splendidly.

Except for Linda Adams. By the time we reached the top of the field, she was out of sight behind us. We waited. Finally, after fifteen minutes, she came up and virtually collapsed on the ground, soaked in sweat and breathing hard. I shot a look at the guide, whose eyes were already on me. "Is she all right?" he asked me in Kiswahili.

"Truthfully," I replied, "I do not know. She's not part of my group, so I don't know her, or if she's able."

He was surprised, having assumed that we were together. We both shrugged, and he started up again. We followed, but Linda remained sitting in the mud, drinking water.

We climbed, we rested, we drank water, we climbed, and we sat. It was steep for even the porters and ranger. But Bob, whom I had been worried about, was going strong, and his wife's attitude was great. Rob and Susan were actually talking and laughing as they trudged upward. I was relieved. We were going to get to the gorillas today, easily.

We breasted a grassy knoll and stopped again. Linda was not in sight. I felt bad, but I also had the responsibility of making sure that my four did get to see what they had come so far for. That Linda was so badly out of shape was sad, certainly, for she had come a long way as well. We waited more than twenty minutes before she and a porter appeared below us, the porter pushing her unceremoniously from behind.

The ranger's eyes met mine. I could tell, without glancing around, that my four were looking at me as well. "If this continues," he said flatly, "we will have to turn around."

There was one option: send Linda back with a porter. We were not even into the hard walking of the upper forest yet, and already we were way behind schedule. At this rate we would be lucky to reach the gorillas at all, and if we did it would be dangerously late in the day. Hiking back down in the dark was not an option. Directly but softly, I said, "Send her back with one of the porters. It is not at all fair that my group does not get to see the gorillas because she cannot make the climb."

He nodded pensively as Linda staggered into our group. Susan Studd and I both offered Linda our water and some chocolate, hoping that a rush of energy would get her over the hump. She was grateful but too played out to be polite, her arms heavy with exhaustion. We plodded on, scrambling over and under moss-covered logs, fighting through tangled vines, each of us falling on the slick vegetation and the

51

slicker mud. At the next stop, only twenty minutes higher up, Linda was nowhere to be seen.

From the sound of her porter's *panga,* or machete, we could tell that Linda was drawing closer. I looked at the ranger, who was looking at me. Linda flopped on the ground, saying nothing. She knew what was about to happen, and it must have hurt her terribly. She had come all the way from California just for this experience, and today, at least, she was going to be denied it. The ranger slid past the five of us and talked with her porter and then directly to her, telling her that he was going to have to send her back. The hard walking, he explained, had not even started yet. She nodded meekly.

We rested a bit more while the porters rummaged through the lunch pack and pulled a box out for her. They added some bananas and a bottle of water, and handed it down the line to her porter, who stashed it in the top of his pack. Awkwardly, we said good-bye. Right or wrong, I know each of us was relieved.

Our pace increased markedly as we turned south and entered the dark wall of forest. We were no longer following a trail, but the thickness of the canopy blocked out so much sunlight that the ground cover diminished substantially. It was no real blessing, for without the plants the soil was more exposed and we slid more often.

I paused and listened to the burring, short rattle of an African broadbill. The male broadbill has got to have one of the funniest little courtship calls and flights of any bird in the world. He sits, all fat and puffed out, on a dead branch, and then, when the mood strikes him, he flies a short and fast circle, maybe a meter in diameter, while letting loose with his loud, staccato buzz. It has to been seen to be appreciated, and chuckled at.

I slid past my four, and told the ranger I was going to find the broadbill. He gave me a questioning look, but I told him to carry on and that I'd catch up. I didn't wait for an answer but started in the direction from which I'd last heard the bird. It turned out to be much closer than I had thought, so I called back to Rob that everyone had to see this bird.

"You want us to see a bird?" he questioned.

"Yeah. You won't believe this little guy. I promise it'll be worth it."

The four stopped climbing and clambered over to me. Eventually all binoculars were on him. "Just stay on him until he calls," I advised. And they did.

I could have figured when he flew, even if he hadn't vocalized, even if I hadn't been looking. We all couldn't help but break into laughter when he hurriedly buzzed his circle, only to land back at his starting point. We waited a minute for a second flight, which stirred more laughter, and then we clambered back over to the waiting Ugandans.

I was lucky, I knew, to have guests who could stop to appreciate this sort of thing. It wasn't the high drama or easy watching of the plains mammals, yet they all found this little encounter worthwhile, in spite of the extra slipping and sliding it had required.

When we rejoined the ranger, he told me that the trackers had found the gorillas' spoor; we should soon reach their night nests. I translated the news to the group and we all peered ahead, as if the gorillas would appear in front of us. Twenty-five minutes passed before we *descended* and found the place where the gorillas had spent the night. Unlike chimpanzees, which climb into trees each evening, gorillas make their night nests on the ground. And nests they are. We were surrounded by a cluster of what looked like oversized, freshly made bird nests, averaging about three feet in diameter. The intense buzzing of small clouds of flies denoted where a gorilla dropping had fallen.

The gorillas move, then stop to feed for a while, breaking small branches, stripping leaves, and stuffing long vines into their mouths like green spaghetti. But the tracking is still an art, not a mechanical skill. You must be wise enough in the ways of gorillas to know what they prefer and where they will most likely head next. In a thick forest, a small broken stem is not all that much to go on in the dim light. We followed the two trackers into a steep gully that headed right back down, paralleling the route we had come up.

I talked briefly with the ranger and he sent a porter off to try to catch up with Linda before she had descended too far. It was beginning to look as if the gorillas might end up way below us, in which case Linda could be led straight across in a long traverse, and possibly still see what she had come for. That would please both her and me.

A low and short series of deep grunts bounced up the gully to our ears. We froze, and then turned to one another, grinning.

My four had never heard a mountain gorilla in their lives, but there was no mistaking that sound.

The ranger told us to leave our walking sticks and lunches here with the porters, so as not to scare or distract the animals. We pulled out our cameras and moved ahead, voices hushed, our eyes probing the greenery ahead. To my delight, the slope became so steep that trees seemed unable to gain a grasp on the soil here. Suddenly we were in sunlight as we slipped and slid down into a treeless clearing, densely matted with only low shrubs. This would make the photography infinitely easier. Thank you, thank you.

Linda Adams came sidehilling across the steep slope and joined us just as we saw the first gorilla, a younger female, sitting contentedly, methodically stripping a vine leaf by leaf. Rob's boyish face was lit up as if it were Christmas morning. Susan Studd's expression said, "Oh, she's so cute." Linda dutifully got out her camera and pushed right past Susan Miller to get the angle she wanted, which seemed to anger Susan slightly.

In virtually all wildlife photography, the trick is to anticipate your subject and get ahead of it. As we worked our way down to the gorillas' level, I assessed their positions, trying to decide where to place my people. The ranger would be strict about how close we could get to the animals — but they could still approach us; and that was the answer. I grabbed Rob by his shoulder and pointed down to an opening on a small game trail just below the feeding female. He instantly understood and rose to move, but the ranger stopped him. I explained where he was going, and when he saw how far it would keep him from the female, he nodded. Rob slid down quietly, pausing twice for photographs.

Susan Studd was beside me, breathing out her oohs and ahhs, and I was very happy. Bob was confident enough to move where he wanted in spite of the ranger's occasional restraining hand or stern look. He had invested a lot to get here and was not about to let the opportunity slip away. Susan Miller was photographing her husband photographing the gorillas. After five minutes, I tapped my watch and showed it to the ranger, letting him know that I, too, was timing our interval with the gorilla troop. For the Ugandans who work here, this is a daily job, but for my people it's a once-in-a-lifetime experience. The difference is not well understood by those in charge of those who pay.

For the next hour or so we scrambled and slid, trying to stay small and inconspicuous as we sought to get clear views of the amazing apes. Both Susans spent a great deal of time playing peek-a-boo with a year-old gorilla that was hiding, with its nonchalant mother, behind a vine-festooned prunus tree. The little male was so obviously being playful that, for all our efforts to stay quiet, we couldn't help but burst into fits of laughter. That little gorilla just knew he was cute.

Bob seemed quite happy with where he was and what he was seeing, so I squirmed on down toward Rob. "Rob, hey Rob," I whispered. He was so intent on shooting the female gorilla before him that he didn't hear. I finally crawled down and tapped him lightly on the shoulder. He jumped. "I thought you were a gorilla coming up behind me," he whispered. He was amazed at how relaxed the gorillas remained in our presence, even the old silverback.

I reminded him that humans arrived to watch them at pretty much the same time every day, as regular as afternoon rainstorms. "Rob, give me the twenty-eight millimeter and give me the eighty-two-hundred. It'll give you a great face shot of her."

"Yeah," he whispered. "Fine. Where's Susan?"

"She's just up the slope and wants the twenty-eight to get a shot of you, the female, and the little valley here."

"Bring me the fifty when you're done, will ya?" he asked as I crawled away.

"Yeah, no worries. You just keep shooting. The light is great now," I said, glancing skyward, "and it may not last."

We were granted five more minutes. The ranger had been fair with his watch, even generous; he had allowed us to move around and stay in the paths of approaching gorillas, and had even helped clear vegetation that was blocking some shots of the ink-black mammals. I tapped Rob on the shoulder, pointed to my watch, and he nodded.

We worked our way downhill, going right through the gorilla family, to meet the porters who had skirted around us and were now waiting below. At least we wouldn't have to climb back up to meet the original path. Here we stopped for lunch. The porters, guide, and tracker ate from old paint cans full of porridge that they had brought from their homes. Their water bottles were each plugged with a banana acting as a cork. The "corks" were eaten and the bottles passed around. We were finally free to talk louder, which we all did at once. The gorilla stories flew, as if each person relating what had happened had been the only hominid in the forest. The garrulous talk slowed only when the first raindrops hit us. Within two minutes it was pouring, forcing us back under a cluster of tall and tightly packed trees.

We didn't wait for the deluge to lighten before we got under way. Our soaked clothes, combined with the wet vegetation, made the hiking even more difficult than the walk up had been. On the path, we saw that the little trail flowed like a brook. The rain and wind now came down on us full force, no longer slowed by the high canopy. Even on the descent, we had to pause repeatedly to give ourselves a chance to catch our breaths and to rebalance our day packs of camera gear. We were muddy messes long before we hit the river at the bottom.

The porters paused to remove their gum boots before wading across, but I didn't even break stride. I was already thoroughly soaked. I dropped my pack on the far shore and came back to help Susan Miller, who had gamely proceeded in on her own, while the porters helped Linda. We headed up the last few hundred meters. It was just 2:30 p.m.

We shook hands all around, tipped the porters, and piled, wet and steaming, into one vehicle. Ten minutes later, at the stairs below camp, Augustus, the camp manager, bless him, met us with both umbrellas, which were superfluous now, and the promise of hot showers, a godsend.

The rain stopped before five that evening. Our little group gathered for a drink by the fire, from which an irregular column of blue smoke circled continually, dousing us each in turn with its pungent odor. I blew on it to get it going until I was dizzy, and the waiter took over after me. Still the smoke belched forth. Exasperated, I got one of the paraffin lanterns from the dining tent and poured the contents of its fuel tank on the damp wood. One match — *whoosh* — and we had instant fire. "Liquid kindling," I said, and went back to my canvas chair. The fire settled down to burn contentedly. Augustus and I had arranged for a local women's group to come and dance for us. I had seen them three times before and admired the emotion and spirit they put into the local dances they demonstrated. Their paid performance for us would help the women become a bit more financially independent, an idea that went down well with everybody, with the possible exceptions of their husbands. At 5:30, right on time, they came trooping up the stairway in matching T-shirts and *kangas,* babies still strapped on their backs.

The thirty-some women formed a half circle on the far side of the fire. Some took their quiet babies and laid them on the grass nearby, but others paid no attention to the pre-toddlers tied to their backs as they began to dance. The drums and the high lilting voices rang clearly in the cold, wet air. Their movements, some charged with power, others more undulating, always had a seductive element to them. We leaned forward, spellbound. During the dancing, I turned to see that the camp staff, all men, had slipped away from their duties to stand behind us. They couldn't help but join in the singing.

Bob had been taking a steady stream of photographs and motion clips of the proceedings on his digital camera. The noise in the camp had reached quite a pitch, and still Linda had not come from her tent to join the mob of us. Her tent, number 8, was the closest tent to where the women were dancing and she could not avoid hearing the drumming and singing. Maybe she was still recovering from the day's trekking.

The fourth dance was a drastic change from the first three, with a new element of aggression and power. The women acted out throwing spears and clubbing one another, some attacking, others collapsing to the ground. Some faces grew ferocious, others scared. I leaned back and asked one of the kitchen men what this was about. He explained we were watching a "war party" defending itself from a raiding tribe from Rwanda. Finally, only one old and very aggressive woman was left alone, circling the fire, celebrating her victory.

The next dance began, which was more like the earlier dances, with one woman starting the singing and the motion, and all the rest joining in and mimicking her. Then several women came forward, took both Susan Miller and Susan Studd by the hand, and led them to the circle by the fire. To their everlasting credit they both joined in, not only without a second thought, but also with enthusiasm. The Ugandans were screeching with laughter, prompting Bob to take even more photographs.

Thirty minutes later, after all the women, white and black, had danced together, with the two Susans swept into the steps and singing along, the performance finally wound down as the darkness rapidly encompassed us all. I thanked the women and tried to explain that they should gather around Bob's computer to see the pictures of themselves. A lot was lost in the translation, but soon Bob was surrounded by sweating women as he loaded up his laptop.

Bob, ever the Intel techie, was in his element. It was great, I thought, that he now had a chance to share his expertise with a culture so different in a world so infinitely far from Portland. A smile stretched across his face as the first picture illuminated the screen. I couldn't see anything from where I was, but I could tell by the laughter and the squealing that the women had beheld themselves. Bob disappeared in a turbulent sea of sweaty green T-shirts. Every thirty seconds or so, another marveling cry rose in the darkness as another image materialized before the dancers.

Rob came around to the front side of the screen in an attempt to get shots on his camera of the women viewing themselves as they danced across the screen in fifteen-second flurries. It was priceless, the ultimate Intel commercial. Here, literally on the edge of the Impenetrable Forest, with no electricity for miles, a group of native dancers were hugging and laughing with people to whom they could not even speak, all made possible by the magic of a computer.

Tragically, those photos would all be lost by 6:45 the following morning. But that was to be the cheapest of the horrible losses that occurred at dawn.

Finally, reluctantly, the women departed and we turned toward the dining tent where a dinner of roasted chicken awaited us. Linda joined us, and we celebrated the dancing and our encounter with the gorillas. I was deeply satisfied to see that Bob was happy about being able to share something with the women's group.

We sat by the fire after dinner, finishing off the wine and staring up at a huge yellow-orange moon that had risen directly over the ridge before us. I could easily see the scarecrow silhouettes of the trees that stood in a guardian row on the ridgeline. The forest was black and silent but I felt its nearness and its size, and both comforted me.

Tomorrow morning we were to trek after the gorillas again. Rob and Susan departed hand in hand, with an over-the-shoulder call of "good night." Bob and Susan would never see them alive again.

March 1, 1999, 6:30 a.m.

I heard the footfalls of the tent man long before he reached my veranda, and before he could speak I called out, asking him to bring the hot coffee inside, which he did quietly. To my surprise, the snowy-headed robin was not bothered by the man's approach and kept up his warbling scales. I was surprised, too, that it was still dark — too dark, I thought, until I remembered that in Uganda we were much farther west than Kenya or Tanzania. Out of habit, I checked my watch. It was precisely 6:30, so we were right on schedule. A few minutes later I was sitting on the veranda outside my tent, listening to the robin, waiting for the colobus monkeys to begin their rollicking calls.

As I inhaled the predawn air, I heard a loud crack. I took it to be the splitting of a huge tree trunk before it tilted and crashed to the forest floor. But why had no colobus or chimpanzee sounded an alarm, the normal response to such a shattering of the peace?

It was quiet again, but then a second and third *crack* split the still air, followed by a staccato volley. I was listening hard now. I knew what rifle shots sounded like; I had heard too many in Uganda fourteen years earlier, when I was photographing the civil war. More shots followed, sporadically, some so close that they ripped through the air instead of whistling or resonating within it.

I grabbed my shoes and ran down the path to the kitchen and dining tents. "What's going on?" Rob Haubner asked me as he ran out of his tent.

"I don't know. Stay put. You and Susan get under cover."

I started jogging down the path. A man appeared some thirty yards below me on the path, striding rapidly in my direction. He happened to be silhouetted by a luminous arc of predawn light shining through a hole in the forest canopy. I saw the bright flash from his raised rifle and heard a single bullet slap through the leaves with a sound like an amplified zipper.

I immediately raised my arms straight up, slowed to a fast walk, and continued down the trail toward a small-framed black man, about twenty years old, bearing a machine gun. I needed to appear harmless, submissive, and nonthreatening. Dressed in gum boots and a fatigue jacket, he had to be a thief, I thought, and the closer I got with my hands in the air, the less reason he would feel to shoot again. I needed him to know who I was.

The man remained motionless, machine gun raised; no words were exchanged as I reached him. Our eyes met briefly; his were flat and cold. The nightmare had begun.

2

Arrival at Last

All field biologists who deal with mammals deal with death; it comes with the job. Or in my case, it came with the love and interest that brought me to this continent in the first place. Long before I was kidnapped and endured an ordeal that led to ten murders, I knew the differences among dying, killing, and murder. Africa, unlike most of the Western world, continually throws these three in your face.

As surprising as it may at first sound, most of my safari guests desire not just to watch lions and cheetahs, but actually to witness them make a kill. They seek to find the predatory feline, follow the stalk, watch the chase, see the prey get taken down, and, yes, die. When you encounter other safari groups during a trip, or get together with them back in Los Angeles or New York, if they saw (or better yet, photographed) a kill taking place, you will hear the full and often gory story.

Neither I nor my guests are bloodthirsty people. We do, however, yearn to be amazed by the astounding eyes, ears, legs, and jaws of the predator at full speed, doing what they were designed to do. That spectacle can only be beheld when they are making their living by killing. The killing scenes I lead my guests to witness, with crocodiles in the Grumeti River, with the lions at Ngorongoro, with the cheetahs at Lake Ndutu, can be difficult to watch, but life is sustained by the bodies of the wildebeest and buffalo and zebra. In the end, we leave those savage scenes with feelings of awe and even respect: predation is the way of that world, and its purpose — simple survival — is pure and blameless. Lions and crocodiles are not keeping score; they are not chalking up victories; they are not laughing. The murders in Uganda, like all other instances around the world of terror perpetrated for despicable purposes of personal and political justification and gain, leave us feeling very differently.

If you live in Africa, you see human death. I encounter a dead body somewhere here on an almost weekly basis. Some have died sad, slow, and painful deaths bathed in malarial sweat. Another death might have been the bloody and anachronistic killing of a poor street thief who stole a ten dollar necklace, was caught, and then beaten to death on the spot. Such mob justice occurred over three hundred and fifty times last year in Kenya, the country I live in, and those are just the ones that were reported.

I have seen killing; I long to see it on every safari and have studied it since childhood. But now I have also seen murder, the senseless execution of human beings by members of their same species. The memory of murder allows me, even now, only three or four hours of sleep a night. I have thought nothing of sleeping on the bare ground in the Serengeti, the Maasai Mara, or Samburu, yet still I am unable to return to the forests of Uganda, because of the murders there that became such a part of my life. The difference is in the dying.

Several years ago I began organizing my notes and my tens of thousands of photographs, and I wrote a proposal for a book about the life and times of a flying safari guide in Africa. As a guide and teacher I wanted to share my experiences of safaris and the unique impact of Africa on the guests who traveled with me, and I wanted to write about the problematic future faced by the large mammals, the predators in particular.

Then, over the course of one brutal day — March 1, 1999 — everything changed.

The atrocities that occurred that day made headlines the world over and the repercussions are still felt. Tourism, and not just in Uganda but in all of East Africa, was dealt a body blow. When and if it will fully recover no one knows. I, and the families and friends of those brutally murdered, must live with this loss for the rest of our lives. We survivors look back with fear, grief, and anger, unending and merciless anxiety, and in my case, at least, a kind of odd guilt. Why them? Why not me? What if . . . ?

A few weeks after the tragedy I returned to the bush alone, in Kenya. When I crept into my tent for the night the terror was overwhelming, forcing me back outside. I returned to lie on the ground beside the campfire, but sleep would not come. For six weeks I did not sleep a wink; and now, nearly two years later, I am still unable to sleep more than three hours straight.

I had come to Africa more than twenty years before partly for adventure, which I had found while living a life of close calls, many on the ground plus a few in the air.

I've trained myself to be imperturbable, and I've almost always succeeded. But now, placing a cup of coffee on the table on my blind side is not a good idea. When my cycle backfires I'm scared out of my wits. I cannot get that day and night in Uganda out of my mind, even for a few hours. The faces of my murdered friends join me every night.

Nine months to the day after the tragedy, I was sitting on the peak of Mount Kilimanjaro. My now-dead friends and I had decided long before that we would ring in the millennium on top of this highest peak in Africa, as our way of saying "thank you" to the continent and its people that we loved so much. After their deaths I thought that I would not be able to do the climb without them, but then I found the courage to do it, out of love for them. If I could not climb with my friends, I would climb alone and quiet.

I left Nairobi on my motorcycle on December 28 and drove down to the base of the mountain near the town of Marangu. I camped in the dense and damp forest, the following night in the moorlands above the tree line, and the night following that I was at the base of the crater itself. New Year's Eve was spent camped in the frozen crater.

Two hours before dawn on January 1, 2000, I stepped clear of my iced tent and was awed, as always, by the deep and endless indigo blue-black of the African night. My thermometer had bottomed out at ten below zero. As I turned to take in the partial moon hanging low in the western sky a brilliant shooting star streaked through the night. It seemed too good to be true, for purposes of the climb; but the Bushmen really do believe that a shooting star is the soul of a person dying and leaving this world for another, better, one.

In the bitter cold, I needed an hour to break my tiny camp, and then another forty-five minutes to trudge through the snow to reach the peak. I was on the summit just before the first hints of the first sunrise of the new era began lighting the low eastern sky. A band of clouds shrouded the Indian Ocean coast, as it does almost every morning at that time of year. Moments after taking a seat facing east I was freezing. My legs, resting on the iced-over rocks, felt like wooden clubs. Soon rays of sunlight began poking over the horizon. The glaciers and rocks of seventeen-thousand-foot Mount Kenya to the north glowed softly in the new light, and four hundred miles to the west pink thunderheads billowed tens of thousands of feet over Lake Victoria. Far below, the rest of the continent was still shrouded in darkness. For nine months I had bottled up my emotions but now I let go: I started to cry, and tears streamed down my face.

And now, this book, which is so different from the book I'd originally planned. Much of it, most of it, is still as I want: stories about the wonderful people and the extraordinary wildlife and land of East Africa, and the safaris themselves. But some of it must be otherwise.

I grew up on a wildlife refuge on the eastern shores of the Mississippi River in Illinois, but I cannot remember a time when I was not enthralled by Africa. My younger brother, Colin, and I would imagine that one particularly large rock was our indestructible Land Rover bouncing along the game tracks of the vast Serengeti Plain. The brother designated as game ranger for the day would jump off and wrestle to the ground the one who was the wildebeest, and then give the struggling animal an injection against some imaginary and rampant disease.

I disappeared into books like Laurens van der Post's classic, *The Lost World of the*

Kalahari, a chronicle of the search for the oldest aboriginal tribe in Africa, the legendary Bushmen, or San people. My ten-year-old imagination took it all in, gathered details that would stay with me forever. On Sunday night, the only night my curiously rigid family was allowed to watch our black-and-white Zenith, I waited for *Mutual of Omaha's Wild Kingdom*, with Dr. Marlin Perkins and his superman sidekick, Jim Fowler. Marlin and Jim didn't always take us to Africa, but they did go there a lot, and when they did it was heaven.

I knew that Africa was the only place on earth I could be truly happy, and twelve years later my dreams were finally realized. I made it to Africa as a college student studying wildlife biology, and shortly after graduating I moved to Kenya, where I've lived ever since. I taught secondary school in a small village, worked as a photographer and stringer for *Time* and *The New York Times*, conducted a steady stream of informal safaris for friends, acquired my pilot's license, and in 1986 began guiding wildlife safaris full-time. In my six-seater Cessna I flew my clients from camp to camp, park to park, in Kenya and Tanzania mainly, but I also led safaris in Zimbabwe, Botswana, and Uganda. This was *precisely* the life I had fantasized about as a young boy while playing my games of Africa.

In December 1977, when I stepped from the plane and first stood in the clear chill of the upcountry air outside Nairobi town, I was literally shaky with excitement. I had studied and dreamed about Africa for years, but those were *real* giraffes and gazelles in the whistling-thorn acacias that surrounded the old runway. Those were *real* antelopes scattering in front of us as we drove along the road toward our hotel, my pounding heart wanting to race right along with them. Minutes after arriving at the hotel, which was miles from town, I was off down the road, binoculars around my neck, bird book in my hand.

I was a twenty-one-year-old student finishing my major and traveling with a group of students who would study for the winter quarter with Judy and Mike Rainy, Americans who had moved to Kenya just before independence in 1963 and ran a multidisciplinary program in-country for a number of universities. Two days after the plane touched down we set off for the semipermanent camp that our teachers had set up on the northern boundary of the Maasai Mara Reserve, west of Nairobi and near the border with Tanzania. They took turns driving one of the Mercedes trucks, while their Samburu partner, Pakwo, was behind the wheel of the other. Pakwo was an impressive sight for the newly arrived students, with his dull-red *shuka* wrapped around him and his *rungu*, a throwing club carved from an especially hard tree root, propped beside his seat. The backs of the two trucks were open to the wind, the weather, and the world. Outside, everything was new to me, but after all the television programs and books I'd absorbed over the years, it also felt completely familiar. My boy's eyes had turned out to be almost frighteningly accurate. The birds that now startled from the bush or soared lazily overhead were generally known to me, and those I could not recognize came from families that I had already studied, so I could easily key them out in my field guide.

We camped that first evening by the Mara River, where I got my first sweet taste of safari tents, which were nothing like the backpacking pup tents I was used to. My parents were teachers, and we had camped every summer since I was three or four years old in the mountains of Wyoming. We didn't stay in motels or lodges, not even on the drive out from Illinois. We cached food for one or two months of hiking and climbing. By the time I was seven I had climbed the second-highest peak in Wyoming, and being under canvas was the most natural thing in the world to me. But these tents on the banks of the Mara River were circus-huge, and the cots with blankets were civilized compared to the sleeping bags and hard ground of Wyoming.

The Mara River is a magical band of red-brown water that hasn't changed at all in the quarter century I've lived in Africa. Its banks are still overgrown and overhung with fig and acacia trees, with thick groves of olive, croton, and euclea growing between them. Untamed rivers are always mysterious and inviting to me, the Mara even more so because of the dark shroud of vegetation that cloaks both shores. Crocodiles or not, the Mara begged to be explored, and that very first night in the bush I gave in to temptation. That first night I also learned a crucial lesson for Africa: around wildlife, ignorance is no excuse.

I knew that all the hippopotamuses we had seen during the day, eye-deep in the river, would be coming out at night to graze, and the only way to photograph their entire bodies was to catch them away from the river during their nightly forays. I was also aware that they are very dangerous in that situation, so my photography session would require a bit of stalking. (Years later I know that while hippos can indeed be dangerous, their reputation as the animal responsible for the most deaths in Africa is perhaps misleading. Quite a few of those deaths result from an accidental collision between a fisherman in a boat and a submerged hippo. If the fisherman then drowns, his death is attributed to a hippo attack, which is not quite true. In Africa, death in an encounter with an animal is almost always the result of human error, if not folly.)

I put the flash on my camera before going to sleep, in anticipation of my waking up at some point, as I always do, and then heading out into the dark to find and photograph these two-ton nocturnal grazers. I had no plan beyond that, but it seemed complete enough. At 1:30 a.m. I woke up, and five minutes later I was walking up the riverbank, wading through the damp grass that was as tall as I was, barefoot and clad only in my underwear, which shone too brightly in the moonlight.

I stopped and listened, and I could hear

the steady and surprisingly fast munching of at least two hippos as they grazed somewhere ahead of me. In the moonlight I could also just make out some large rocks, somewhere near the hippos. I decided to get up on top of one of those rocks, and from that vantage, safe from hippo ivory, I could take my sweet time and get the shots I wanted. I pushed on through the dense grass, jumping high to relocate the rocks, then crouching a bit low for no particular reason. Twenty yards on, I stopped and listened again. Now the massive, mashing, noisy jaws of the hippos were almost right in front of me, but still hidden from my sight. A jump revealed the rocks very close by, slightly to my left. I angled in their direction, but when I reached where they should be, they weren't there. I jumped again and saw them to my right.

I was the new kid on the block, but it finally dawned on me with a sickening reality that the two smooth boulders I had planned to use as observation posts were in fact the smooth and slightly arched backs of the hippos I had hoped to observe. I made the first good decision of the night. With slow steps and racing heart I retreated to my tent, entering quietly enough not to awaken my tent mate. I didn't want to explain my unwise expedition.

The following days were exactly what I had always known they would be. We were only the second group of students in Mike and Judy's charge, but you could never have convinced me of that. I was overwhelmed by their mastery of the territory around the park, and by their ability to teach. Mike was a biologist who really knew his "backyard" and could teach anyone about it. He was a *field* man, not a lab or classroom man. Every day he and Judy had us out on the tracks and trails before the sun rose over the multihued, greenish peaks of the Loita Hills. We drove, stopped to scan the wide grasslands, then moved on to the next likely viewpoint. Every morning, we came across some feline predator, whether cheetah, leopard, or lion, within the first thirty minutes of our expedition. Mike had written his dissertation on one of the gorgeous antelopes of the savannah, but he was also an expert on the predators, and the lions were his favorites. He had cataloged most of them in the reserve and knew their territories, groupings, birthing cycles, and hunting preferences. We learned about the unique whisker pattern and ragged ear notches that are used to identify each cat. (A chart of the notches is called an ear-clock.)

These were not just generic lions. Moshe Dayan was the huge male with one eye (hence his name), the dominant male of the Miti Miwili pride, and the female over there was Sheeba, who gave birth in late September to the three cubs that were now harassing Moshe. The other two cubs were age-mates, but of a different mother, Mfupi. She was always shy of the trucks and stayed well back in the croton, but she did allow her cubs to run with Sheeba's. Mike knew who liked to sit near whom, which female tolerated which cubs that weren't her own, who paired up for the hunts. He could even tell his students, as any given hunt progressed, which lion would use what technique and what cover to get near the selected prey. In school I had studied the lion's social system, but in the wild it was even more defined than I had anticipated. Africa was the most astounding classroom I could imagine, Mike's illuminations held me spellbound, and he ran safaris for a living. That point was not lost on me.

After an incredible week, we pulled out of the Mara camp and headed hundreds of miles north to Samburuland, where Mike and Judy lived. Our camp there, set classically beneath umbrella acacias, was very different from the lush landscape of the Mara. This was semi-desert, and though the bush buzzed with life, it was generally of a smaller scale than the large herds of antelopes encountered farther south. The birds, especially, fascinated me as we drove through the great and sandy Samburu Reserve. Mike and Judy were as comfortable and at ease here, among the rising mountains and flat deserts, as any Samburu born and raised in this ostensibly inhospitable country. Mike spoke Maa, the language of the Maasai and the Samburu, and he and Judy had eventually even had their son circumcised in the traditional Samburu ceremony. I knew almost immediately that they lived and worked the way I wanted to live and work. Everything about the land, its wildlife, and their way of life was working its inexorable power on me.

The Ewaso Ngiiro River flowed through the parched land, bisecting the adjoining reserves of Samburu and Buffalo Springs. Its ribbon of red-brown water was also a ribbon of life. The doum palms and acacia elatior lining the banks sheltered miles of wildlife as well. Reticulated giraffes, Grévy's zebras, beisa oryx, and elephant after elephant all crowded into the green shade by the dark water as we watched. On the game drive one morning I suddenly realized that a face had been staring out at me from the center of a saltbrush bush. By the time I had run across the truck bed and pounded on the cab roof we were forty yards past what I had seen. Michael's head appeared out the right window and craned up to look at me. I excitedly told him that we had just passed a hidden cheetah. He questioned the sighting, but I stuck by my call and convinced him to back up the heavy truck.

We could see nothing in the bush, but I kept watching, and Michael was a patient teacher; a few seconds later the spotted face raised up in exactly the same gap in the bush. Michael saw it instantly and gave me a long smile. I think, looking back, that this was the moment our relationship changed. In the following weeks he would frequently ask me to do this, go there, or remain behind while he took the group on ahead. And then one morning he tossed me the keys to the Land Rover, and my life was forever changed.

My instructions were to get out of camp and not come back until night. Beyond that, I was on my own and told nothing.

"But I don't know the park, Michael!"

"No, you don't."

"I'll end up lost out there for sure."

"Yes, you will. Just take a lot of drinks along, and get out of camp. Take Tad and Phil with you if you want, or go alone. But be gone." He turned back to the dining tent, his baggy shorts making his legs look spindly and bowed. He called over his shoulder, "Make it back tonight, no matter what."

I tore to my tent to get my camera and enough film for the day. I forgot everything except my field guides to the mammals and the birds and my ever-present binoculars, hanging like a medallion of honor around my neck. Suntan lotion, hat, water bottle, and jacket were superfluous items and remained behind. I then ran to Tad and Phil's tent. They mobilized in seconds while I ran for the kitchen, grabbed a handful of bananas, a box of biscuits, and half a dozen bottles of soda water, and bounded for the Land Rover. Of course I didn't know how to drive the 4 x 4, with its wrong-sided steering wheel and gearshift, but no matter. I headed straight for the wide and winding Ewaso Ngiiro River. In this dry, semi-arid region, the wildlife would be forced to concentrate along its shores. That's where the action would have to be.

We were still several miles away from the river when we came upon a herd of elephants that required our investigation. From watching Michael, I knew better than to drive straight into them, so I slowed and approached at an angle, like a sailboat tacking upwind. From the swinging heads and occasional soft trumpeting blast, we knew that the elephants were aware of our presence, but they continued to feed on the acacias, so I kept easing the Land Rover closer. Soon the elephants were all around us. I left the driver's seat and joined Tad and Phil on the roof.

For thirty minutes or more, the elephants fed as we took pictures and whispered among ourselves. Suddenly one female, a small baby underneath her, ripped a trumpeting blast and charged us hard from fifty yards.

I had no idea why she was charging and waited a few seconds, thinking it was probably just a threat, as Michael had told us so many elephant charges are. There are exceptions to every rule, however, and this female was charging onward, smashing through the flimsy acacias. Phil and Tad were yelling at me to drive away, so I shot back down through the roof hatch, and I reached for the starter lever. I couldn't find it. Hell, I couldn't even locate the steering wheel. In my rushed descent I had forgotten the Land Rover was the right-hand drive model. Phil and Tad were yelling at me to go, but I wasn't even in the correct seat yet. When I tried to scramble across the bench I was held up momentarily by the tall gearshift lever, and when I was finally positioned behind the wheel, the truck wouldn't start. Absolute silence from the vehicle. As the yelling from the roof reached fever pitch, the starter finally engaged, the engine fired, and the clutch dropped in the same instant. I heard two solid crashes when Phil and Tad went flying backward as the 4 x 4 went flying forward. The looming elephant I never saw. A few hundred yards down the track I stopped, tears in my eyes, laughing uncontrollably, and turned to face the others, who were also out of control.

When we'd calmed down to the point of breathing I said, "The book says elephants can run twenty-five miles an hour. Let's go back and find out."

There was a fair amount of serious protesting, but it gradually died down as I started backing up.

"I'll keep the motor running and stay behind the wheel this time. You guys just tell me when to hit it and I'll floor it. We'll try and keep her close and see what she can do."

"Oh my God!" Tad said. "We're all going to die."

Phil joined in. "This is it. I can't believe we're going back."

But they were both laughing softly as they got their cameras ready. The elephants hadn't moved, and seemed to have forgotten the commotion of a few minutes before. They were off breaking branches and stripping them of thorns and leaves, destroying just about everything in their peaceful manner.

I identified our female almost dead center in the group, her back to us, her baby just behind her. I stopped for a second in order to go up through the roof hatch to look for a route back toward her, and a route out. The only obstacle in my path was a red termite mound. I sat back down, nudged the gear into reverse. The boys grew quiet, and I tried to keep the engine running quietly as I skirted the termite mound and bounced over a dead log I hadn't seen. At the crunching sound the old female turned halfway toward us but kept chewing on the strip of bark stuck in her mouth.

I eased back another sixty feet and held up. With the engine running, I came up through the roof, camera in hand. It all seemed quiet as I drew down on the old female and brought her into focus, but just as her rumpled skin became clear in my viewfinder, she charged. Phil and Tad, in unison, yelled "Go!" I stayed behind the camera and brought the focus way forward. I had been shooting wildlife for years and had learned how to focus "closer" than a running subject and then to fire the shutter as the subject ran into focus. I waited, finger lightly on the shutter release, while Phil and Tad yelled. I took the shot as the elephant "snapped" into focus, spun around and dropped to the seat, mashed the vehicle into first, and we were safely away. I kept it going hard, changed into second, and turned back over my left shoulder to see what was happening. The female was still coming fast. The speedometer showed twenty miles an hour, and I held it there, wanting the elephant to close the space between us. I was afraid that if she wasn't right on us she would break off the chase early and we'd never get a reading on her speed.

I looked back again and saw her bulk right behind us, and Phil's voice was coming in loud and clear over the noise of the truck and the trumpeting elephant. I gunned the accelerator, then backed off as the needle touched 25. The truck jolted hard, followed by a crashing sound and flying glass. I stood on the pedal and we skipped off the edge of the termite mound and ran crazily out onto the smooth sand of the track.

When I looked back the elephant was not in sight, and Tad was rubbing his head, shards of glass sparkling on his shoulders. Phil had a death grip on the back of my seat as he crouched and looked behind us, bits of glass on his shirt. I could figure out none of this and slowed to an easy speed. "What happened?!"

Phil showed me the damage: the elephant had caught up with the Land Rover, reached out with her powerful trunk and simply torn off the bumper. She had then thrown it at us, shattering one rear window. "Well," I said, "either the book or the speedometer is wrong."

I read a passage from my guidebook out loud that stated that impalas, when chased by a hunting predator, can jump ten feet in the air and sail thirty feet or more horizontally. Later, we drove in on a bachelor herd of some twenty impalas. They looked peaceful in their big-eyed silence, but then stiffened and bunched closer at our approach. Antelopes are not nearly as intimidating as elephants, making bravery easier to come by, so I pulled closer. Tad and Phil raised their lenses, and on the count of three I revved the engine and we whooped and yelled, someone slamming a flat palm against the truck's roof. The impalas did fly off, an incredible sight from such close range, and I took off after them with the accelerator to the floor, only to fall steadily behind as they bounded off in high and suspended flight and entered the taller grass. Tall grass often signifies an increase in ground moisture. The extra water is what allows the plants to grow to the greater height. A spring, a small rivulet, or even a narrow river can supply the moisture. This can be true in the desert as well as in the savannah, but I didn't know this yet. Suddenly we, too, were airborne, but going *down,* not skyward like the impalas. We also hit a great deal harder than they do, hard enough, in fact, to badly bend a tie-rod.

Phil and Tad were mad at me again, but

I simply hadn't seen the river, and I pointed out that they from their elevated perches hadn't either. After three tries we got the Land Rover back up to dry ground. There we dismounted and stretched out by the river and waded in the shallow and surprisingly cool sandy water, taking turns on "croc watch." I sat back, tilted my head up, and ran my eyes up and down a doum palm, studying the cluster of orange fruit high up where the leaves blossomed outward. I listened to the birdcalls I already knew and tried to memorize the new voices that cut through the hot air. Downstream a herd of oryx tentatively approached the far bank. I watched as they finally got down on their knees and put their tan muzzles to the flat water and drank. I would have to remember to ask Michael about this herd behavior, too.

As I concentrated on the sounds alone, it dawned on me that this bush radiated with a life of its own, always humming, buzzing, clicking, whistling. Insects and birds filled the air to bursting with their songs and voices — a beautiful symphony. I had spent a great deal of my life out-of-doors, but this was the first time I had ever focused so keenly on just the sounds of a wild place. It has since become a lifelong habit I treasure, one I practice every opportunity I get. I can have a wonderful day *listening*, never seeing an animal larger than an unstriped ground squirrel. I try to induce in every client on my safaris the same appreciation. A long time passed and I was overwhelmed with the peace of feeling so small and so safe in so grand a place.

But where were we? Leaving camp, we had tried to keep up with landmarks and twists and turns, but that had proved hopeless as a method of navigation. After all the chasing around, all I knew was that camp was downstream and several miles away from the river, somewhere out there in the heat-dancing distance. After an hour or so, we stumbled back and found Mike standing by the other trucks, waiting. For some time, he had seen our white dust cloud winding its way haphazardly but ever toward him. He didn't have to ask how the day had gone, for just a quick look at our faces told the story. I waited for a few minutes of excited talk to die down before I pointed to the rear window, apologizing. Mike just shook his head and laughed loudly, as we explained how it had happened. Pakwo had walked up and joined in with his typically understated Samburu laugh, almost childlike in its enthusiasm.

When the other students appeared, my gang low-keyed it. That night I took my cot out of the tent and dragged it under the nearest umbrella acacia, where the bright light of the moon cast a wedding-dress-lace of shadow through the sparsely leafed trees, a pattern so fine and delicate and dimly lit it could not be photographed, but only smiled upon and committed to memory. I lay back and listened long into the inky-indigo night, thinking about the elephants and wondering what they were doing, how they lay or stood as they slept. A hyena called from somewhere down-stream and near the trees by the river. Deeply satisfied, I slept long and well, still waking before dawn but not before the calling doves.

After another week, our mobile class-room pushed north out of the Samburu Reserve proper and farther into the terri-tory officially designated as the Northern Frontier District. The road got bumpier and drier and the country got tougher, more parched in the dry areas and more rugged in the mountainous ones. There was no electricity up here, no towns, no commerce, and even few villages. The NFD, as it was locally known, conjured images of wandering bands of Somali *shifta* (bandits), camel-running Samburu, cattle rustling, and open warfare. All of which, I would learn, was sporadically true. The white caliche dust swirled up behind the truck's "duals" and swept over those of us sitting in the back. We slowly turned a ghostly white, from head to foot. It seemed the perfect way to be entering these notorious badlands. We were earning our stripes.

Our destination up north was Mike and Judy's permanent camp, where we were greeted in the heat of the afternoon by the amazingly dressed Samburu going about their various tasks, or no tasks at all. In their red and blue, purple and white cloth and their wide necklaces they looked like brilliant Christmas ornaments against the dull greenery of the tents. They were to be our hosts for the next few days in their own cow-dung *bomas*. I was worried about my inability to speak their language, but otherwise I was ready to go when Mike introduced the students to our respective hosts. As we had been taught to do, I respectfully held my own wrist as Ole Sempele's long and powerful fingers gripped my hand and held it awhile. After barely a word between us, Sempele hoisted my day pack and started off on his slim and skinny legs with long, springy, ground-eating strides. His brother Kasoi accompanied us with similar legs and stride. I hustled on my short legs to keep up.

Not a word was attempted for the next few hours as we walked hard across the baked ground toward the hills on the northern horizon, with a half-domed mountain, Neibor Keju, a striking landmark to the west. At the base of the hills we entered a woodland of low acacias and thick bushes. Now Sempele said something to me, but I didn't understand what he was trying to communicate, so I just nodded and we walked on across another plain, much smaller than the one we had just crossed. I could see on the far side tiny plumes of blue smoke rising from behind a wall of thorn branches. It was Sempele's *manyatta,* or village. Just then a cluster of small forms slipped through the wall and started running toward us.

Only when the children reached us did my Samburu guides finally stop walking for a moment. They touched each youngster on the top of the head when the little ones bowed forward. Then we all started off again, our pace finally a bit slower. A few children held hands with the men, and a tiny set of slim black fingers crept into my hand, too. In my childhood home in Illinois, even out camping in the mountains during the summers, there had been no such touching, so I was extremely uncomfortable holding hands even with a small Samburu boy who was only seven or eight years old. But I managed a loose grip until we reached the settlement, where I stood somewhat awkwardly to one side as my hosts greeted all the adults in turn, not stopping their rolling conversation as every child in the place eventually presented his or her head to be touched. The little ones stood stock still until the hand was placed on their heads, but the second it was removed they shot off like bolts of black lightning.

I shook hands all around and followed my hosts into their hut. Coming inside from the strong light of the afternoon equatorial sun, I was completely blind. It was pitch black within the dung walls. Minutes went by before my eyes could make out anything in the smoke-filled interior of my temporary home, and I was startled a few minutes later when I looked over and saw an ancient face framed by beaded ears gazing serenely at me. I instinctively extended my hand and was startled again by the force of the grip that returned my greeting. It was Sempele's mother, whose age no one knew. She had been born in the year that the calves died, this was all that was known. Dying calves, I would realize later, are hugely significant to a pastoral people whose very existence is cattle, but for now the description just added to the mystique I was experiencing.

Tea was prepared over the tiny fire that idled silently in the middle of the hut. In spite of the stifling heat, the hot and smoky liquid, thick with fresh milk and sugar, was incredibly refreshing. It brought a dew of sweat to my skin, but if I relaxed completely and held still, I cooled down. The cup was taken from my hands the moment it was empty, to be refilled and offered again. The second serving was even more refreshing and cooling than the first. Sempele gently proffered a thick banded blanket and tugged briefly on my hand before he bent low and shuffled out of the hut and into the bright and smokeless sky. I shook hands with the old woman, nodding and saying thank you as I returned the enamel cup to her withered hands, and followed her son outside. Sempele then led me outside the *boma*, weaving through the cow dung to a position to the left of the gap that served as a gate in the thornbranch wall. His black eyes gazed toward the south, where I saw nothing significant enough to merit his rapt attention. I could, however, barely hear the distant *gonging* and *tinkling* of hollow bells.

Blankets thrown around our shoulders, we stood in the silence and the coming cool for fifteen or twenty minutes before a narrow white line emerged from the trees on the far side of the small plain. As it extended onto the open ground, it broke into numerous dots of varying color. Cattle, I realized, and sheep and goats, all gently driven by four or five boys no older than seven. Sempele and I watched their approach in silence, and I was amazed at how the line fanned out as it crossed the plains, only to funnel back to a single file as it neared the *manyatta*. As the herd filed before us, passing into the corral inside the thorn fence, Sempele studied each animal in turn. The goats and sheep hardly seemed worthy of his gaze, but not a cow went by unnoticed. Once the last young bull had passed through the gap we followed them, leaving the cut tree that would "close" the gate lying on the ground outside. As we circulated among the standing, steaming cattle that were the family wealth, Sempele pulled on a leg here to examine a lower foot, twisted a head by the horns there to look at an eye. Each beast submitted mutely to his touch, making no effort to move off. Two women began to milk two of the cows, directing the thin white jets directly into an old calabash gourd burnished by years of milking hands.

The light was fading fast now, and I needed some clean air after the smell of smoke and dried dung had assaulted me for so long. I signaled to Sempele that I was going for a stroll and indicated with my wristwatch a thirty-minute sweep. I draped my blanket over the fence as I walked through the gate. I was five minutes beyond the *manyatta* before I left the smoke and cow odor behind me and suddenly stepped back into the untouched desert air of the north. It was like passing through an invisible wall. A low, blue-gray haze hung above the plains and trees, the suspended moisture gathering in the cooling air and scattering the low sunrays, as if a pale gauze dressing was about to be draped over the surrounding land.

Returning to the *manyatta* I found the cattle settled peacefully, their widespread girths touching hide to hide in the crowded enclosure, their sweet smell ascending. The wind had died and the descending moist air seemed to be taking the strong smells to ground with it, for the odors were not so overpowering now. Or maybe I was already becoming comfortable with the new environment. I couldn't see Sempele, so I turned to the left and called "hodi" before ducking down to enter his hut. My eyes didn't need to adjust as much this time, so I didn't have to embarrass myself by mutely standing there. I took a tiny wooden seat and sat mutely instead. Sempele poured me a cup of tea and handed it directly over the flames to me. I could smell the sparse hair on his arm burning, but he ignored the sensation, if he felt it at all.

The tea was followed by a larger enameled mug full of a curdled mixture of blood and milk. I have a tough stomach and knew better than to decline the dish, but it still took a closed nose and a hard head to get started on the pink yogurtlike mixture. It got easier after the first few swallows, and I was able to finish the mug with gusto, and Sempele grinned widely as I handed the cup back to him empty. I was afraid he might fill it again, but I was let off the hook and received sweet tea instead.

I listened carefully as he and the others slowly discussed matters of importance to them — cattle, grass, rain, and women, as I learned later, and in that order. Their voices filled the round space with the soft and rolling sounds of the Maa language, which sounds somewhat like Spanish, somewhat like gentle white water. The warmth of the hut, my very full stomach, tired legs, and the exciting day had my head dropping and snapping back to attention before the slowly dying fire. Two other men Sempele's age entered the home and the conversation picked up for half an hour, until suddenly it was time to sleep. Without a word to me, Sempele and the other two men moved onto a raised section of the floor, wrapped their blankets around themselves, and then lay backward, legs straight out, arms crossed over their chests like Egyptian mummies.

I stared for a while at the three tiny pieces of wood that burned so economically. Three young boys stole in quietly and lay down. I wasn't sure what to do next, so I crawled over and lay down on the opposite side of the raised pallet from the other three men. I was too hot with the blanket over me, so I used it as a pillow for a while, figuring the small room would cool down eventually. I felt cramped and woke up repeatedly, but I slept fairly well until exactly 2:15, when a confusing flurry of voices and movement and dancing flashlights roused everyone. The fire was kicked into gear and threw a horror-film light over the chaotic scene. Sempele grabbed his *rungu* and his spear, paused to look at me and say, in English, "Lion!" and followed the kids outside.

Lions. I couldn't believe my good fortune, and ducked out into the night. The corral was a confused and rushing mass of man and beast, charging back and forth. I stayed against the wall of the *boma* for fear of being either trampled by a cow or speared or shot with an arrow by a Samburu adolescent in his quest for everlasting glory. Then Sempele was standing directly in front of me, though I hadn't seen him approaching. In English, *good* English, he told me that a single male lion had jumped onto the roof of one of the huts that was built into the thornbranch wall. From there he had dived down into the terrified herd, locating a calf before he was forced back by the overwhelming Samburu. However, he had taken the calf with him when he charged straight back through the thornbranch wall. This had astounded even the seasoned Samburu. How brazen a lion, and how desperate as well. It was a high-risk way to make a living, as the calculating animal had to know.

Sempele gently turned me by my shoulder and propelled me toward the hut entrance. I didn't protest and led the way. Once inside a cup of tea was once again pushed upon me. Sempele talked with his mother, presumably relating the story of the stalk, the charge, and the miss. Soon Sempele returned to the pallet and his mummified position, and I did likewise, though sleep itself was distant. I lay in the warm silence and imagined the small boys running around in the moonless night, armed with spears far bigger than themselves and with arrows far smaller, knowing that a lion was somewhere near with a stolen kill.

In the morning, still wrapped in our blankets, Ole Sempele and I assumed our positions beside the *manyatta* gate and watched the same boys lead the long line of cattle and trailing smaller livestock back outside, across the plains, and into the bush on the far side, heading toward the larger plains beyond. Once they had all filed by, the men sat down to discuss the lion and examine the bull calf it had carried out through the thornbranch enclosure but then dropped. The mauled calf would be killed and eaten that night, since it looked highly doubtful that it would survive. The meat would be consumed in honor of the boys who had charged without hesitation into the night after the lion. Their intentionally raucous search among the herd had forced the predator to abandon its prey.

That evening we sat outside, quietly eating the roasted meat, the children solemnly accepting what was offered to them, and never reaching. If this was some sort of celebration it was a serious one, I thought. No laughter or spontaneity broke the quiet and composed faces. I ate my meat and drank my milky tea in silence too, watching the boys who never raised their eyes, marveling at a life so orderly, so clearly defined, so vastly different from my own. In just two days I already felt more sure and secure here than I had ever felt in my own house in Illinois as a child. I then realized how hard it would be to return to the United States, having stepped over the threshold and been welcomed into a world I knew I could treasure, no matter what it offered me.

3

The Welcome of the Bush

A wise man once said that the problem with visiting Africa is that you feel forever an exile after you have left. After my studies with Mike and Judy Rainy, I returned to the States and finished my B.S. in wildlife biology, along with a B.A. in secondary education. It was 1978, and I planned to teach or join the forest service as a biologist. First, though, I returned to the summer job I'd held for several seasons, fire fighting in the mountains of Washington and Montana. The following winter I built a mountain cabin for some friends. But Africa was always in the back of my mind, and after the fire-fighting season in 1979 I returned for a tour of West Africa that concluded abruptly when I took the night train from Abidjan back up to Ouagadougou, in Upper Volta (now Burkina Faso), and on to Timbuktu when it derailed. My back was broken in three places, my sternum was crushed and my skull fractured, and my right arm was badly burned and cut to shreds. Six months later, my body had healed just enough to allow me to join my fire-fighting crew in the summer of 1980.

The new season started off dramatically on May 18 with the explosion of Mount Saint Helens. The U.S. Forest Service, like all government-action bureaus, I suppose, has a manual for every contingency. For firefighters, a certain fuel type on a certain slope at a certain moisture content requires an exact attack, specific equipment. All of us had been to fire school, seen the films, and personally fought many types of fire, but the U.S. government had yet to write a manual for a volcano. It was a firefighter's dream come true, improvising fire-fighting techniques to contend with a volcano. Based out of Hood River, Oregon, for the first few weeks, we flew daily missions out to Saint Helens and took on whatever job we were assigned in whatever manner we saw fit. We worked seventeen-hour days, raked in hazard pay, overtime pay, per diem pay, and free room and board on top of it all. The volcano was a windfall for me and my team, and I got out of debt and well back into the black. It was the perfect time to acknowledge the inevitable and return to Africa for good. Under the auspices of the Peace Corps, I took a three-month immersion program in Kiswahili (the language of a small coastal tribe that was adopted as the de facto language of record when Kenya achieved independence from the British in 1963) and then taught science at the local school in Gakindu, in central Kenya, about eighty miles north of Nairobi.

For more than two decades, Kenya has been my home. Time and time again when I meet prospective clients during the planning stages of a safari I'm told that they have always, *always,* wanted to come to Africa, but they find it hard to explain why. In spite of its wars and poverty, Africa is a huge playground for adventure and discovery, and sometimes men (more rarely women) will cite this spirit of risk and danger and the lure of the big game. More often, though, and almost always with women, my guests acknowledge that in some recess of the heart they are drawn to this continent. There is the sense that Africa is basal *bedrock* in some deeper sense. It has a primal draw that may truly be genetically hardwired. I felt that way from the moment I stepped off the plane the first time, and most of my clients leave with the same feeling.

It is, of course, possible that my clients are different and self-selected in this regard. Of the roughly half million tourists who visit Kenya every year, three-quarters (most of them European) go straight to the beach hotels on the Indian Ocean and stay there. They are wonderful beaches, and Lamu and Mombasa and Malindi are fascinating towns, but they are not the heart of the real East Africa, which is upcountry and in the bush. Most of the tourists who do venture upcountry go the minibus route. I don't begrudge these safaris, by any means, because they are the only way many people will get even a taste of the real Africa. I just don't want to operate that way. I want it slower, deeper, more involved.

In the game parks, my group usually *is* the first out and the last in. The guards at the national parks in Kenya close the gates at sundown, and I eventually ran out of half-baked excuses for them when we kept pulling up an hour later. One day I started telling the truth, which, amazingly enough, worked much better. When I told the uniformed guards toting AK-47s that we were tardy because of a great cheetah chase we had watched, or because the light on the river had been too beautiful to pass up, they would charitably wave us through. My guests do put in the time in the field. We put in the time *on the ground,* literally. We get our knees dirty; we try to create our own luck. The bush or any wild place becomes alive and meaningful only when the information, issues, and events become personal, when you get to know and somewhat understand a given leopard or lion after hours of patient proximity. From the first day and the first observation, I slow down with my people. We'll be with the first cheetah we see for hours, unless he's fat and happy and punched out in the shade. If we find lions on the move in the morning or the evening, or playing with their young, that's where we'll spend our day. A herd of elephants that's not in transit? We'll stick around and see what develops.

At home we "read" our pets, and not just their moods. After years of living together, we can often predict when the dog or cat is going to roll over, yawn, jump onto the windowsill, or flop down to sleep. I've lived long enough with a host of African animals to know similar behavioral traits. I can almost always tell which cat is going to yawn, who is going to greet whom, and where they are going to lie down. It's not a magic trick, but the product of intimate, unending hours in the field, and it becomes the bread and butter of any professional guide.

On one occasion a few years ago my group was discussing this point as we bounced along a shaded road in Meru Park, a remote and relatively unvisited park northeast of Mount Kenya. At that very moment I noticed that the bush was suddenly still, as if on cue. I asked my driver on that safari, Kimani, to stop the truck. Without the rattling diesel, the bush was abnormally silent. Moreover, we had a small cluster of Grant's gazelles before us and a pair of Kirk's dik-diks almost beside us, and these ungulates were frozen as well. No one browsed or grazed, no one walked or lay down. Something was amiss, and I said so. The more I observed these prey species, the more convinced I became that there was a predator right beside us, somewhere. My searching induced everyone else to look. For minutes we didn't find anything, but this didn't change my convictions in the least. The gazelles stayed too tightly bunched, and the dik-diks neither bolted nor fed.

I asked Kimani to pull forward, thinking

that our view of the predator might have been blocked. The shift produced nothing new, despite all the probing eyes. Kimani returned the truck to its original position. Still nothing. I knew the group was getting frustrated and was probably thinking I was wasting time or showboating, but I just knew we were on top of something, so I begged for patience. I asked Kimani to pull for a second time around the cluster of trees beside us. Five minutes later I could fairly feel everyone's eyes boring into me. Frustrated, I decided to move on — but then I was interrupted by the high, sneezing alarm note of the two dik-diks. Everyone heard it, and they knew we were onto something. They looked at me, while I quietly explained that this sneeze was the dik-diks' alarm call and that we should look where the pair were staring. Only the diminutive antelopes were staring in two different directions, and neither sight line showed me anything.

A fallen log about twenty-five feet off the road drew my attention for the cover it provided. I followed its corrugated bark up and down and up again, but saw only the deadwood. Finally I got down off the roof, opened the door, and stepped onto the ground. "Just going to check this tree. I'll be right back," I said. All eyes followed me. When I was still fifteen feet from the tree a dark yellow explosion erupted before me as a large leopard launched himself from his hiding place alongside the tree trunk. Everyone got a brief view of his fleeing form. I was overjoyed.

Knowing when to stop requires more time in the field than something more "flashy," like picking out which individual wildebeest a charging lion is going to try and take down, or which gazelle is destined for the gaping jaws of a croc as it tries to swim the Grumeti River. The leopard sighting did not come about because of something I had read in a book or picked up from another guide. It was simply the result of years spent slow-dancing in sync with the habitat. Time in the field, and no end of patience, will get you what you're after. That, and a little luck.

Every predator selects his or her home territory for very particular reasons and needs to know it well in order to be successful at the killing game. Skills, knowledge, and genetic design are required for a predator to kill and live. A lion cannot just stroll out onto the Naabi Hill plains and make a living at killing. He will have to establish, mark, and maintain a territory to survive. He needs to know who's there and when, what geographical features he can use to his advantage, what encroaching competitors he may have to deal with or even kill. He need not have grown up in his chosen territory, but he will need to put in enough time to learn it intimately and to be aware of its continual changes. This approach works very well for me, too. I have to be out there enough to learn the *Who's Who* in the wildlife social roster of any given park or reserve. The big cats are not just scattered around at random. Each species has a carefully defined social structure that dictates, in the case of the leopards and the lions, a ferociously defended network of territories. (Cheetahs are not territorial in this way.)

The African plains of southern Kenya and neighboring Tanzania, and even the desert country to the north, are dynamic worlds, with continual battles waged among the predators for territory, water sources, prey species herds, and good cover in which to raise offspring and find refuge. The situation on the ground is always changing, so after an absence of any time I need to catch up on the latest developments among my long-term acquaintances. As I get ready to meet a new group of guests and then depart for the bush, I will mentally run through my checklist and pull out my field book to refresh my memory on who I should be catching up with during the safari. I know that besides the familiar feline faces I will, hopefully, make the first acquaintance with new faces that will, in turn, develop into long-term relationships. The territories and home ranges now occupied by these "friends" will eventually become vacant, through death or abandonment. The system cruelly and impersonally flows on and on in that way, and I can't wait to meet the next tenant, though I often rue the passing of the last one.

In August 1987, my group camping in the Maasai Mara repeatedly crossed paths with a solitary lioness. She showed obvious physical signs of pregnancy and she had re-moved herself from the pride as well, a trait typical of either pregnant lionesses or mothers with cubs less than six weeks old. Two weeks later I was back in the Mara with another safari group, two couples from New York, the Ealys and the Perezes, and I was excited to find out if the female had given birth. We spent hours the first evening driving the upper Olare Oruk drainage, looking for the tattered-eared lioness, but with no luck. We searched again the following morning on our drive out, but still saw nothing. On the way back to camp for lunch, driving down the winding dirt track below the Mara Buffalo rocks, she suddenly materialized, strolling casually with the loose paws and rolling shoulders of a lion without a care in the world. She was padding along in our direction and stepped off to the side of the track, flopped down, and eyed us closely as we pulled up beside her.

As a general rule, the big cats become accustomed to vehicles; often they seem not even to see them. A large hunk of metal is foreign to their world in the unadulterated wild, but it's not foreign to their world in the game parks, where they may encounter vehicles quite often. The cats, not in spite of their intelligence but because of it, will allow Man to come right up and join them as long as he stays relatively quiet, relatively low in the truck, and does not violate nature with sudden moves or loud noises. Finding the predators in the first place may be a challenge, but getting near them once you've detected them seldom is. Cheetahs, in particular, are well habituated to trucks and often think nothing of hopping up for a better view into the distance. I've had three at a time on top of the truck. More important, the cats have no associations between danger and a big truck, which therefore serves as excellent camouflage for humans; but should you step outside the vehicle and be seen for what you are, the most dangerous creature on the planet, everything changes in a flash.

Although we had driven up behind this lioness and gotten away with it, it's better to be *first,* ahead of the lion. For almost all wildlife, in fact, the difference between approaching from behind and circling around to the front so that the game then *comes to you* is unbelievable. If the animals are walking along and just happen upon you — even though they've obviously seen you, heard you, and smelled you — they are as calm and relaxed as can be. You are just a part of their morning, you are not causing them to change either their direction of movement or their behavior. That's the ideal, and for all the right reasons.

We stayed near the lioness for a few minutes, pointing out the unique whisker pattern and ear cuts of this female, as well as her late-pregnancy condition. I was greatly relieved to see that I hadn't missed the birthing. Her nipples were not swollen, and the hairs around them were not dirty or worn down. We left her lying on her dappled flank only a few hundred yards from our camp. After our 4:00 p.m. tea we opted to head north, toward the short-grass plains, in hopes of picking up a cheetah. On the way out I thought we would just swing by the lioness and see how she was getting on. When we found her almost where we had left her four hours earlier, she merely raised her head, gave us a brief once-over, and lay back down, exhaling heavily. We left it at that and continued on our way to higher ground. We had no luck with cheetahs that afternoon but did spend a long time watching a family of bat-eared foxes as they high-tail-bounded back and forth from one burrow entrance to the other, tackling and tumbling over one another en route. On our return to camp we spent a few minutes with the pregnant lioness, who was now stretched out horizontally on a lichen-colored slab of phonolite, a volcanic rock with, often, a beautiful gray-green hue. She looked benignly at us and then returned her searching gaze to the grassland beyond, perhaps sizing up prey possibilities before darkness fell.

Two days passed, and the lioness could not even be bothered to look at us when we showed up. She appeared not to have eaten, or, if she had, it was not a large kill, for her chin and throat were always clean, never sporting the pale pink wash of blood that a recently satiated lion almost always carries. On our final morning in the Mara, a clean and clear one, we wove our way up the now familiar track to see how our lioness had fared the night. We arrived at the usual rendezvous just in time to see her striding with a gunfighter saunter into a grove of trees three hundred yards away.

We pulled up near the trees, turned the truck broadside, and started scanning in an attempt to get a fix on her, not knowing that she had a fix on us instead. Less than twenty feet away, the lioness sat up and started walking directly toward our truck, head held low, feet carefully placed one directly in front of the other as she picked her way forward. And between her huge canines, swinging gently from side to side with the rhythm of its mother's pace, its tiny tail curled up, was a kitten at most a few hours old.

We were ecstatic. Firing away with our cameras but afraid that we might alter the lioness from her course directly toward us, we tried desperately to keep quiet and move slowly. Ten feet from the vehicle she stopped and, while still holding the little kitten in her mouth, scraped away the leaves and deadfall and made a nest into which she lowered it. Without so much as a backward glance at us, she turned about, left the kitten crying there, and returned to the grove of trees. Just as we were about to lose sight of her, she lowered her head, then picked it back up and turned toward us with a second kitten tenderly grasped between her gleaming yellow-white teeth. She deposited the new kitten in the nest alongside the first one. After a few seconds of crying, the kittens curled up together and fell silent. The lioness rounded the front bumper of our truck and walked off across the plains toward another forest grove, simply leaving us and her kittens behind.

I was deeply puzzled, and very disturbed, by the lioness's behavior. Why had she brought the kittens to us? And why had she left them there and simply walked off? She was supposed to keep these new kittens secluded for about two months before bringing them out into the open and introducing them to the rest of the pride. At that age the cubs can keep up with the adults and know when and how to hide themselves if danger threatens. They are also past the age when the males might commit infanticide. The lioness's behavior did not seem to bode well, and now we really had no choice but to stay and baby-sit until the mother returned. It was not a sure thing that she would, and the little ones would be easy prey to hyenas, jackals — even raptors. As minutes dragged into an hour or more, we scrunched down in various ungainly positions in the truck and continued scanning for the lioness.

Suddenly Kinyolo, the driver, shook my shoulder and pointed with his chin toward the right. Across the plains, loose-pawed and low, came the female back toward her newborns. She circled the truck, never giving us even a glance, and went directly over to her kittens, sniffing and licking and occasionally moaning softly to them while they cried. Then she picked up the darker kitten, a male, and carried it off in the direction from which she had first come that morning. She didn't return for several anxious minutes, but then emerged from the grove, went directly to the remaining kitten, a female, and mouthed it a few times before getting a comfortable grip around its head and returning with it to the safer darkness of the trees.

I didn't see this young mother again for two months, which was as it should have been. When I did see her next, the cubs were tumbling and stumbling along in their mother's golden wake. They had distinctly different coloration: the male was darker and less spotted, while his sister was a golden-honey hue, dappled with white on her round little belly. In concert with my clients at the time, I had named them Dusk and Dawn, respectively. I watched Dusk endure his adolescence and join up with eleven other males as they started their nomadic years. A day arrived when I came across that mob of males feeding on a female giraffe. I scanned through the lions one by one until I found Dusk, who had crawled halfway into the now hollow carcass. I wonder whether my group believed me when I told them all about this animal, who was around two years old, and about his mother, who had trusted us to baby-sit him and his sister while she went to clean up and get a drink of water. That story always makes me smile.

On another day, in another place (the southeast Serengeti), I was overcome with even greater delight as I measured three cheetah cubs with the tape I always carry with my camera gear. A cheetah hunt is a rare enough thing, but during my twenty-odd years on safari I had seen far more cheetah kills than I had newborn cheetah kittens. Lions, hyenas, poor nutrition, and poor mothering combine to decimate their population. Some 97 percent of all cheetahs born on the Serengeti Plain do not live a single year. At breakfast that morning I had picked up a cheetah some two miles distant, coursing back and forth across a massively wide basin. After breakfast my clients and I packed up and we started slowly toward the place where we had last seen the cat. The coursing action was indicative of a hunt, so we kept our distance, partly for the cheetah's sake, but also for our own. We didn't want to blow our opportunity.

We stayed off to the east about seven hundred yards as the hunter continued to sweep the plain. It seemed to me that the cheetah was searching for either a hare, which is not unusual, or a newborn Thomson's gazelle that it had seen drop down into hiding. We stayed back, patiently waiting for the outcome, but time slid by with no resolution. Finally I decided that we would move right in, get a series of close-up photographs, and the cat would either hunt successfully or we would leave and search for another.

At our approach the cat sat down, but soon stood up to continue slowly on its way. Only then, at this near range, did I realize that it was a female, very heavy with milk. She was searching for her *cubs,* and that was why she had been peering into every depression and hole. Furthermore, and much more exciting to me, she was not calling them with the birdlike chirp that is so well known with cheetahs. Her cubs, therefore, must be too small to come to her.

By 3:45 we had lost sight of her. In no rush, we repacked the vehicle and slowly headed west to where we had last seen her, and as we came up a gradual slope toward a low pile of granite, there she was, with her head and front paws in a narrow hole, working her head back and forth. When she raised herself to a standing position, she held in her jaw a tiny, semi-curled cheetah tyke.

My group was frozen with delight, but my training had me switching lenses and capturing the images on kodachrome. Imagine how shocked we were when she walked *toward* us and dropped the kitten on an open patch of ground not fifteen feet from my door. I was speechless, and I wanted to explain, but I also wanted to take pictures. I fired away with my camera as the mother, seemingly disinterested in us, turned and walked back to the hidden holes and again walked toward us carrying a second kitten, then turned to the hole and returned with a third and final kitten. The eyes of this last one had not even opened yet. It had to be less than four days old.

The mother circled the cubs a few times before lying down almost on top of them. She then took them one by one in her incisors, pulled them to her, and licked each in turn. The last kitten out of the hole got very little attention and seemed lethargic. The other two didn't appear overly thrilled with bath day either, but at their helpless age they had little choice but to submit, though we could hear them vigorously voice their complaints as they tried to belly crawl away from the raspy tongue and the indignity of it all. Using her oversized front paws the cheetah then pushed the kittens toward her belly, squirmed down in the grass, and allowed them to nurse. The kitten with its eyes still closed either didn't know where to go, lacked the energy to get there, or was not well and just lay at the mother's slowly heaving side, making no attempt to take any milk.

After an hour or so alternately bathing and nursing her kittens, the mother rose and left her little ones where they fell as she strode purposefully off to the north. Instead of following her on her evening foray, much as we would have liked to watch a hunt, we felt obligated to stay with the exposed kittens. The two more active ones immediately, though slowly because of the thick grass, crawled toward one another and wrapped themselves in a knot of gray, gold, and tiny black dots. The last kitten lay on its side, unable or unwilling to join its litter mates.

When I was absolutely positive that the mother had crested the rise and was out of sight, I stepped from the car and measured the kittens. I was careful not to touch any of them, though it was difficult to suppress my desire to bring the weak one to the warmth and comfort of the other two in hopes that it might survive, too. As I retreated to the Land Rover I pushed down a prominent clump of red oat grass that partially screened the kittens from our sight, and almost on cue the sun finally settled at a low enough angle to shine out from underneath the gray blanket that had kept the kittens in such low light. It was as if the switch for the stage lights had been thrown. The change in color and intensity was so great that all of us in the truck looked to the west as the orange ball emerged, wondering what had happened. We were more than an hour from our camp by the alkaline lake, but we waited a tad longer, until the mother had returned to the circle of short grass. Then, as the sun came to rest momentarily on the great wafting sea of grass that is the Serengeti, we fired up the motor yet again and headed south and home, massaged by the soft sunbeams, overwhelmed and over-joyed.

I would get to see these kittens next month, the month after, and even the month following that one — if they lived, that is. I jotted down the date in my book.

I have now outlived every single terrestrial predator that populated the woods and plains when I first arrived in East Africa. The one-eyed Moshe Dayan, the very first cat Mike Rainy introduced to me, was eventually driven out of his territory and gradually starved. The son of the first lioness that ever walked into my Serengeti camp, a massive, black-maned dominator, is himself dead of old age, and his son has come of age in a territory that has shifted sixty miles over a decade. These lions now have to share the plains with a pride that has pushed, or been shoved, south from the rolling grasses of the Gol plains.

One August in Samburu I was looking for a leopard I'd followed for four years when I realized that the very tree in which I had first seen her was now collapsed on the ground and serving as the ignoble camp for a baboon troop. The discovery gave me pause. I had never expected the trees themselves to die right out from under me. I found myself thinking of the animals I study and introduce to my clients as a living time line, and I realized that the "somedays" on that time line are ever more rapidly becoming "now." Change remains the only constant, a truism that must include me within its compass.

The good news was that the leopard, a slim female, had adjusted to the new circumstances perhaps better than I had. On our second evening in the reserve, we found her stretched out in her usual relaxed arboreal posture, her back legs straddling the trunk, her muffed front paws gathered underneath her necklaced chest. Instead of being safely twenty feet above the world, she surveyed her kingdom at this moment from a fallen log a mere six feet off the ground, but this lesser vantage appeared to bother her not at all. We were quite happy with her selection as well, being able to photograph her at eye level instead of with the neck-craning shots into trees that are the norm when photographing leopards. However, this female would pay the penalty for continuing to use such a lowly post. The next time we saw her on this log she had an impala fawn with her. When she had finished with her kill, stashed it, and then slid silently off toward the river, the baboons who had been barking intermittently at her for more than thirty minutes immediately moved forward with swaggering strides, and two males didn't hesitate to leap onto the fallen log and appropriate the remaining meat. (The books say that baboons eat only meat they have either killed themselves or have watched being killed. I have never seen a contradictory case. Maybe these baboons had witnessed the kill.)

When I met this leopard four years earlier, I was camping in Samburu by myself and trying to get clean tape recordings of the various birds of that rich habitat. Late one afternoon, I heard vervet monkeys barking in a grove of acacia elatior trees. It was probably too late in the day for them to be raising an alarm over a bird of prey, so there was most likely a cat in the neighborhood. I drove over to investigate, found the vervets easily, and gazed where they were looking. Nothing showed immediately, so I sat down on the roof to wait, and for some reason, my eyes came to rest on a dead elatior branch long since stripped of its corrugated bark, now table-top smooth. Lying there was a honey-colored apparition stretched low and long, partially hidden and well dappled by a shadowy lace of leaves. I don't know how long the leopard had been there, but there was no question she was there now. I watched her, fixated as if *she* were the prey, when she suddenly raised herself up and slid off the tree like mercury slides off paper, only to rise up magically on another tree almost beside me. I was of no apparent consequence to this leopard as she surveyed all that was around her, studiously ignoring the barking vervets. Her eyes paused on me briefly during one of her head swings, but the wide orbs did not linger, and I realized I was holding my breath unnecessarily. I also noticed a feature that would serve me for years to come. This female leopard had a distinctive little slit in the outer top of her right ear, cutting in perhaps a third of an inch. And so I met Msikio Kulia (Right Ear).

I was back in Samburu two months later with two eager families from Colorado, and we set out in separate trucks. I made a point of being back at the same grove of trees at the same hour of the day that I had first come across Msikio Kulia. We had been circling and sitting for only fifteen to twenty minutes when the vervets sounded off again, exactly as they had months previously. We drove over and arrived in time to find the leopardess walking up to a huge elatior tree, then with three bounding leaps effortlessly vaulting almost twenty feet up to a branch just the right size to stretch out on. I called the other vehicle on the radio and declared in a deep voice, "We have leopard!"

It turned out that this rather small female had the habit of coming down to that very same area every three days or so as she patrolled and hunted within her territory. I usually camp in Samburu for at least three days whenever I visit there, so during the course of my stay I would usually encounter her at least once if I came to that acacia grove between 5:45 and 6:30 p.m. She was incredibly reliable, to the point that even when she mated and had her cubs, she stuck to the routine. I know this because I was waiting for her appearance one evening when a monstrous male I had never seen before showed himself as he walked along the grassy riverbank. When he looked in our direction we could see that his right eye was completely clouded over with glaucoma, but this didn't seem to affect his abilities. He was fat-bellied and thick-necked and on a mission. Moments later Msikio Kulia showed herself on another fallen tree trunk, and the one-eyed male headed directly toward her. Instead of scrambling down and scooting for cover, the female benignly watched his advance and accepted his presence when he effortlessly sailed up beside her onto the log. We remained with the two leopards as they caroused until dark, knowing that they would be mating that night, and perhaps for a few more nights to come. I jotted down the date inside the back cover of my mammal field guide and added one hundred and ten days, and she did not disappoint me, in the end.

Some months later, in November, I was back in Samburu between safaris, just kicking around the park with a good friend, Neil, and his girlfriend, Emily. Neil is the executive chef at a nearby resort and knows birds well, assuming they are under glass or covered with sauce. Every time I pointed out some avifauna he described in detail some colorful sauce that he thought might go well with the bird's plumage. On our first evening game drive I told Neil and Emily about the little leopardess as we bounced slowly down the southern bank of the Ewaso Ngiiro River. Leopards will stick with a given post for life, ten or more years, so it was very possible we'd find her there three months after my last sighting. Driving down the river, we didn't, but the return trip was a different story. As we neared the fallen acacia we saw not the leopard, but three lionesses who were traveling the open road as well. They sauntered down the track, looking neither right nor left, unhurried by our vehicle behind them. And we weren't eager for them to hurry either, because I have never met anyone who does not love to watch a lion's beautiful stride. From behind, especially, you can see clearly the shoulder blades rise and fall in counterpoint to the swinging legs. I always find myself fascinated by the loose paws, which flip up and out and then reverse before touching the sand again, landing perfectly straight and perfectly flat on oversized pads. Each step looks like a stretching exercise; the graceful stride hypnotizes me.

The road forked a hundred yards ahead of the three lionesses, with the right fork leading down to a wide tree-filled shelf by the river. The leopard's fallen log was also on this shelf. I thought these cats were on the move, most likely looking for the rest of their pride on the open planes, and would therefore go straight, rather than swing right toward the cover. But they did, probably only to prove me wrong, and suddenly, all three froze at precisely the same moment, their heads up, ears forward, and backs rigid, a fascinating simultaneity of reaction. Scanning with the binoculars I could see the leopard sacked out beyond them on her personal log, head curled on furry paws in sleep. The lions stayed motionless for an eternity, and then, almost imperceptibly, lowered themselves silently to the sand.

I swung the huge 400-mm telephoto onto the roof and asked Francis, who was driving this trip for me, to move on up the left track and find a spot where we could watch all four cats at once. Lions don't play favorites. They will kill competitive felines if they can catch them, and this little leopard was low to the ground and still sleeping. With a patience I possess only for fishing, wildlife photography, and teaching, I waited. They began to stalk, their bellies held scant inches above the lion-colored sand as they moved. Their front feet extended straight out, step after step, as if on rails. The legs moved with the steady and controlled motion of machines, the paws no longer flipping but staying motionless at the end of the thick forearms, showing individual motion only as they were placed on the sand and adjusted to conform.

Lions, and the other cats as well, can stalk in complete silence, but *something* tipped off the leopard. She suddenly woke up and rapidly swiveled her head in the direction of the lions, who were still forty yards distant. She kept her body low, stretching only her neck as she assessed the threat. When the fact registered that it was death in the form of three lionesses coming toward her, she wasted no time. She didn't slide off the tree in the usual fashion of a leopard but rocketed down and ran. The lions charged at the same instant, throwing explosions of sand behind them, but compared to the lightness and agility of the dashing leopard they were linebackers, heavy and clumsy. A second later the leopard was on the trunk of another acacia, but a vertical tree this time. She pulled herself up effortlessly, slipped into the wide fork of the first major horizontal branch, and casually walked out fifteen feet before lying down. The lionesses had gained the base of the tree by then and were looking up longingly. Once up, the leopard couldn't even be bothered to cast her eyes down. She curled her stocky head onto a well-furred foot and closed her eyes once again, completely secure in her surroundings.

We relaxed, knowing that nothing would happen now, and the lions wandered off upstream and out of sight. I confirmed, by her split right ear, that it was the same leopard that used to rest on the fallen tree, and Emily and Neil had their first chance to admire the physical qualities that make a leopard so supreme a feline. Three of the four wide and fur-lined feet hung loosely in the air, occasionally twitching for reasons known only to the leopard. Her white whiskers, unlike the short bristly facial hairs of the cheetah and the lion, were incredibly long, spanning a width exactly as broad as her shoulders, allowing her to navigate in total silence as she stalked her prey. Her thick tail, such a good counterweight when sprinting, dropped straight down off the near side of the wide branch, its white under-tip flicking occasionally. It was only when Neil returned my binoculars to me that I noticed she was lactating. Even in the splattered shade I could clearly see the unnaturally tan circle around each nipple, shaped by the damp and dirty mouths of little leopards. This we would have to follow up the next day, when there was a distinct possibility of seeing her cubs.

We didn't, however, find the leopard the next day, much less her little ones. In fact, I left Samburu without seeing her again, and two months passed before I was able to provide Neil and Emily with an update via telephone. I had been in the Samburu park for two days and had driven by her log four or five times, stopping to show my new clients, ornithologists all, the deep and sharply angled V-shaped claw marks left behind as the leopard ascended and descended the now barkless log. I traced my fingers along the bark, and pointed out that the spacing between the marks was too narrow to be that of a lion, and too sharply angled as well.

On our last night in Samburu we looped one last time past her fallen tree, parked a discreet distance away, and soaked in the sounds, the air, and the feel of this subtle environment. It did not feel right to break the stillness by providing names and identifications. The human voice would have been polluting, so we sat in silence, sipping coffee and wine, doing absolutely nothing. As I often do, I closed my eyes to enhance my senses, and when I opened them the leopard was on the log. She had arrived without the smallest sound to give her away. I cautioned everyone to wait for their photographs. We would move in much closer after giving her a little time to settle. Four long and excruciating minutes later we sidled up to her as quietly as a one-and-a-half-ton diesel truck can. After fifteen minutes of fairly steady shooting everyone was slowing down, taking the time to view this animal without the interference of a lens.

A small motion pulled my eyes off her and down into the tangle of black branches below, on either side of the trunk. Again I saw motion but could make out nothing. I knew it wouldn't be a dik-dik, a six-pound antelope common in this park, so I guessed it must be an overly confident crested francolin that wasn't put off by the leopard's proximity. The motion moved slowly to the right and revealed itself to be a solitary leopard cub picking its way with infinite care between the long thorns of the deadfall. I was flabbergasted, and so was everyone else. As with the adults, it is much more rare to see leopard cubs than either lion or cheetah cubs.

The cub, only three or four months old, eventually summoned the courage to climb up beside its mother. Perhaps fortunately, it was too dark to photograph the pair, so we contented ourselves with marveling at them through our glasses until the blackness was almost complete and the two cats mere shadows, then we returned to our camp on the riverbank. I had known from the beginning of the encounter that this would be another night when we'd be late returning home, but I thought I could count on the rangers' benevolence, given the circumstances. I was right.

The two leopards were almost impossible to find for many months after that, perhaps because the mother became shyer as the little one began to follow her more and more. They could have been using a different part of their territory for a period, allowing the game along the river to build in numbers and confidence during their absence. I frequented her log during every safari in Samburu, but her absence was confirmed by the lack of fresh claw marks on the tree. I was disappointed and concerned.

Finally, in June, when the grasses were still tall and abundant from the rains of April and May, my clients at the time got lucky. We departed camp early and decided to head away from the river in search of Grévy's zebras and gerenuk, the slim and long-necked antelope of the dry north. On our outbound departure, my driver, Ndiema, turned left by mistake after crossing the bridge instead of heading straight on toward the more open high ground. He realized his mistake, apologized, and said it was just a force of habit that made him turn. No problem. With Ndiema, it's never a problem, because he's one of the sweetest guys I work with. Clients fall in love with him, and I have tremendous respect for him. A lot of drivers, frankly, are terrified of elephants and rhinos, but not Ndiema. A lot of drivers are boringly by-the-book, but Ndiema will "push the program" in terms of fudging on the rules about darkness, for example. We have worked together about half a dozen years and know each other well. If I happen to be exhausted one day I can ask him to give me a plan, and he'll do it, and it will be a good one.

Since we'd turned left, I thought we might as well follow the river for a little bit and then swing away when we reached the two huge acacia tortillis trees. I wasn't particularly thinking about the leopard, her cub, or the fallen tree. Then there she was, just like that, though her cub was out of sight. I signaled the clients — all professional photographers — who were sitting on the roof, to drop down inside the truck in order to give the leopard time to adjust to our presence. We would be far less intimidating standing up through the open roof hatches than sitting exposed on top. Inside the truck everyone was scrambling as quietly and as quickly as they could to get the lenses that they wanted on their cameras, their bean bags repositioned, and even extra clothing shed as Ndiema moved us closer.

Finally, I came back up to "periscope depth" and started to bring my lens into focus, loving that moment when the cat would become crystal clear in my glass, all its detail magnified and beautiful. I had fired off perhaps ten frames before I felt Ndiema reach back with his long arm and tug on the hem of my shorts.

"That isn't the same leopard," Ndiema whispered, and he was right. In my hurry to get organized I hadn't even noticed that this was a different female. "This is her daughter," he continued. "She has inherited that same black spot on her neck that her mother has."

I never did see the adult female again. I think she had already died by the time we saw her daughter on the log. Recalling all the hours I and my clients had spent watching her feeding, climbing, and sleeping, I was glad that I never saw her dead, unanimated, perhaps mutilated body. It would have seemed so unleopardlike.

Instead, sometime soon I'll be back in Samburu with Ndiema and clients, and we'll drive across to the other side of the river in the evening and sit quietly with wine and coffee and listen for the vervet monkeys to bark a warning of her daughter's coming. We'll then wait, give her time, and finally come forward to introduce ourselves to the heir apparent of this log throne and the stretch of river and trees that it governs.

★ ★ ★

Sometimes, however, no matter how comfortable you are with a situation on the ground, no matter how patient you have been, no matter how dirty your knees, you not only fail to create your own luck but also court a natural disaster instead.

This happened to me and my group some years ago at Lewa Downs, a private game reserve north of Nairobi. The scene is almost as vivid in my mind today as it was then and there. We had paused as we reached a rise in the road that affords a view of the beautiful valley known locally as the valley that belongs to the coal-black leopard. On the west side, the valley rises slowly to a ridge that winds toward Mount Kenya, whose black-and-white rocks and glaciers loom silent and still. To the north, the valley rises slowly to the mountains, where we often find a small buffalo herd; to the south it rolls down to the old camp-site, flattening out just before meeting the Lewa River and its bordering line of yellow-bark acacias. Across the river the ground rises steeply at first but soon flattens out into a vast plain stretching to the south. The open land is perpetually dotted with herds of both Grévy's and common zebras, as well as with eland, impalas, and giraffes. At this distance, even those giant grazers seventeen feet tall and weighing three thousand pounds look like ants scattered across a pale green picnic blanket. A herd of elephants grazed peacefully along the west side of the valley. They, too, were tiny at this distance, appearing as dark loaves of bread left out to cool on the hillside.

The slow-moving herd might provide us with a good opportunity to watch the complex and little understood family dynamics of these seemingly expressionless giants. On this private land, we could sit for as long as we wanted, undisturbed by other vehicles and unrestricted by any park rules, and slowly gather a bit of insight as to how they functioned and interacted during the normal course of their day. My longtime friend and favorite Lewa driver was behind the wheel: Mungai with the all-seeing eyes of an eagle, good knowledge of the animals, encyclopedic awareness of every pothole on every mile of dirt track at Lewa, and fluency in English, Kiswahili, Meru, Kikuyu, Luhya, and Kalenjin.

Mungai and I have worked together for years, seeming to have a special affinity for finding leopards when we pair up, helped by the fact that half a dozen or more of the cats have staked out accessible territories. He shares my thinking about how our guests should encounter the wildlife. He will drive where many drivers fear to leave tread marks. Immediately Mungai aimed us off the main track and down a steep side track that led through a narrow and rocky valley up toward the broader slopes. I had already judged the stamina of the six people with me and decided we had an unusual opportunity to get out of the truck and truly be on the same level as the elephants, in every sense of the word. Cynthia and her husband, Mac, along with Len, were psychologists from Colorado, all very athletic and fit. They skied, they ran, they hiked, depending on the season. Len's childhood friend, Pete, was also in good shape and didn't appear to pose any problem. My only real concern was for Chris, a young laboratory technician from California, who seldom saw the actual light of day due to her work and her workload. But her friend, Elaine, from New Jersey, seemed physically and emotionally able.

Discussing the question briefly, all six were very much in favor of walking. We had already successfully stalked rhinos, and everyone had enjoyed the adventure immensely and behaved beautifully. This experience looked to be more of the same, but this time even safer, because the elephants would be below a small cliff and we would be above it, out of harm's way. I knew that just a few months earlier a single elephant in the Maasai Mara had swatted down three people like flies and had then stayed around to make certain they were dead, running through each body with her massive tusks and crushing it repeatedly with her broad forehead. But I was determined not to deprive my clients of all relatively close encounters with elephants, and was sure we were not running any serious risk.

Mungai took us to the south end of the cliff, to the point where it first jutted out of the hillside. I went over how we would proceed with the group, slowly reviewing the rules for stalking any animal: Stay absolutely quiet. Stay close to me. Walk on the outside edges of the shoes, heel to toe, so as to be quieter. No talking. Take no pictures until I say it's all right. Stay behind me always. Go where I tell you. Do what I tell you instantly and without question. It's all simple and straightforward enough. Basically, any guide has to run a benevolent dictatorship while stalking. There's no other way to do it. Everyone nodded his or her head. In this instance, I took the extra precaution of quietly asking my friend Adam, who was along for the ride, to stay by Chris and be ready to take her physically by the hand in case anything happened. In single file, walking on the outside edges of our shoes, we started down the game path along the top of the cliff. We paused a number of times as we got closer, giving the aware elephants a chance to get adjusted to our presence. I'm sure they didn't see us, but the wind was swirling erratically in the narrow valley and they undoubtedly had picked up our scent. And quiet though we were trying to be, I'm sure they heard us as well. Only Adam and I were used to stalking game on foot, and it's almost always impossible to convince novices of just how much noise they are making, in spite of their efforts to the contrary. We were also walking on broken, flat sandstone slabs, with loose sand and dry leaves scattered across the rocks, so some sound was inevitable. But we proceeded well. After a stalk of only twenty minutes and perhaps five hundred yards, we were safely positioned on the rocks thirty feet above the herd feeding about two hundred yards away. An elephant would occasionally stop and raise its trunk to get better wind of us, but generally the herd kept feeding and very slowly and peacefully moving along the bottom of the cliff.

Two hours later we were still perched on the sandstone slabs watching, completely entranced by the massive gray animals directly below us. The little elephants were casually eating, some even nursing, while the large females and the two sub-adult males browsed as they strolled. The sun sank slowly lower and Mount Kenya turned from black and white to a muted mix of grays, then grayer. The herd kept browsing and slowly trundling along, then stopped feeding and started to move with more intention to the north, paralleling the cliff from which we viewed them. But the cliff petered out to the north, fading back into the hillside, leaving only steep ground between us and the silently walking hulks below us. So I gathered my covey and told them we would have to start walking back toward the vehicle if the elephants started even the least bit up the slope. As the fourteen elephants reached the end of the cliff they did indeed turn almost straight uphill, and further surprised me by picking up their pace. I immediately told everyone to head back toward the vehicle, where Mungai sat waiting for us. I shot a knowing glance at Adam, who then took Chris by the hand, and started her back toward the vehicle immediately, leading the rest of the group. Out of habit I hung back, taking the last position in our retreating line.

And then someone up ahead paused and took a final picture. Even at two hundred yards, if not more, the lead female heard the camera shutter and the motor drive and instantly trumpeted and began to charge, flat out. She came straight at us, and at a thundering speed. I yelled to everyone to run for the vehicle, and as the group bolted I waited a bit longer to see if this truly was a charge or just a noisy bluff. It was surely for real, so I turned, too, and sprinted to catch up with the group.

As I spun back around to the left, I caught a glimpse of Cynthia out of the corner of my eye. She had apparently slipped on the coarse sand on top of a slab of rock and hit the ground. The thunder of the screaming elephants was now deafening and had frozen Cynthia solidly where she lay. Two hundred plus yards may seem like a long way, but the elephant could cover that distance in twenty seconds, probably less.

Cynthia lay transfixed on her side as the enraged herd bore down on her; by this point the matriarch was clearly aiming for Cynthia, her head down and her trunk rolled up. A double-trunked acacia tree directly in her path snapped like a twig as she glanced off it.

The elephant was now very close to Cynthia. Everything was chaos, noise at a fever pitch, and I was terrified. My only chance at saving my guest was to divert the charging elephants away from her prostrate, motionless form and, therefore, toward me. I ran back past Cynthia and stopped fifteen or twenty feet away, near the edge of the cliff. I jumped up and down, screamed and yelled and clapped my hands over my head in a crazed and desperate attempt to draw the first of the elephants' attention and then their charge. If it worked, I thought I could then sprint over the cliff to safety.

It did. All fourteen elephants swung toward my commotion, missing Cynthia by twenty feet or less.

I waited, desperate, as long as I possibly could, yelling and waving all the while, and then turned and bolted for the edge of the small cliff, gratefully sailing off into peaceful space. As I left the rocky ledge, a huge, gray-brown shape swung past my right shoulder, missing me by perhaps ten inches, and then I was clear, falling toward the silent, rocky ground and patchy grass thirteen feet below (as I later measured). I thumped to the earth, falling forward on my knees, catching myself with one hand while holding my camera with the other. I was fine, but one of my homemade tire sandals had come off, and I turned back to look for it.

Stopped by the cliff, had the herd swung back toward Cynthia or the others? This fear passed through my mind in a flash as I turned toward the rocky cliff face to find my missing sandal, just as the female elephant in the lead came over the cliff. But this was impossible. She couldn't be coming down that drop-off after me. Like giraffes, elephants are not supposed to like going downhill, much less down-cliff. This angered lady had apparently not read the research. Nor had the rest of the herd, which immediately followed her example.

Forget finding the sandal. I began racing with just one down the valley with this huge elephant looming only feet behind me. I had been scared many times in my life. I had been scared scarcely a minute before, but now I was truly terrified. I still couldn't believe that she had done it, that she wanted me that badly. I was running for my life and knew it. I couldn't afford the luxury of looking back, nor did I need to. The crashing and thundering were right on my heels.

Maybe three hundred yards down the valley I slowly realized that the elephant wasn't right behind me anymore. Or maybe she was, but I simply no longer had the awareness. Either way, I dove under a bush and crouched down. Everything was still except my panicked heartbeat. The elephant was no longer after me, but farther below in the valley I could hear rampaging pachyderms bellowing and smashing their way through whatever was before them. I stayed crouched and waited, almost crying with worry over what may have occurred or might still be occurring on the cliff top. But all I could do at the moment was wait quietly where I was and give the elephants time to move off and settle down.

Fifteen minutes later I could see them progressing at a slow walk up the other side of the valley, as if nothing at all had occurred in the previous quarter hour, as if this rampage were a casual and daily episode for them. I anxiously and carefully started back up to the cliff face, finding a gap through which I could ascend. My one bare foot was torn and bleeding, slowing my climb, but I was desperate to know what had happened, if everyone was alive, if Cynthia was safe and sound. There was no one at the top of the cliff so I started working back toward the vehicle. As I rounded an umbrella acacia tree, I suddenly saw the truck with people standing inside, Mungai at the wheel. I rapidly counted eight heads and felt weak with relief. No one had been killed. No one had been hurt. My head dropped to my chest and my pace gratefully slowed to a limp. I could feel their eyes on me, but whether with relief or anger I couldn't say.

I suppose that my first reaction, out of fear and relief, was to make light of it all and diffuse some of the pressure. I was trying to find out what had happened uphill, above the cliff, while my group wanted to know what had happened to me down below. Until Adam spoke up, saying he had seen the female swing her trunk out at me, tossing me into the air and over the cliff, I didn't realize that they had thought I had surely been killed. As I had sailed off the ledge, the lead female had indeed swung her trunk at me, and from my group's oblique position it looked as if she had made solid contact, knocking me out into the open sky. When that same elephant had then proceeded over the cliff, followed by all the others with such an unholy commotion, they were sure she was coming down to finish off what she had started. Then all they knew was what they heard, the horrific noise echoing out from the valley. My delay in returning to the vehicle had further reinforced what they thought they already knew. In fact, Adam had just decided to leave the group and the car to look for my evidently flattened and broken body when I had appeared over the brow of the rock face.

A game scout employed by Lewa ran up. He had heard the infuriated elephants from over a mile and a half away and knew something was horribly amiss. I imagine it was a combination of his worry and relief that caused him to let loose on me, but I was simply not in the mood to take his outburst, and I cut him off.

Mungai fired up the engine and we started slowly back down the mountainside toward the main house at Lewa, talking animatedly at a thousand miles an hour. But our raucous group grew inexplicably more quiet as the ride went on and night overtook us. As the vehicle descended, the warm air was split by our faces like glassy water by a ship's prow. It flowed past our cheeks and eddied around our ears before returning to the night. In the black void to the south the canine tooth of Mount Kenya bit seventeen thousand feet into the sky, as if trying to devour the stars. But we saw nothing outside the headlights' cone and heard nothing but the diesel truck on the dirt road.

After dinner we sat together in somewhat forced conversation, carefully avoiding the incident of the afternoon. We broke early and headed for our cabins, Len and Pete in one, Cynthia and Mac in another, and Chris and Elaine in the last. I slowly walked back out on the road for a mile or so. For several hours I hadn't been able to get my mind around what had happened, how suddenly the situation had changed, and how drastically. Now the realization swept over me that I could have easily caused the death of six clients, perhaps Adam, and even myself. I was safe now, as were my people, but my heart did not seem to want to accept what my head knew as fact. Perhaps my heart was wiser. In spite of my training and my years and years with elephants and a certain close call still fresh in my memory, I had intentionally walked those unknowing and trusting people into that situation. Mungai had years of experience as well, as did Adam, but all my attempts at rationalizing and assembling logic did me no good.

I did not sleep that night and was often on the verge of vomiting. I got the shakes every time I allowed myself to relive the scene one more pointless time. When the white-browed sparrow-weavers started their chittering calls at 5:30 a.m., I quickly accepted the invitation to rise and walk out on the road once again, where I ran through the whole, nearly disastrous scene one more time, hoping not so much for peace, but for understanding and learning that would help ensure my clients lived through the next encounter a bit easier than this one.

This group had always gathered by the fire or at the breakfast table around 6:30 a.m. By 7:30, when no else had shown up yet, I finally mustered my courage and went down to Mac and Cynthia's cabin. Cynthia had had more than just a bad night. Mac and Len, her fellow psychologists, had spent hours working with her, helping her to get over the images of her own imminent death. She told me in her cabin that she had just known she was going to die. "I could only lie there," she said, "seeing that charging elephant bear down on me." She had never imagined being killed by an enraged elephant. She had been resigned to death and had lain there waiting for it to happen, yet now she was alive and also stuck with that mental and emotional picture.

Elaine and Chris were better off, but extremely somber and serious. It seemed to me that perhaps the best thing would be to get back out on a game drive, be out in the daylight with the wildlife, and try to get our safari back on track. So that is what we did, with a quiet Mungai at the wheel.

Not two miles from the ranch house we came across elephants, the same elephants, now feeding along the Lewa River. Mungai braked us gently to a stop and we discussed going down, and to everyone's everlasting credit we were unanimous in our decision to get close to the elephants once again, only this time staying within the safe confines of the Land Cruiser.

We silently coasted down and came to a stop along the outer edge of the fourteen animals who had tried to kill us the day before. The lead female was easy to identify and we noticed that she had a still-bleeding wound a third of the way up her trunk. It looked like a classic bullet hole, with one small entry and one large exit wound. We discussed the possibility — the likelihood, I thought — that the click of the shutter and then the motor drive yesterday afternoon had been associated by these elephants with the chambering of a bullet by a rifle bolt. They were all feeding peacefully now, but we took no pictures.

Three days later, on the first day of this group's camel safari at another camp, we found ourselves once again on a cliff face above a different but even larger group of elephants passing below us. This time we were heavily armed, as always when on an "official" walking or camel-back safari. We were also as silent as church mice in house slippers, but some tiny noise alerted the herd to our presence. Suddenly, and literally in mid-stride, all sixty-odd elephants froze as one, some with a foot in the air, an amazing display of simultaneous perception on the part of the animals. The only sound was the rhythmic crashing of our human heartbeats. After an extremely tense thirty seconds or so, the herd finally commenced walking again, and we turned and tiptoed slowly back up the hill in the direction from which we had come.

4

At Home in the Fields

I was where I preferred to be, sleeping out on the ground, when the first lion roared at 4:00 a.m. Snug under the weight of my blankets, and sheltered from the heavy dew by the entwined branches of olive trees, I held my breath while a lioness joined her voice with the old male's. We were on someone's turf. If these lions were on the move, if this area wasn't their territory, the female would not have joined in; we would have heard only the deep voices of nomadic male lions tentatively laying claim to the territory.

They'd call again, and I'd have them. The only problem was having to sit up and tackle the freezing air in order to get the fix. I knew where I was in camp, which way I faced lying down, where the Isiria Escarpment was, where the Mara River flowed, where the track exited camp, but this still wasn't enough when I was lying down. I waited. Five minutes later the two lions let loose again. Now I'd have about fifteen roars to get them pinpointed before they again fell silent, but that was more than enough. I swiveled my head to be sure. Yes, they were up over the ridge line, perhaps even across the plain with the hyena den, maybe as far as five miles away, down to the dead grove of croton. If we could find that pride this morning, I would have enough teaching material for hours, enough information and entertainment to occupy us for days. And once again I could illustrate through experience the truth that you don't have to be a stranger, an outsider, in this environment.

At 5:00 I threw the blankets back and dressed as quickly as I had undressed six or seven hours earlier. With the air moist and the grass wet, the cold was deeper now. By the time I had passed the guests' tents, picked my way through the tall grass, and reached the new flames, my feet and lower legs were soaked with the dew clinging to the red oat grass. I pulled a chair from the dining tent's veranda, where it had been stored during the night to stay clean of dew. I placed the front legs of the chair well into the ashes, almost into the flames, and sat down carefully. Within seconds, my shins heated up to the point of burning, but I remained there, letting the welcome warmth soak into my chest and face while my shins got hotter and hotter. With no word spoken, Mwangi, the cook, put a tin cup of coffee in my hand, cream already in it; I leaned forward, feeling the heat burn in my legs, gazed at Venus through the patchy roof of leaves, and slowly exhaled. Soon it would be time to merge with my people into the day. Flashlights danced like fireflies beyond the canvas walls as they searched for whatever they didn't organize the night before. Last night, as usual, I had visited each tent before turning in, turned over the shoes and placed them close to the zippered entrance, flipped over glasses, and poofed out their lanterns with a soft breath. So their searching right now shouldn't be too tough.

As they came up to the fire and plopped into the sagging camp chairs, biscuits, neatly nested in napkins, were already on the little side tables and Mwangi offered tea or coffee. No one really wanted to disturb the quiet blue-black veil of the night just yet, so we sat quietly, transfixed by dancing fingers of flame, side by side yet alone.

Ndiema, my driver, had opened up the

roof hatches and wiped down the moist windows. The night before he had brushed out all the dirt and wildebeest dung that we surely tracked in during yesterday's driving. As I started herding my little group toward the vehicle, I cast a quick glance at Ndiema, asking without words if he had already loaded the coffee, hot chocolate, and biscuits. He answered with an all-knowing smile. Of course he hadn't forgotten the obvious.

The moment we started, I went up through the roof hatch to sit on the roof, alone, soaking in the dawn and ducking low branches as we headed out of our camp, trying to keep my eyes from watering to the point of blindness in the cold air. It was a tad too breezy at the moment for anyone else to muster the energy required for spotting, and though Ndiema heard the lions, no one else did, so it was hard to convince them the lions could be close and that now was the time to start searching for them. I knew not to expect any other attitude this early in the safari. In another week, however, the guests would be pushing me, and anything I missed that they found I would most definitely hear about. But that's what I was striving for, so I could hardly complain.

Out of camp and across the first small plain, high in red oat grass, I saw nothing but zebras, impalas, and a few toepis. As we breached the top of the ridge, weaving through the rocks past the tilted leopard tree, the hyena clan was just coming in from the night's work. Apparently the pack had had a successful hunt, for each was covered in dried blood, now brownish-red, from tip of nose to base of neck. They cantered slowly past, throwing disdainful looks our way. With their heads low and their shoulders high, it was easy to see why so many people almost instinctively hate them, but if you catch hyenas up close and not fresh off a kill, they provide a different story. They are clean, and the little ones are as cute as teddy bears. As parents, hyenas excel. Maybe not this early in the day, but sometime on this trip, I would teach my clients about the hyenas' attributes. They have an intricate social system and complex vocalizations, and most important, in terms of correcting human assumptions about them, hyenas are *not* scavengers. They are predators, and as such are phenomenally *effective*, much more so than lions or leopards.

Clients are always amazed to learn that lions, not hyenas, are the greater scavengers. The initial misunderstanding arose because the earliest researchers on early-morning game drives saw lions on a kill, with hyenas on the outside waiting to steal it. One researcher, Wes Henry from the United States, wondered what data he might gather if he studied the situation at night, at the actual kill rather than hours later at 6:00 a.m. And what he learned is that the hyenas are making most of the kills, but their noisy yapping and yelping attracts the lions, who then scavenge the kill. It's a numbers game. I have a picture of seven lions trying to protect their meal from thirty-five hyenas. The hyenas finally won. They were smaller but had far stronger jaws. A single lion can handle only three or four hyenas, depending on the motivation of each side.

Ndiema pulled the Land Cruiser to a halt before we dropped down to the rocky crossing that led to the next ridge top of short grass, and at that moment I saw them. A scattered, dull-yellow line of faint forms was leaving the plain and working down toward the taller trees and the cover they offered. These were our lions. Even in this dim light I could easily see one of the huge males halfway back, lumbering along with loose paws and aged shoulders rolling with his gait, with cubs on both sides of him. I dropped down through the hatch and told Ndiema and the group that we'd scored. Lock and load cameras, check the film roll; if you're near the end just burn it off and reload with fairly fast film. The sun was still twenty minutes on the Indian Ocean side of the horizon, so it was going to be tough light for a while, but we had everything we needed here: three litters of cubs, females young and old, scarred and clean, and, of course, the two old gunfighters themselves. You can't really call them anything else. Look at that loose swaggering walk, the heads slowly swiveling from side to side taking it all in, evaluating the most benign movement, the most casual sound. There must have been close to thirty-five years of experience between them, no trifling factor in this world of predator and prey, where every season takes its mortal toll. Smooth rounded ears become gradually more tattered and scarred from brawling, chasing, and killing. (Thus the ear clock used by researchers for identification.) The wide flat nose bridge, the brow, and the cheeks pick up deep scratches that serve as badges of matings past. I had been following this pair since they were in their prime, strong, clean, striding with heads high as they patrolled their territory and ruled their prides.

The myth that female lions do all the work and males are lazy thieves is another misconception. Females do most of the *hunting,* but not most of the overall work. The males spend far more energy and risk more than females while maintaining their territory and defending it to the death. As a result, they have a shorter life span — 33 percent shorter, in fact, a span of ten years for males versus fifteen for females. In sum, it is harder to defend a territory than it is to hunt within it. Few animals other than humans will fight to the death over territory. We do it all the time, of course, and lions will as well. I've witnessed horrendous fights between males, but no death, which is usually accomplished by crushing the enemy through the skull after biting the lower back and paralyzing him. I have, however, seen paralyzed lions pathetically dragging their useless hindquarters across the plains.

The gang in the Land Cruiser was wound up and excited now. In spite of the many years of similar experiences, I was pumped up as well. I tried to politely tell everyone to talk softly and move slowly and smoothly, but the speed with which I was pulling my own camera gear up, checking film, switching lenses for something shorter, something faster, was sending another message.

"Tutajaribu mbele ya hawa, karibu na mti ile, iliyekufa. Nakumbuka kuweka gari yetu kando kabiza kwa sababu ya jua, na photos ya wageni wetu." I told Ndiema that we would try to post up in front of the lions, near a dead tree, and I reminded him to park completely sideways, so the angle of the sun would be right for photography. I explained to the group that the cardinal sin for wildlife photography is not being close enough. Moreover, candid shots and behavioral photographs are infinitely better than portrait work, and we had to let the lions be lions to get that action. So quietly, slowly, our bodies below the silhouette of the truck, nothing sticking out of the windows, we joined the pride. My guests were behaving perfectly, probably too scared to do much else at this point. The pride was right on top of us. My folks would relax soon enough, and by then the lions would have accepted us, so we just had to bide our time.

Soon the mothers flopped in the shade around the high ground of a termitarium, right next to the dead tree, and right next to us. The cubs naturally followed suit, but couldn't just lie down; there was no drama in that. Instead, they flung themselves to the ground with decidedly audible grunts and sighs, dying like gut-shot gunfighters in some cheap Western. Kittens are kittens the world over; these cubs just had to make a game out of everything. This particular area was short of bones, so a stick had to serve as the ultimate object to covet, and the game was on. Around the vehicle, even under it, the cubs were chasing the little boxy-headed boy who had the stick clamped in his jaws. Eventually he was outnumbered and surrounded, and after a ferocious, guttural growl, deeper than his few innocent months belied, he lost the wood to a small female, much slighter and slimmer than himself. Round two was off to a literally roaring start.

A small, solitary cub wouldn't join the ruckus over the branch and sat forlornly a meter or two from his mother's tail, watching the others with huge round eyes and wrinkled brow. Suddenly the female's tail twitched in an effort to dislodge the annoying flies, and the lone cub's ears tilted forward and his little paws aligned themselves. A short stalk found him sitting at the tail tip swinging at this "prey" with all the accuracy he could muster. Right and left the fat little paws cut an arc in the air, catching nothing at all. Finally he scored a hit and instantly scooped the tail tip into his mouth and clamped down. This surprised his mother, who reacted with a snarl and whirled around, slapping the little aggressor and sending him rolling smartly backward into the gully. He was out of sight down there, but we could hear him crying clearly, and eventually he pulled himself back up to lie in the grass, staring bewilderedly at Mom.

Mom's tail again swished at the flies, and the cub reemerged and started slinking in. He missed in rapid succession, and then had another score, another chomp followed by another snarl and another slap. Again the cub was somersaulting back down to the ditch. No crying this time and no delay either. Two black-tipped ears appeared over the edge and he belly-crawled back toward his target, focused and waiting for the tail to move. The female's ears were pointing backward, so we knew she heard the cub and was aware that he was coming again, but she pretended to sleep as her little killer moved in.

A sudden thump jostled the truck as one

of the sleek golden-yellow females threw herself over in our very shade, hitting the tire and sliding down to the ground. Within a few minutes, two cubs came over to nurse, which she allowed without complaint, even though they might not have been from her own litter. Communal suckling is the norm within a pride.

One of the old males sat down, carefully, keeping his head up and alert, though when he slid down into the dappled grass he was suddenly, completely gone except for dark eyes and ear tips. A tiny cub moved in. This was probably not going to be a good idea for the cub, so I tipped off the group to swing their cameras around and prefocus on the big male, who saw the little cub clumsily stalking through the short grass, stopping every three feet to raise up and check his direction, only to instantly flatten on the ground with deadly seriousness. The old man didn't turn but raised his head imperceptibly, showing us his gapping, drooling jowls and yellow, worn teeth. His eyes swiveled left to follow the two-month-old aggressor as he stumbled closer. At a grand distance of four feet, the cub finally launched his deadly attack, right at the throat of the 450-pound male. To everyone's surprise, the huge male toppled under the weight of the ten-pound killer and, groaning loudly, fell over flat, taking the cub with him. The little boy wasn't even slightly deterred. He had known he had this kill in the bag right from the start, so up he climbed on the neck of the mammoth male, got a sharp-toothed grip on his neck, and shook it for all he was worth, which, granted, wasn't awfully much. The old man groaned, pawed the air a little, and died. Off went the cub, bouncing toward his next prey, whereupon the dominant male raised himself back up and resumed his vigil as if nothing had occurred.

And thus the hours evaporated before us. I couldn't help but quietly ponder the thought of this stocky little male some day becoming very much the male he just "killed." There would be months of joyful play before that eventuality, however, and I reminded myself to be happy with that.

Mungai, the head driver, has worked at Lewa Downs Wildlife Conservancy for a decade and a half, and he knows his "back-yard" intimately. It was he who first intro-duced me to Gilbert. Like most bull elephants, Gilbert led a mostly solitary ex-istence vis-à-vis other elephants. Only occasionally would he join up with a breeding herd, and then only long enough to systematically check out the condition of all its female members for breeding status before moving out on his own again. He was christened Gilbert because he appeared at Lewa about the same time the hurricane of that name was bashing the east coast of Florida to bits, but Gilbert confined his destruction to vegetation. For reasons of his own, he became very social with humankind. But his friendliness did not help him; the fate of this huge elephant with the telltale divot the size of a Frisbee cut out of his lower left ear is a cautionary tale about the future of the wildlife of East Africa. The situation has changed dramatically in the more than twenty years since I first began studying with Mike and Judy Rainy, and I think it will change even more dramatically over the next twenty, as the human pressure on wildlife increases with a continuing explosion of human population.

My clients are surprised to learn that more than 70 percent of the wildlife in Kenya live *outside* the national parks and reserves of the country, shoulder to shoulder with the twenty-nine million people who in the year 2000 had an average annual income of $310. Only 10 percent of the land in Kenya is arable, and the remainder is seldom better for most animals than it is for crops, so the vise created by the human population can only clasp tighter and tighter around the free wildlife. Today, there are more leopards and lions in Kenya than ever before, but the abundance will not last. A single leopard needs fourteen square miles of territory and maybe *four times* that much from which to make his choice. The land is shrinking, and the cohabitation of people and animals is uneasy. For the Maasai and Samburu pastoralists, there's nothing romantic about losing a prized cow to a lion. Pull out a newspaper in Nairobi any week and you'll read about some farmer who has lost his entire grain crop to a few elephants within a matter of hours. We Westerners can afford the luxury of romanticizing the wildlife, but the average East African cannot.

Inevitably, I believe, in only a few decades Kenya will have little oases of wildlife confined to the national parks and the private game reserves. These oases are not utopias. In a confined space, even one as large as Tsavo near the coast, the Kenya Wildlife Service (KWS) cannot just "let the system run." The artificial borders make this impossible. The elephants would eat themselves out of house and home, creating a fruitless desert. Pressure created by tourists must also be controlled. When I first started as a part-time guide twenty years ago, we could camp anywhere in the parks, but that has changed radically. We are now restricted to certain established campsites.

The privately owned game reserves, of which there are about twenty, are also not natural environments with only natural borders. Electrified fences surround most of these reserves. Owners bring in so many elephants, so many leopards, so many cheetahs, so many zebras and giraffes, and then have to move some of these animals when the predator/prey ratio or one of the predator/predator ratios falls out of whack. Like other owners, the Craig family, who own the sixty thousand acres of Lewa Downs, are working closely with the Kenya Wildlife Service and many neighboring villages to institute a coordinated plan of village improvement and animal conservation, a setup known as a group ranch.

And into this little world stepped a certain elephant named Gilbert. At first he would merely tolerate vehicles near him, but in time he reached the point where he would hear a vehicle slowly working its way closer and then save you all the trouble by walking over to you instead. Elephants have a very complex and sophisticated vocalization system, so I was never surprised when, like Mungai and Will Craig, I called Gilbert by name and he responded. My clients, however, were surprised. I don't think the elephant necessarily knew what was being said, just as I don't think a dog necessarily understands the words, but Gilbert certainly understood that you were talking to him. He'd never hesitate to come right up to the vehicle — and I mean right up to the side of the open vehicle. The extremely close proximity could be very intimidating to us puny humans crammed in the Land Cruiser, especially if my clients were new to Kenya. Elephants are peaceful by nature but they do weigh in at five to six tons, all of it potential power and destruction. We'd sit there, generally frozen solid, while we looked at a massive elephant leg a mere five feet away. The leg led upward to a deep belly and vast chest. Above that, framed by blue sky, were two thick, though short, tusks, and the most massive, solar eclipsing ears, the left one with that identifying scoop cut out of it.

Gilbert would stand beside you, pretending to eat or fiddling with a branch or bush to occupy his time while he waited on you. Most of my clients were, at first, a bit too intimidated to feel free to move around and use a camera during those opening moments in his presence, but over the two or three days that we would stay at Lewa they would loosen up until they were photographing Gilbert and even talking to him, mimicking his own incredibly, bottomlessly deep and rumbling voice. With one group of clients, just off the airplane and astonished by Gilbert, I took one of their cameras, slid quietly out the side of the truck away from him, carefully backed up about fifteen feet, and took a shot of the group as they turned away from Gilbert for a moment to smile at the camera — the entire background was blotted out by Gilbert in all his gray greatness. Those families used that photo to pass along their message of peace and goodwill that Christmas.

Unlike me, Gilbert would never snap at anyone or do anything that he regretted in afterthought. He was always a gentleman with humans but just hell on trees. A year, maybe a year and a half after Gilbert first showed up at Lewa, he joined three other male elephants, and the four of them left only a tornadolike path of shattered trees in their wake. It became obvious that something had to be done, and there was uncomfortable talk of relocating or even shooting Gilbert. But his personality protected him. He had become such an integral part of Lewa Downs that everyone was always asking about him or relating to others their own "Gilbert experience."

It would have been impossible for the Craigs to shoot such an old friend, such a great ambassador of trust. The decision was made, therefore, to tranquilize the other three elephants and move them off Lewa to a national park where they would have more room to roam, thereby spreading their path of destruction over a far greater range. The plan was carried out without undue stress on any of those three animals, but it had an effect on Gilbert no one had anticipated. Without his old cronies he seemed lost. He took to wandering far abroad, perhaps searching for them. Lewa Downs is fenced except for one twenty-foot gap on the western side through which elephants and the other animals can pass over a low rock wall; many elephants do so because they prefer the sandy soil of Samburu over the sticky black soil of Lewa in the rainy season. Gilbert might have moved north to Samburu or Buffalo Springs, where larger numbers of elephants circulated. But I was up in those national parks every month, for days at a time, and kept an eye out for him, without luck.

Then one day or night about six months after his disappearance, Gilbert was killed on the unprotected ground that connects Lewa Downs with the Samburu reserve. He had been speared or shot by a local, probably, and not for his tusks, which were far from impressive in spite of his hulking body. His friends surmised that he had probably seen, heard, or smelled a human and had come sauntering up in all his grandeur. Without knowing about Gilbert and his friendly ways, his killer probably struck down the dangerous-looking elephant out of fear and a sense of self-defense. Gilbert was in the wrong place at the wrong time. They found his huge body awkwardly prostrate. I picture his telltale massive left ear lying like some wrinkled gray blanket spread unevenly across the ground and am glad I wasn't there. Humans, even in Africa, seem unable to share their tenure on the land.

★ ★ ★

Gilbert was locally famous in Lewa Downs. A female leopard in Maasai Mara named Half-tail became world famous, perhaps the most widely photographed and commonly viewed leopard of all times, and she, too, paid the ultimate price in the end for her symbiotic relationship with human beings.

Half-tail got her name because she found herself in just that state of disrepair after an extremely close encounter with a troop of irate baboons. (No animal would initiate such an encounter. Baboons are unbelievably strong and, when pushed to the wall, vicious. A large group of males is more than a match for any predator. Half-tail the leopard was fortunate to have that much of an appendage.) Surprisingly, perhaps, her trauma at the hands of baboons didn't affect her attitude toward their close relatives, human beings. She was incredibly patient with us and not shy in the least. When I would meet up with other guides in Nairobi someone would usually ask if Half-tail had been seen and, if so, where, and what had she been doing. One evening in Vancouver, British Columbia, at a slide show I gave for a crowd of about five hundred, someone asked if the leopard in

Maasai Mara with only a partial tail was alive and doing well.

I first met this leopardess before she had her run-in with the baboons. At the request of an exhausted group of safari-goers, I had left them in camp and gone out by myself for the afternoon game drive. Thirty minutes later I was passing below an outcrop of basalt rock, and there, unnaturally exposed, was a leopard walking back and forth across the jumbled little cliff. I pushed in the clutch, shut off the engine, and coasted down-slope to the base of the black rocks while trying to pull my camera out at the same time. The leopard ignored me. At the bottom of the cliff, I slowly rose up through the roof hatch and set my long lens across my jacket. Still she ignored me, and I realized she was searching or hunting for something concealed within the black rocks. Her head and shoulders would descend into one rock crevice, come back up, and move on to the next one. Sometimes her whole body briefly sank out of sight. During the whole process she never gave me so much as a fleeting look. Finally she laid down and cleaned herself with typical cat fastidiousness.

Back at the evening campfire I told the group about the leopard, and my excitement over her easy manner and apparent acceptance of my presence proved contagious, as I had hoped it would. At six o'clock the next morning, with blankets and coffee on board, sleepy but not too uncomfortable in the dampness of an unusual late-August rainfall, we were waiting for the dawn to break over those rocky cliffs. When it did, the leopard was missing — and stayed missing. We took a vote and decided to wait until 10:30, and then return to camp for a late breakfast.

At 10:13 a.m., I heard a silver-backed jackal deliver a series of barking yelps somewhere on the flat ground above the cliff and a little to the north. This was encouraging, I assured my group, for jackals usually reserve that alarm call for either leopards or cheetahs. We popped open all the dripping roof hatches and poked up into the flat gray air and waited. Now the barking approached from behind us and to the right, steadily gaining in volume as it neared. Then, as if it was the most normal thing in the world, the female leopard strolled out of the woods, came up behind our truck, sauntered past with those heavily rolling shoulders and incredibly loose paws, and bounded effortlessly onto the rocks.

As she started the very drill I had watched the previous evening, peering into a little crack or cave, then into another, the eastern sky finally lifted high enough for a surprisingly strong sun to light up the whole basaltic face. The leopardess vaulted back down to a wider grassy ledge and gave a soft series of grunts. There was a blur of slow motion a yard in front of her and, miraculously, an oh-so-tiny leopard cub stumbled bleary-eyed into the bright daylight. Fearful that the cub would rapidly retreat into the crack, we were jabbing one another and trying to point without making any motion — an impossibility. But the baby bumbled forward, eyes almost shut against the spotlight of the sun. Then a second cub came forth, and again we squirmed and tried to point without moving. The mother made no move, either, but let them approach her, licking each in turn.

In the truck we were speechless but no longer inactive. My motor drive practically overheated as I hurried to capture the cubs on film. That morning we were blessed, truly blessed, and the patience of my group had paid off. It was close to noon before the mother cat led the two little dappled balls of wadding into a wide crack in the rocks, her tail accompanying them into the dark. Instantly all of us began talking at once. For me, it was an amazing beginning to an enduring relationship. Along with many other guides, drivers, and clients, I watched those two cubs develop and come into their own. Both grew up in the inevitable presence of safari vehicles, but they endured the situation well and allowed us the same interactions with them that we found so remarkable with their mother.

And then the long friendship with the male cub ended. One day a vehicle from one of the lodges found the young but mature male up a tree, sleeping away the afternoon. A quick radio call to other drivers out on their treks soon produced a covey of cars surrounding the tree. Passing lions stopped by the scene, probably knowing from experience that such a gathering of vehicles could signify a kill, or perhaps it was just feline inquisitiveness that drew the pride near. Either way, they were immediately aware of the male leopard up the tree.

Lions will always go after leopards if they have the chance. They are mortal enemies, and the pride began pacing and moaning below the tree. The male got more and more nervous. Unable to stand the pressure any longer, he leaped from the tree and was instantly set upon and destroyed by the resident pride. Quite a show for the tourists in their trucks. I wasn't there, but it was painful for me to imagine the scene.

The female cub stayed within her mother's territory for almost two years before setting up her own on adjacent ground. Not long thereafter the mother leopard also died at the hand of man, and directly so. The facts are unclear, but apparently Half-tail killed a Maasai goat one afternoon, and that was all the excuse the Maasai needed to hunt her down. I doubt much skill was required for that stalk, considering how trusting this leopard had become of humans. For the price of a goat she was run through with a spear.

You want to spend $100 a day and go everywhere by road? Or you have ten days and you really must see at least six different game parks? Or you have eighteen good friends from your fraternity lined up for the trip? Then I'm probably not your man. My basic safari is geared toward four, five, or six people who have about sixteen days in-country and who want to stay in only three, maybe four places, flying between lodges on private wildlife reserves and, within the parks, staying in my personal mobile camps, as they are called in the trade. Some of these campsites are set on open savannah, others in deep forests, but all are heaven. A favorite camp of mine in the Serengeti in Tanzania is open and expansive, but with just enough shade provided by the lacy branches of the tortillis trees. The view down and across to Lake Ndutu, the occasional drumming thunder of a herd of wildebeests running past, and the sounds of the lions and hyenas echoing every night make this camp exquisite. A hundred miles to the north in Maasai Mara is an entirely different type of site, not exposed to the scene at all but tucked back in a thick forest grove of olive and croton trees. The Mara River is close but hidden in the valley below our private forest. This camp has an inviting mysteriousness thanks to the density of dark vegetation surrounding it on three sides.

In my early years taking groups of friends and their friends on safari, we slept wherever we could and it didn't much matter. But for my clients coming from the States, often with families or friends they've talked into joining them, expectations are higher — much higher. I mentioned earlier that I like to work slowly and deeply. Well, the comfort we can provide is a tremendous asset. My people come to Africa for the wildlife and the experience of being on the ground in this primal place, but if I can keep them fat and happy at home, so to speak, they are willing to trust me when I ask them to wait ten hours for that cheetah to finally start hunting. I love teaching and live for it. By raising the comfort level, I also mysteriously raise the trust level in my teaching.

While I don't want to guide the entire Sigma Chi house, I will accept the challenge of two families with four attitudinal teenagers who have seen it all. I have the nifty airplane, I have the big Land Cruiser, I have this amazing camp in the middle of nowhere, and I can probably put them so close to an elephant or a buffalo their hair will stand on end and they'll decide, wait a minute, maybe I don't know everything after all. Maybe there is something to learn and love here.

And so it was with the family of Bernard and Vicki DeWulf, in-country from Georgia. At the ripe age of eleven, Cappucine was the oldest of their three children. A teasable, expressive, and joyous girl, she loved everything and everyone around her. To my initial amazement, that love even extended to her younger brothers, to the point that she was often commenting to me, or to my staff, how good they were, how clever, how smart. This was delightful new territory for me; in my house growing up, the Ross children evolved as a deadly competitive group. Dean was a year behind Cappucine and a small, serious boy who already seemed to have taken on a lot of responsibility, including the welfare of both Cap and his admiring younger brother, James.

Children trust. They will naturally do what I ask of them and naturally want to be good, be loved, and be loving. This puts me in a wonderful, but delicate, position on safari. A little girl is definitely not afraid of *E. coli* in the water. A boy does not give a thought to what else may be in the mud that he desperately longs to stomp through. I must protect them, but I never want them to end up fearful. I can use their joy. If I want the parents out on top of the vehicle to feel the morning air and smell the buffalo or elephants as we drive by, I simply grab the nearest youngster and plop him on the roof. Suddenly a parent's head will appear through the roof hatch wanting to be a part of that child's experience.

I think it was Dean who focused on the heavy, wet soil beckoning to him from the spring in the yellow-bark acacia forest alongside the road at Lewa Downs. I only needed to glance around at that time of day to make sure no elephants were near, and then I stopped the car and encouraged him to jump out. Both Bernard and Vicki looked at me quizzically, but neither said no or questioned me too hard. This was a safe playground, and mucking about in that black mud, in this setting where we had seen rhinos, elephants and giraffes, would make the kids feel even safer. So they jumped into the mud — black, sticky, squiggly bottomed, unknown, deep. Cappucine, ever the little lady, was not in too great a rush to wade in, but her brothers were having such an obviously delightful time that soon she had no choice but to bend to the voice of her heart and get the mud between her toes. Bernard, Vicki, and I sat in the shade of a large acacia and watched. As the time slipped away, the afternoon game drive was forgotten. Children being children and Africa being Africa, this seemed like the perfect expenditure of time. By the end of that safari we had seen dramatic predators and had exciting encounters with huge mammals, including a charging buffalo, yet all of us, even today, also recall the mud pit that Dean had found beside the dusty road.

From Lewa we flew down to Maasai Mara and my private camp tucked back into an olive grove, surrounded on all sides by animals and opportunity. I immediately bet Cappucine that we could find all five of the major predators in the Maasai Mara in just one day. Not the Big Five big-game animals — leopards, lions, elephants, rhinos, and buffalo — but the five major predators: leopards, lions, cheetahs, hyenas, and wild dogs. The lions, cheetahs, and hyenas, I knew, should not prove to be too hard, but picking up leopards and wild dogs would be a challenge and require some luck as well. If I lost the bet Cappucine said I would have to wear my hair in pigtails for a day. If I won, I told her she would have to sleep outside the tent, on the open ground alongside me. So the deal was struck and the day started. By 11:30 that morning we had spent time with lions and hyenas, who, as territorial residents, were relatively easy for me to locate. On the way back to camp for lunch, we had the blind luck of seeing a leopard shooting across the track in front of us, darting from one forest patch to another. Three down, two to go. I grinned at Cappucine.

At four o'clock, as customary, we enjoyed tea and cake and were back perched on the roof hatches by 4:30. A drive way south into the main part of the park produced a cheetah with cubs, and we spent most of the remaining daylight with them. Four down, one to go. I continued to tease Cap unmercifully, telling her in great detail what it would be like to sleep out in the open. She teased me right back, saying how she was going to take a picture of me with my pigtails and send copies of it to all of my guide friends in Kenya, to show them what I really look like. The parents joined in with me, warning Cappucine that she was in for it, and she'd better start getting ready now. But she was carefree and confident as we turned for camp. We both knew we still needed a wild dog.

As we descended off the ridge and dropped down toward the west and our cozy canvas home, I looked back in the direction of the high ground and saw a rather odd silhouette under a distant acacia tortillis tree. We drove on a bit before I decided to turn the vehicle around and check out what I had noticed. It could well have been a family of black-backed jackals, just coming out of their den, and getting ready for their evening foray. Or it could just as easily have been the outline of bat-eared foxes, but I wasn't aware of a den of theirs in that area. Or it could be wild dogs.

With a shriek, Cappucine's hands shot to cover her mouth and she dropped through the roof hatch like an anvil when we saw the three wild dogs casually grooming one another in a patch of red oat grass. I started poking her unmercifully. "You're sleeping out with me. You're sleeping out with me," I kept chanting in a sing-song rhythm.

"No, no, I take it back, I take it back," she said. "I'll do anything else you ask, but don't make me sleep outside."

I was deliberately unmoved. "A deal's a deal, and you're out with me."

Somewhat to my surprise, Bernard and Vicki backed me up. Their daughter had made a bet and lost so she had to live up to her word. Cappucine squirmed on the seat, her arms wrapped tightly around her legs. James casually spoke up just then and saved the day. "I'll sleep out with you guys," he said. Then Dean said he would too, and this seemed to placate their sister.

When we got back to camp, the four of us dragged our bedding, bed frames and all, out of our tents and walked them forty yards out into the open plains and lined them up, side by side. I'm sure the staff thought I had gone off my bean.

After dinner we all sat by the fire, exhausted from the day, slightly burned by wind and sun, tired from the excitement of all we had seen. I pulled out the book I was reading every night to the children. After only a few pages they were almost asleep, smooth faces glowing in the firelight. The adults finished another cup of coffee in silence, the idling fire throwing a blanket of heat and light over us, the distant calls of all the Mara's night predators completing the ring around our camp.

Since everyone was so tired, I had decided that the children could sleep out another night, but when I got up Cappucine roused and asked me to wait for her. Then James and next Dean also roused, so we all headed off across the grass to the beds and our little adventure. Cappucine said she had to be in the middle, so I took one side and Dean said he'd take the other, leaving James by his sister. To our surprise, Bernard suddenly appeared, dragging his bed along, and announced that he'd decided to join us. His children were thrilled, and told him to sleep on the other end of the row, opposite me, and beside Dean. Now they were all yelling back up to the tent their mother was in, telling Vicki to come out under the stars too. She said there wasn't the slightest chance of us getting her out there, not in a million years, but just as everyone had finally settled down and a night's sleep looked like a possibility after all, Vicki called out from her tent plaintively, "It's lonely in here now. Someone come and carry my bed for me."

Bernard and I got up, trudged back through the dampening grass and carried Vicki's bed out, putting it in the long row inside of Bernard's. After another fifteen minutes of chatter, I heard the heavy breathing of someone finally sleeping.

In the morning, the camp staff couldn't contain their smirks and grins as they went down the row of beds in the grass offering coffee and hot chocolate to hands reaching out from under the dew-heavy blankets. We still had three days of camping here ahead of us, which would give me chances to take the group walking, have picnic lunches out in the bush, play by the river, even go fishing for the catfish that lay on the muddy bottoms of the river pools. A few miles out of camp on the morning game drive, paralleling the Mara River, Bernard saw something in a greenheart tree some four hundred yards uphill to our left. Neither our driver, Nganga, nor I had noticed any movement, but we could have missed something, though that was highly doubtful in Nganga's case. He'd been driving for quite a number of years now, and was incredibly sharp; little passed unnoticed before his Kikuyu eyes.

But Bernard was right. We had missed something, and something significant as well. When we were still a hundred yards from the two dense greenheart trees that grew as one, the outline of a leopard became fairly obvious. As we drew quietly up to the trees, we could see a medium-sized cat crouched over a kill, an impala, on a wide protruding branch, a little less than halfway up the tree. We finally got all the children's eyes and binoculars on it and settled down to photograph and watch.

Perhaps fifteen minutes had passed in silence when, to our total surprise, a little leopard cub about three months old crawled out from under a croton bush and somewhat clumsily pulled itself up the tree to snuggle against its mother beside the meat. Cameras clicked and flashes popped and the kids oohed and aahed as the cats fed, taking no notice of us whatsoever. Another Land Cruiser passed by on the track down by the river, stopped, and altered its course to join us, which is standard operating procedure in the parks and can result in a dozen vehicles being camped around one scene. We really didn't want to share "our leopards," so we quickly schemed a plan before the interlopers arrived.

"Habari zenu?" The driver of the other vehicle greeted us. How are you all?

"Tuko sawa, asante. Na ninyi, inaendelaje?" Nganga replied. We're all right. And how does it go with you all?

"Vizuri, lakini bado kuona kitu leo. Mmekuwa na bahati?" the driver said. Good, but we haven't seen anything today. Have you all had any luck?

"Hapana. Tunatafuta ndege tu." Nganga replied. No. We're just looking for birds.

Fortunately, the group of white heads sitting on the seats did not come up through the roof hatches to follow the foreign conversation, so the leopards not thirty feet away went unnoticed by them all. They thanked us, turned their wheels back toward the river, and drove west again. The DeWulfs couldn't believe the other group had not seen the cats in the tree, but neither Nganga nor I was particularly surprised. The average visitor to the game parks does, sadly enough, just sit passively in the vehicle until the driver stops and points something out for them. This leaves everything up to the driver, and if the driver . . . never mind.

The two leopards soon descended from the greenheart tree, the mother in long, effortless bounds, the cub clutching and scratching for dear life and dropping the last few feet in a soft thump to land unceremoniously in the tall grass right beside our truck. We were all dead silent and motionless, and the mother's eyes swung slowly down the length of the vehicle, seeming to assess each face in turn. The cub sat on his fuzzy little butt beside her dappled flank, curiously waiting to see what would happen next. The leopardess lay down and commenced to clean herself up after her breakfast and the cub did likewise for a bit, before his curiosity got the better of him and he decided to stalk our left front tire, very carefully placing one paw at a time, inching snakelike through the grass, closer . . . closer, until he was near enough to push his little face out as far as it would possibly go while keeping his body back as far as he could while he sniffed the black rubber. His nose suddenly convulsed and he jumped back, returning to his mother's safe presence, where he again mimicked her cleaning motions.

We eventually headed out, and, surprisingly, neither mother nor cub shot for cover when we cranked up the engine and backed away. They simply stopped grooming and watched us benignly as we eased back from their trees. We returned at lunchtime, and they were still there, but back up in another greenheart tree, sound asleep, barely able to raise their heads at our approach. And late that afternoon, they were there still, but with a different attitude regarding our presence. To my utter amazement, after just a few minutes the cub slowly backed down the trunk, groping at branches and bark, and dropped in the greenery at the base of the tree. Seconds later his spotted head poked out of the tall red oat grass, and he carefully walked up close to our green truck while his mother remained in the tree, watching.

The six of us crammed ourselves into the left side of the truck, filling the windows above the little leopard, who sat in the grass less than ten feet away, looking at us, a disarmingly quizzical expression etched on its young face. It seemed that we had a curious new friend on our safari.

We saw lions and cheetahs during the next few days and went out to Lake Victoria, where James caught a fish that outweighed him by four pounds, but checking on our leopards became the priority, our time with them overriding all else. We adjusted our routine as we departed and returned to camp, and mother and cub adjusted their routine a bit for us as well. When we arrived, the cub would be on the ground waiting for us in the patch of grass that the truck had pushed flat. There was no doubt about this, because once, when we first came around the broad curve that put us in sight of the tree, we stopped to watch through our binoculars. The rumbling diesel must have gotten his attention, for he was already staring in our direction. Then he started his mad and clumsy scramble down the tree and was patiently waiting for us long before we drew near.

On the third morning, Cappucine said we had to name this "sweet little cub." Sugar is sweet, and sugar is *sukari* in Kiswahili. That afternoon, as if our naming him had broken through any remaining barriers, Sukari tried to join us in the Land Cruiser — literally. He strolled up confidently and circled our truck, studying each human face in turn, taking us all in. As he came around to the front passenger window, I watched him sit down, gather himself together, back legs coiled underneath, front paws close together. His head swung back and forth in slow motion, like a hypnotizing snake, and it suddenly dawned on me he might want in. As smoothly as I could, I reached around Vicki and rolled up the window most of the way, and none too soon. Seconds later Sukari launched himself and smacked hard into the glass. He fell back to the ground, landing on his backside and falling over, very undignified and uncatlike, and looking affronted. He regained his composure and pulled himself halfway up, looked at all of us with a tremendously hurt expression, and then fell back on his side.

We could no longer contain ourselves. The DeWulf children seriously wanted to let him in. "He wouldn't think of hurting us," Cappucine said. "I just know he wouldn't."

"No, he certainly wouldn't do it on purpose," I agreed. "But he might by accident. And besides, it's his mother I'm worried about, not really Sukari."

"But," James piped up, "she's not even

looking at him or watching what's going on." Which was true. She just lay in the tree, facing slightly away from us at an angle, sleeping, or appearing to, as the kids pleaded with me. For a few unwise seconds I actually debated rolling down the window. Then I told the children we just couldn't do it. Sukari listened intently to the dialogue, then proceeded to walk to the next passenger window and coil himself for another attempt. Before he could embarrass himself further, I slowly put an opened hand against the window glass, and spread my fingers wide to fill as much space as possible. He stared at my hand and cocked his head in that engaging sideways manner of his, but he relaxed his stance and finally flopped down altogether, both disgusted and resigned.

On the day we were to leave the Mara and fly back to Nairobi, we had to go the long way around to the airstrip so we could say a sad good-bye to our friends, particularly the little one. He was waiting, of course, and then, when we started to pull away, Sukari began to walk toward the retreating bumper. The cub paused as Nganga turned the vehicle around, but as soon as we had begun to drive off he came to his feet and started following us. Dean and James were at the back windows, and the rest of us were on the roof, following Sukari's progress. Vicki and Cappucine were almost in tears. And, unfortunately, he was keeping up. Little cubs are granted no immunity in Africa; on the contrary, any lions or hyenas that picked out his form as he walked through the grasses would certainly kill him.

I told Nganga to speed up, which he did, but Sukari broke into a canter and kept with us, perhaps even slightly closing the distance. Vicki and Cap were almost beside themselves, the tears flowing, but Sukari was getting dangerously far from the safety of the trees and his mother. Then Nganga really stood on the gas. We had to make sure that Sukari stopped now, while he was still within range of the protective forest. Smoke pumped from the exhaust as we picked up speed, and Sukari fell behind. We stopped half a mile away, at the far end of the plain, and I leveled my binoculars backward and could just barely make out a gold-and-black irregularity weaving through the tall grass stems between our tire tracks as Sukari worked his way back to his mother in the greenheart trees.

Not long ago, I pulled from my mail an

envelope that I took to be an invitation, with its satin color and finish and elegant, raised lettering. The return address was the DeWulfs' home in Atlanta. Moments later, I held a wedding invitation in my hand. It was Cappucine's. I couldn't believe that many years had elapsed since I had read to her by the fire and made her pay her debt by sleeping beneath the stars in the Maasai Mara.

At the bottom of the invitation, Cap had written just five words: "How is Sukari? Love, Cappucine."

Unable to leave Kenya for the wedding, I mailed back my RSVP with regret and added a few words at the bottom as well: "Sukari is a bit ahead of you, I should think. He must have grandchildren by now. Love, Mark."

5

Good Intentions

Like all children, I grew up with certain potent sayings of my parents forever ringing in my ears. Whenever one of us kids had tried and failed at something, my mother would declare, "The road to hell is paved with good intentions." I did not expect this adage to be a truism in relation to how we conduct ourselves around African wildlife, but time would prove it so.

August in Samburu can be a dry, windy month. As strong currents blow down from Mount Kenya and the higher, cooler escarpment to the south, we are often forced to restake our tents time and again. But this particular camp had held up well, and so had my group, which included a mother, Eleanor, and her thirty-eight-year-old daughter, Marie. The younger woman had just completed a successful month trekking in Nepal and was reveling, justifiably, in her healthy vigor. After the high cold of Nepal and the cold wetness of the mountains near Mount Kenya where we had camped previously, the warm and thick air of Samburu must have been a joy in itself.

Late one morning, easing back into camp, we came across a breeding herd of twenty-one elephants lazing away the early heat of the day by standing tightly clumped under the thin shade of an acacia tortillis tree. The mammoth sun-speckled shapes swayed gently back and forth, with two little ones lying flat on their sides safely surrounded by a forest of thick, gray legs. The elephants had obviously been at the nearby river, the Ewaso Ngiiro, for they were no longer the reddish color of the soil, but the gray shade of freshly cleaned elephant hide. As we were only a few hundred yards from camp, we paused to take some photographs and soak in the peaceful scene. We then drove the short final distance back to our riverside camp, where lunch and an afternoon nap were waiting for us. My camp manager, Lynn, greeted us as we disembarked, little clouds of sandy dust exploding from our clothing as we jumped down. Marie then asked if we could go back on foot and spend a bit more time watching the dozing herd.

In one context or another I hear that question often, and my answer may be the most critical one I give on that safari. On a game drive, getting close to wild animals in a vehicle is one thing, sometimes even difficult and exciting, and sometimes the only alternative. But stepping out of the vehicle, however briefly, drastically changes one's perspective for the better. It changes one's very reality. Those moments when I can get people out of the truck and involved with the land, almost invariably end up being the true highlights of their safari. It does not have to be a self-inflicted "near-death" experience that suddenly allows one to feel finally and fully alive. Far from it. It could be flat-water rafting or calmly canoeing on the Zambezi River, or walking across a tiny bit of the endless Serengeti on foot, or a week's horseback trip through the Maasai Mara. Just sitting on the ground a mere fifty yards from the truck and watching the sun sink over the Chizarira escarpment in Zimbabwe can work wonders. Or stopping suddenly and suggesting that one person in the group walk one hundred yards in one direction, another person one hundred yards in another direction, and so on, and asking them to sit down, or lie down, and simply make no sound for half an hour. They love it. What's going on? Nothing, nothing at all, except unfiltered Africa: you and a continent.

Sometimes, however, there is a risk. We have an inherent craving to experience life cleanly, purely, and intentionally stalking animals is as good as it gets in this regard on safari, but the wild animals are just that — wild. They are also bigger, faster, stronger than us, and they have at least one or two senses that are much sharper than ours. In their own environment, they're designed to get the better of the encounter most of the time. So the trick is to create an honest adventure and to get people intimately involved with wildlife while keeping them safe at all times.

The key is gauging the setting. *Surprise* is not a good thing. If, for example, a lion lying in the grass sees you approaching on foot from a distance, he will naturally assume that you see him. He smells you, and he assumes you smell him. But you don't, and you keep walking toward him. When you're seventy-five yards away, he growls, but not loudly: "Go somewhere else." But you don't hear him and keep coming. At twenty-five yards he growls again, but still you're deaf to his warnings. At fifteen feet, he feels it's too late, he's pinned down, so he has no choice but to charge. The newspaper headline reads, ROGUE LION ATTACKS TOURIST, forcing the rangers to drive out and hunt him down. But that lion charged out of defense. A couple of years ago in Zimbabwe a young man heard lions prowling around his tent and panicked. Inside the tent he was perfectly safe, but he ran outside and induced a charge.

You and I are not a prey species for predators in Africa or anywhere else. We humans are to be feared, a reaction that is by now genetically hardwired in these animals after millennia of experience dealing with us. We're only trouble. In a car, on a camel or a horse, we're usually ignored, maybe even accepted; on two feet, however, we can be dangerous. Why would a buffalo want to kill you unless somewhere deep in his synapses you signal danger? After all, he eats only *grass*.

In some cases the animals may be used to human presence, but they are individual enough to have their own good days and bad ones, times when their patience has no end and times when they easily become fed up. Animals that have previously encountered humans will undoubtedly judge the rest of us by the quality of those first encounters. Who knows what has happened to a given herd of elephants? Who knows how they will react? I can often tell when an elephant is going to pause right there in the road and give our Land Rover a good ear-flapping and shake of the head before he proceeds, but I can't *guarantee* what he will do thirty seconds later. I must read the situation minute by minute, second by second, or animal by animal, but I can't predict what the elephant might do *instead* of flapping his ears. A herd of elephants feeding peacefully for two hours can turn for reasons unknown and try to kill anyone nearby. That is, for reasons unknown *to us*. I've had to shoot a lioness who came at us from six hundred yards. We walked into it in tall grass, heard it growl, and immediately backed up for maybe fifty yards. Then we turned around and walked in another direction, assuming she had stayed put. But six hundred yards later — we measured the distance, after the fact — she charged. Hidden in tall grasses, she had followed us without our knowing it. She seemed to want us. It was very unusual behavior, but understandable from her perspective: she had four cubs tucked away. Even after being shot, she came through the line of people, her momentum was so great.

And human behavior can be just as unpredictable. In a tight situation you may catch yourself by surprise and see a new, perhaps flawed, facet of your behavior, abilities, or character. If you don't get killed or kill someone else in the process, the incident might teach you something and make you much stronger. But what if someone does get killed? Africa does not suffer fools gladly. No place where life and death exist cheek by jowl does. Even on a mobile flying safari experiences continually bring you up against yourself. Clients haven't been under that kind of pressure before. Telling them not to run, or to run in a certain direction, is one thing, but compliance may well be another.

When I weigh a situation or a request such as Marie's, my instinct is to get the people out of the vehicle and on the ground. My parents, by placing me in physically challenging situations all the time, and especially during our summers in the mountains, helped me develop into a physically confident and able individual. I am not a parent, but being a guide must be somewhat like being a parent at times. I fear for my clients, naturally as well as professionally; this fear is part of every guide's job. Like parents, I am frequently forced to evaluate physical, mental, and emotional abilities. Like parents, I usually get it right, but sometimes get it wrong.

When Marie asked if we could set out for the nearby elephants on foot, I'm sure I paused at least momentarily before I said, sure, we could go back, assuming the elephants were still there after lunch and still sleeping. And I knew she was tough and physically strong, gauging that she'd be quick and responsive in a tricky situation. During lunch the conversation again came around to Nepal and the joys and difficulties of trekking in that remote domain. Marie had loved every moment and hadn't even minded the bouts with sickness from the physical stress. Walking among such cathedral-like mountains had been worth it all. We finished eating and Marie went back to the truck to select the camera gear she wanted to use should we get close enough to the sleeping elephants. I told her we certainly wouldn't end up all that close, so she'd probably better grab her 300-mm telephoto, or at least her 80-200-mm zoom. She opted for the zoom and exchanged the film in her camera for a full roll.

Because there was not much cover on the near side of the herd, we would go around to the far side, the upstream side, which had much thicker cover provided by the salvadora, or toothbrush, bushes. As we walked along I told Marie the rules for stalking any animal and she understood. When we got closer we would evaluate how relaxed the herd was, but since they had barely awakened when we drove right beside them an hour earlier, I didn't expect much change now. She would most likely be free to shoot all the photographs she wanted from the dramatically low angle of the ground. If the elephants did charge, I said, I would remain behind to give her a head start, and she should run back down the same route we were going to use for our approach, but not run so fast as to risk tripping. I knew she was fit and didn't seem the least concerned about being on foot rather than inside the four-wheeled safety of the Land Cruiser.

After we wound through the bushes for a few minutes, I whispered directly into her ear that she should remain here for a few minutes while I went ahead and scouted out the exact position of the elephants and got a better idea of how precisely we could approach them. She was fine with the idea of remaining by herself, which I took as a very good sign. I left her crouched by a huge acacia elatior tree as I gently and silently picked my way forward, straining for that first view. We had guessed exactly right. The path that we were on led me to a position seventy-five to one hundred yards upstream of the group and still well-covered by the protective wall of greenery. This was an ideal setup, with room enough on the path to photograph and plenty of room in which to turn around and retreat when finished, and at a distance that would allow for the accidental misstep or whispered conversation. But as they say in investing, "If it's too good to be true, it probably is."

I quietly returned the way I had come, met with Marie, and carefully laid out in hushed whispers the direction of the track, where we would end up, where she could stand, and how we would depart the area. I also told her again that if all hell broke loose she was to retrace her steps. "This path," I said, "you'il go right down this track."

She looked back the very path on which we'd just arrived. "But that's where we just came from."

"That's right. So you know how to get back to camp."

She shrugged.

"If I tell you to run, that's where you'll go."

She nodded absentmindedly, already thinking ahead to her photography.

I went on. "You wait for me only when you're back in camp. Nowhere else."

"Nowhere else," she echoed.

I thought these instructions might all be regarded as somewhat overly dramatic, so I added that stalking on foot, particularly with the larger animals, was like aviation in that you hoped for the best and had a contingency plan for the worst. She nodded in assent, a brief smile creasing her face, and we turned and started our approach.

When we arrived at the predetermined spot at the edge of the open, sandy country, the elephants were right in front of us, seventy-five yards away, still sleeping, rocking slowly and rhythmically in the intense afternoon heat. For the third time, with my lips brushing Marie's ear, I reminded her to run immediately if I told her to. I even took the unnecessary step of physically turning her by the shoulders and showing her the path that she had just walked up. If you've driven only one way up a road, or walked one way up a path, the reverse view can be substantially different, even completely unfamiliar. Marie

214

glanced briefly down the path, nodded in agreement, took the lens cap off the zoom, stepped from behind me, and raised her camera to her eye. I rested my hand solidly on her shoulder. She took the time to focus carefully, balance the metering by turning the aperture ring on the lens barrel, and even swinging the 200-mm back and forth a bit, deciding on her composition. In spite of the harsh midday heat, the elephants should photograph well, with the widespread acacia branches reaching out past their massive forms. A beautiful black-and-white shot, I thought, though Marie had loaded color. Finally she was happy with her preparation and was ready to shoot. I still had my hand on her shoulder when the shutter fired and the motor drive advanced the film.

At that precise moment, the world erupted and the ground thundered beneath our feet. I could literally feel the thudding through my sandals and into the bones of my legs. My stomach turned. I glanced at Marie and saw a frozen form, camera half lowered from her face. Her mouth was parted, her eyes focused on something in the near distance. I turned back to follow her gaze and instantly understood why she was spellbound. The entire herd of elephants that had been sleeping just seconds before was now charging directly at us.

I waited a few tense seconds. Most elephant charges are merely bluff, a mock charge to get a point across. Their point here was well taken, but the distance between us and them was rapidly diminishing. My hand still rested on Marie's right shoulder, and I picked it up and gave her a very solid thump and said with deliberate vigor, "Run now!" I really wasn't convinced that the charge would continue, for the whole herd was on the run, even the little babies that had been sacked out on their sides. I waited, fairly sure that all this noise would die down and the herd would angle to our left, out into the openness of the sandy flat ground. Why would they charge into this dense foliage? So I stayed crouched behind the edge of the bushes as long as I could make myself wait and then turned to run down the path toward the river, where Marie should have been by then.

As I did so, I glanced back at the elephants, who had indeed turned toward the open ground. What a relief. I came back around, still watching the lead female, and was puzzled to see her lower her head and gather her trunk underneath her chin — classic signs of a serious charge. Something was just about to take a deadly pounding. But what? I turned a bit further around to my left and, out of the corner of my eye, saw a form running away from me, right out in the open, heading *away* from the river and the safety of the covering vegetation.

For some reason Marie had run not back down the path, where she would now be perfectly safe, but across the rocky packed sand right in front of the herd. And she was making slow time with short, babylike steps. Elephants can run at least twenty-five miles per hour, maybe faster. These elephants were closing ground with every stride. Without thought, preparation, or choice, I sprinted out as well, parallel with and ahead of the herd, yelling at Marie, "Turn to the left! Turn to the left!"

But my calls were drowned out by the ear-splitting trumpets and the thundering feet of the infuriated herd. I kept yelling and running, finally catching up with — incredibly — a *bare-footed* Marie just before the elephants did. We had run over two hundred yards, the last thirty or so with the herd right on us. Marie was fast running out of gas and starting to cry.

Out of sheer desperation, I reached down and scooped up a handful of sandy soil and turned back toward the female at the front of the charging phalanx. I screamed and threw the sand into her face, and she jammed her legs straight down and literally skidded to a stop, other elephants crashing into her. Marie went down too, touched by nothing that I saw. I grabbed a second handful of dirt and flung that at the stunned elephants as well, while I yelled and screamed and waved my arms.

The elephants bolted away from us, to our left, still in a tightly packed mass of flapping ears and trumpeting voices. I picked up Marie and trotted toward the bushes and the safety of the river. Seconds later I could hear the elephants coming again, crashing right through all the small trees and bushes in their way. Still carrying Marie, I slid off a little edge and down into a sandy gully, cut six or seven feet deep by the previous season's rains. I crouched down there, imploring her with words and eyes to be very, very still. In their own panicked run the herd tore right past us along the lip of the wash. As if by magic, everything was suddenly quiet and deathly still; no sounds anywhere, not even a bird. We waited and waited, and I tried to slow my breathing to a point where I could listen carefully. Marie was no longer limp but anxiously looking around and starting to breathe in almost tearful gasps. Again I implored her to be quiet: "We can't let them find us."

Finally, I let her slide out of my arms to sit on the hardened sand and cautiously stood up to peer out. I could see nothing but a distant cloud of dust about four hundred yards upstream, blowing crosswise away from us. I bent back down and inspected Marie's feet. They were nothing but bloody shreds. It turned out that she had badly blistered both feet during a previous day of wet hiking, leaving just one paper-thin layer of useful skin after the calluses had peeled off. This layer had then peeled like an orange during her run from the elephants. The exposed meat was bloody and embedded with particles of rock and bits of thorns. I was astounded that Marie had managed to keep running as long as she did and grudgingly admired her strength.

With her on my back, helping to hold herself in position, we regained the path and headed down to the river and continued toward the camp, where everyone was waiting anxiously at the edge of the clearing. They had heard the tremendous din of the trumpeting and running, and of trees snapping in front of the stampeding elephants, but they had not a clue how close Marie and I had come to being killed.

My camp manager, seeing the state Marie was in, wisely poured two half-tumblers of straight gin for her, and the crew brought a plastic basin of hot water full of the disinfectant dettol in which Marie soaked her feet. I was furious but managed to contain it. Why hadn't she run the way I'd told her? Why had she run directly *into* the danger? And where were her goddamned shoes, anyway? I suppose I was scared, as well as deeply upset with myself for having gotten into that predicament with a client.

After the fourth tumbler of gin I pulled up a chair opposite Marie, withdrew one of her feet from the grayish water, and started cleaning it with a pair of tweezers from the medical kit. But there was so much sand driven into the raw flesh the tweezers were worthless. I scooted my canvas chair into position beside her, wrapped one of her legs with my left arm, held the ankle in a solid grip, and proceeded to scrub with my own toothbrush, occasionally stopping when she couldn't stand it any longer. Marie was brave and, surprisingly, not at all tipsy, much less drunk. Her metabolism must have been running at such an overload that the alcohol had no visible effect whatsoever.

She held her mother's hand and talked a blue streak. We carried Marie in her chair to the fire, and she stayed on the hard stuff all that evening. I wanted to ask over and over again, "Why did you run the wrong way?" But she had no idea: she simply couldn't recall the initial charge or my thumping her shoulder and telling her to run. She did remember what the plan had been, but that was about it. And the shoes? She thought that she would probably be faster barefoot than encumbered by footwear.

On the night after our arrival there another group of travelers came in from Samburu, bringing with them a harrowing story about a small herd of elephants that had been harassed by Somali bandits just outside the reserve four days earlier. One member of the herd had apparently been speared. One day later, the day after we arrived in Samburu, that same herd had caught and trampled to death two Samburu warriors as they returned from washing at the river. So, a couple of days after that, this was the herd that had charged us, provoked by the simple click of the shutter in Marie's camera, a click that almost got us killed.

"Rhino!" Mungai said sharply, pointing to the animal clear across the valley at Lewa Downs. The dirt track leading toward the rhino wound across the basin, up the far side, and then disappeared around a sizable hill before it climbed the slope above where the animal now fed. He suggested that I go in on foot from below with a few of the group — two families from Denver — while he took the car around and met us above the scene. It was a good plan, and I immediately had two volunteers who wanted to stalk. The young teenagers Big Ben and Little Ben would walk with me while their respective parents and sisters rode around to the high position with Mungai.

It was a white rhino, which is, along with the black rhino, severely endangered throughout East Africa, the result of poaching for the benefit of the young men of Yemen, who use rhino horn for the handles of their treasured daggers. The population of both species in Kenya has decreased from twenty thousand just twenty years ago to about four hundred today. Lewa plays host to about fifty of these. The distinguishing names have little to do with color, although guide books say that the white is a slightly lighter gray than the black. The "white" derives from the Afrikaans word "weit," or broad, which suggests the wide, square muzzle that makes this herbivore a grazer, while the black rhino, with its long prehensile upper lip, is a browser. The white rhinoceros is the second largest land mammal, after the elephant, approaching four tons, yet it was a slightly smaller black rhino that is credited by authoritative sources with derailing a train.

Both white and black rhinos, I explained to the boys, depend on their ears and their noses. Their eyes are almost vestigial, but their other senses more than make up for it. We were downwind of this creature, so she wouldn't be able to smell us. The difficulty would be trying to move in absolute silence. I don't believe the often heard assertion that rhinos' hearing is keen enough to pick up our heartbeats at close range, but their ears are phenomenal. We scanned our approach route with the binoculars, noting the trees along it that were big enough to get behind or up into, should the need arise. The two Bens agreed to do absolutely what I said and when I said it, and to do nothing else. They understood the ground rules. While we were going over all of this, Mungai interrupted to point out that the rhino had a tiny, tiny baby with it, one so small it looked like a warthog.

We set out on the stalk. The first three hundred yards were easy; we didn't even have to worry much about being quiet. We didn't sing and dance, but we were still out of range of even a rhino's superb hearing. A little farther on we dropped into a drainage, and as we came up and out of that we were then on the same slope as the two rhinos. We paused here, partly to get our breath and partly to go over the plan again. Both Bens were good athletes, and I had no doubt that they would be capable of a sprint to safety, probably leaving me in their dust. We moved off again, unnecessarily bent over. You don't walk any quieter when you're hunched up, but everyone seems to do it anyway. In a few more minutes we were about thirty or forty yards straight downhill from the two animals, with a solid acacia tree in front of us.

Neither mother nor child had any awareness of our presence. Even when we started taking pictures the sound of the shutters either went unnoticed, which I doubted, or it just wasn't enough to alarm the mother rhino. We fired a few more frames and then stood still, just watching the baby as it head-butted its mother and "sprinted" in tiny circles before her massive hulk.

Mungai, meanwhile, had brought the truck all the way around and was now coasting down the rock-strewn slope toward the rhinos, the engine shut off. He bounced over the occasional boulder, but none were big enough to bring the Land Cruiser to a stop. I was relieved that the six members of the families who had stayed behind in the truck were still getting a good view of the small calf. It was a rare encounter, and everyone needed to have a chance to see and film it. The mother rhino, some two tons of her, stood stock still while her calf danced exuberantly, blowing off steam as he charged aimlessly around. Occasionally he would run back in and go for his mother, who would simply lower her massive head, allowing the calf to bounce right off the stout front horn.

Mungai kept steadily coasting in closer, and still the rhinos ignored him. They did so, in fact, until the moment he rolled over a large dead branch concealed in the yellow grass. The branch snapped like a rifle shot, and then half of it flipped up against the truck with a great whanging echo.

Instantly the rhinos, with the baby in the lead, came charging downhill directly at us. They weren't actually charging us, but rather were running away from the source of the violent and sudden noises that had torn the silence. Their racing retreat just happened, by unlucky coincidence, to take them directly into our path.

I grabbed one Ben in each hand, taking a solid grip on their collars, and waited, ready, knees bent, eyes on the racing rhinos.

As the baby reached the acacia we were hiding behind, I threw both Bens under its thorny branches and dived in behind them. The small one zipped past us, its mother thundering on its heels, literally shaking the ground. Just below us, and now therefore downwind, she skidded to a stop, undoubtedly smelling us for the first time, debating what to do next.

We had nowhere to run, so our fate for the moment was up to her. After a few tense seconds, she turned and rumbled off down the hill to catch up with her calf, her tiny tail curled up on her wide rump.

I extricated myself from the wait-a-bit thorns, as they're called, and pulled out first one Ben, and then the other. Both were scratched, blood welling up in the thin lines etched by the curving thorns, but otherwise fine. I had a scratch, too, right down my forehead to a point just between my eyes. We started up the hill toward the car, laughing, the rhinos long gone. We could see the four parents and the two girls all standing up in the Land Cruiser, looking down the hill in our direction. I'm sure Mungai was looking our way as well. As we drew near, wiping the dusty blood from the scratches, one of their mothers cut loose on me.

"What the hell were you doing out there?!" she shouted at me. "You could have gotten them killed!"

Mungai sat in the front seat, studiously keeping his eyes on the speedometer, his shoulders jerking slightly up and down as he chuckled. I replied evenly, "We were doing just fine until you showed up, weren't we?" I paused, then continued, "We didn't have the slightest problem at all until you all came rolling down and chased the rhinos into us."

We looked at each other, temporarily out of wind and words. Then one of the girls spoke up and softly asked, "Did you guys see the leopard?"

We stopped, surprised. "What leopard would that be?" I inquired slowly, unbelieving.

"The one that took off out from under that bush," she indicated with a raised arm. "Are you serious?" her father asked, not sure whether to believe or doubt his daughter.

"Yeah. There was a leopard that ran out from there, or at least I think it was a leopard. Some big cat, anyway."

I asked Mungai if he'd seen anything, but he said no. Nobody else had seen the cat, and I guess the doubt showed on everyone's faces. The girl who'd spoken up was starting to feel bad, I could tell, so I suggested we go over and have a look at the bush she had pointed to, just as a way to defuse the situation.

At the bush I crouched down on my knees, and there was no question about it. Four neat prints, symmetrically paired, were indented in the ground beneath it. Connecting the two pairs of impressions was a single, large impression, where the cat's belly had been pressed down into the soft soil. Mungai crawled in beside me and carefully pulled out a few hairs that had remained behind in the belly print when the leopard had fled as the rhinos charged past.

Mungai turned and handed the hairs to Heather, who was now standing behind us. "Leopard," he said, and started silently back uphill to the truck. I could see only the back of his head but knew there was a broad smile on the other side.

The rhinos I have encountered that were raised in captivity don't seem to start out all that tough or all that mean, but the charge of a wild adult is for real, a guaranteed adrenaline rush as the tonnage comes at you. However, it can usually be turned aside by yelling and waving. With the Bens, I didn't have the time, or I would have tried this. The vast majority of elephant charges are false charges that end in bluffing stand-offs. The elephant may even inexplicably back off, as did the ones who were chasing Marie in Samburu. Lions, too, are usually bluffing and can be stopped in their tracks with a lot of noise. The one thing you don't want to do is run. Running instantly converts you, in the lion's eye, from predator to prey, and then, most assuredly, only a bullet will keep you from going down before them. Leopards, cheetahs, hyenas, baboons, giraffes, and the antelopes will flee your two-footed presence except under exceptional circumstances. Baboon troops can be aggressive and, if so, very dangerous. And hyenas have certainly caused trouble with sleeping people.

Cape buffalo is the one big-game animal whose charge, in my experience, is never a bluff and can never be turned. They seem singularly lacking in curiosity and humor. Or maybe they just play rough. In any event, when charged by a buffalo you need a Plan B. Even the little ones just keep on coming, as I found out one November down in the Selous Game Preserve in Tanzania. I was with my Italian friend Guido Rossi, a professional photographer and author, who was not going to let any animal stop him from getting whatever picture he was after.

We had just finished shooting a group of young lions as they had tried again and again to bring down a yearling wildebeest. For half an hour the clumsy and fearful cubs had danced around the spinning calf, too scared of its stubby horns to step in and simply knock it over. Four adult lionesses, amused, I'm sure, had watched placidly from the shade of a doum palm that rose out of the dried mud along the edge of the pan. When the cubs, by force of numbers rather than by skill, finally brought the dizzy wildebeest down, Guido and I left the scene and circled the broad dry lakebed as we wound our way back to camp. On the far side a seasonal river flowed into the pan. It was dry now, and only a line of darker mud gave any indication of its whereabouts, but we carefully avoided the dark soil anyway, knowing that the vehicle's weight could break through the dry crust on the surface and leave us mired in the wet and sticky mud underneath.

Passing by the hidden mud, Guido spoke up and requested a halt. He raised his lenses and focused. When he stated that there was a young buffalo trapped in the mud, I raised my glasses too, surprised, but Guido was right. We could see just the head and back of a small buffalo almost buried in the mud about four hundred yards down the bed.

Guido regularly hunts buffalo in Zimbabwe and has hunted in other areas of the world as well, so I was now surprised a second time when he said we had to get this one out of his predicament. I told him the youth would die anyway, as the herd had long since moved off, apparently, but I knew I was wasting my breath. Guido wouldn't change his mind. He's every bit as stubborn as I am, which may explain why we get along so well. We stripped off all cameras, binoculars, and vests and started across the cracked soil of the dry riverbed. The only other animals around were a distant herd of now-alert impalas.

The little buffalo was well and truly stuck. A cursory look of the tracks showed how the entire herd had come pouring out of the woodlands at a gallop and emptied onto the pan looking for water. The larger, longer, and stronger legs of the adults had been able to plow right through the mud in which the calf was now mired. As with most of the ungulates, the herd at large had not given a second thought to the one that was missing but had left him there, as they had to. The mud, caked and dried to pottery shards on the calf's back, formed a pattern almost identical to that of the dry mud we had just crossed. But underneath the calf's belly it was still wet and sticky, the suction holding him firmly in its black grip. Not waiting for my lead, Guido pulled off his boots, so I slipped out of my sandals, and the two of us waded in, breaking through the crust past our knees. The black mud belched out a rotting odor each time we sucked a leg free to move forward, and in no time we were painted black. When we finally reached the animal we buried our arms and dug around its legs and hooves and gave it our best shot, but he barely budged, much less came free. In fact, we were only pulled down deeper ourselves.

"We're going to have to dig under his belly," Guido said. "Then let's grab each other's arms and try and raise him that way." The mud covering his mouth, and his strong Italian accent, rendered him almost unintelligible.

We tried this as the calf rolled his eyes back to watch us, bellowed, and vigorously shook his blunt head in defiance. I distinctly recall how his stubby horns ricocheted the sunlight like granite striking flint. He bawled softly, too worn down to do much else. Guido jumped as my fingers grabbed his wrist in the mud below the buffalo's rib cage.

"It's only me," I told him. "Lordy."

"I know, I know, it just surprised me, that's all."

We took our time, bent over so far that

our chests were in the black mud, and tied our grips together with interlocking fingers. We worked the handholds until we both were set, and Guido said, "Pull!" We leaned back and slowly raised up, grunting and straining. We sounded like weightlifters in a gym, getting a rhythm and blowing out hard with each increasing pull. A steady, drawn-out sucking sound issued from the mud gripping the calf, but our grips held and as our backs tensed again the calf popped up and out, its legs flailing weakly in the air.

"Hold him! Hold him up!" Guido reminded me in a muffled voice, his face planted in the mud-matted hide. We waddled forward, dragging the calf's legs, but holding his body above the pit he had just escaped. His legs were unsteady when we set him down, and he collapsed in an awkward heap, one front leg folded under, the other protruding forward at an angle, the knee locked. We rested, panting heavily, while the young bull sat quietly, unable even to gather himself. When I tilted my head up and caught sight of Guido I had to laugh, and he reciprocated; we were covered in mud aside a Cape buffalo.

Our next move was to get him to the shade one hundred yards away. High on his front leg we gripped a handful of hide apiece and easily raised him. He wobbled and kicked his feet uselessly until he got them organized. We still held our grips, giving him time to test the ground and get some feeling back in his limbs, which had been useless for more than a few hours, judging by the tracks of the adults.

"Slowly, very slowly," Guido instructed me, and I gradually eased off with the pressure that was holding him up. He lurched but stayed upright, and Guido and I stepped back, proud parents of one filthy and exhausted child. Like so many children, he showed no gratitude whatsoever. The buffalo looked at me, his large round eyes almost too heavy to hold up. He turned to the left and sized up Guido with the same melancholy eyes, and then *charged!* He butted me, almost knocking me over backward, bawled softly and charged again. I rolled out of the way, pushing his ungrateful head sideways as he came past.

"Bloody hell," I exclaimed. "Can you believe this? He can barely stand but he charges into the first thing he sees."

"How typically buffalo," Guido said. The tiny bull now ran at him on jerky legs, but it was soon too exhausted to continue the pursuit and just stood there wobbling and panting. I tried to push him from behind and get him going in the direction of the sheltering trees, but as soon as he felt my hands he turned and had another go at me. I adopted Guido's method and danced left and right, staying just ahead of the two-inch horns that jutted out at an angle from above his wide ears, enticing him closer and closer to the woods, and finally left him there.

By the time we got back to camp, the mud had dried on us like terra cotta cement. It pulled at the hairs on my arms and legs as I walked, forcing me to move stiffly and with small steps and a little swing to my arms. Guido walked as if he were on ice as he moved toward the dining tent.

Benson, who ran the camp, was laying out teacups on the wooden table next to the fire. Always the solemn one, he sized us up and then returned to whatever was so interesting about his teacups. He had run this camp for years, also worked the hunting camps sometimes, and had perfected the "seen-it-all" demeanor of veteran service workers the world over.

"What was stuck this time?" he asked in his deep monotone. "Another buffalo?"

Truthfully, Benson pretty much had seen it all. No doubt he remembered the last time I'd gotten involved with a buffalo and returned to camp bathed not in black mud but in sweat. That camp was on the Olare Oruk drainage in the Maasai Mara. My group was returning from the Mara River where we'd been watching panicked wildebeests during their desperate crossing, and just where the ground opened up above Leopard Gorge we practically drove into a solitary male buffalo surrounded by patiently circling hyenas with their heads hanging low. A Maasai spear had been thrust right through the bull's incredibly thick neck and protruded out both top and bottom. Horrified by the scene, we stopped and evaluated what we might be able to do. A rule in the bush is that the animals should be left to their own devices. It's a good rule, but, like many of us, I sometimes break it. I saw no harm in saving the buffalo. Humans had been the cause of this disgusting scene, so it seemed fair for humans to try to rectify it. The Maasai themselves were long gone.

I was with regular clients, a group of Canadians who were adventurous, a hardy and game lot, like most of the Canadians I've run into. We had spent hours stalking and watching a herd of bathing elephants only a few weeks before, trying to get low-angle shots. If the spear could be removed, we reasoned there was a possibility that the old bull might just be able to carry on. Animals (although rarely prey animals) can carry on with grievous-looking wounds. I've seen an elephant get by with half a trunk, and both lions and hyenas with three legs. It's no coincidence that these are not solitary species, and not prey. This big bull was certainly alert and still capable on his feet, as he ran at the hyenas intermittently to keep them back. The real question was how to remove a spear from the neck of a wounded, and therefore highly dangerous, Cape buffalo bull.

I decided on the tow rope. If we could rope him and then topple him over with the truck, there was a good chance he would stay down, exhausted, long enough for us to pull out the barbless spear. All we had to do was go out on foot and rope the buffalo.

Fortuna, North Dakota, was where I learned what meager roping skills I possess. I had worked there on an angus-and-wheat ranch during high school. I hadn't been any good at lassoing then, and I didn't figure that twenty years without practice had improved my timing, touch, or aim, but I certainly couldn't ask a client to do it. Not that they were volunteering. I got the rope out from under the back seat and tied a slip knot in the stiff polypropylene.

"This," one of the Canadians said with a grin, "I've got to film."

As I walked gingerly toward the bull he turned to face me, and before I was even remotely close, say thirty yards, he charged. I was not surprised — I knew it was their nature. We were in an open woodland, and there were many options: I chose an olive tree and stepped behind it. The bull stopped, stared at me briefly, and then turned back around as if he were expecting the hyenas to attack from the rear. The hyenas just hovered in ever-increasing numbers. I approached again, and was sent off again in much the same manner. Pumped by the buffalo's exertion, fresh blood flowed down his heavy neck and collected in the line of black, wiry hair that ran down his throat. My plan was going nowhere fast and would end up killing the buffalo just as surely as the hyenas would.

On the third try, chased yet again, I headed for some large basaltic boulders at the base of the slope that ran parallel to us.

I skittered onto a sizable rock, one too large for the buffalo to mount, and I threw the tow rope from there. Amazingly, I caught one horn, but in a fit of anger the bull tossed his head and neatly flipped the rope back off.

I was running out of patience, though the clients jamming the roof hatches seemed to be getting full value out of it all. When the bull chased me on my next approach, I dodged and jinked toward the truck. Without time to open a door and climb in, I dove onto the hood and slid up to the base of the windshield with my running momentum.

The truck shook violently as the bull smashed into it broadside, denting it just ahead of the front door post. He backed up and came on again, crushing the wheel well over the left front tire. On his third and final charge, he managed to catch one of his long and graceful though scarred horns on the underside of the wheel well, which briefly held him prisoner. I stood up on the hood, opened the lariat, and simply dropped it over first one side of his rack, then the other. When he finally raised his head free of the metal, he was roped. He charged off and I leaped down, quickly taking three wraps with the free end of the towrope around the bush bar. I hung on to the rope tail and leaned back against the coming tug.

Naïve. As the bull reached the end of the rope he simply kept going, snapping the bush guard off the car and badly burning my palms and fingers as the polypro shot through my pitiful grasp.

In camp forty minutes later, I eventually worked up the nerve to ask Benson for the iodine. He brought the bottle and some clean gauze pads and waited to see to what purpose it would be put. I turned my palms up, showing him the burns and the finely peeled skin.

"Did you get stuck out there today?"

"No. We tried to rope a buffalo."

"They're big."

I nodded. Benson waited as I tried to open the bottle. Finally he took it, gave the cap a quick turn, and handed it back before walking away.

"They're big," he said again. "You'd better stick to rhinos."

Rhinos?

"Benson, why did you say rhinos? They're bigger than buffaloes."

"Didn't you and that Colorado group try and get a rhino or something last July?"

Now I knew that he was referring to the

episode with Big Ben and Little Ben at Lewa Downs. "No," I answered indignantly. "We were just walking in on a rhino and calf, and they bolted in our direction. Very different. A whole other thing."

"Oh. I thought you'd tried to rope that, too. I must have got it wrong."

"You did," I emphasized.

The next day we retrieved the bushguard and found the remains of the buffalo.

6

The Story in the Sands:
Safari on Foot

The lion track was only four or five feet from the fire. Judging by its size, the print had been left by a male who had slipped in and out of camp during the night, quietly strolling across the leaf-scattered ground, making not a sound. But his right front foot had landed between the leaf litter for just one step, and I had found that track. The wind, which had been blowing down-slope all night, had barely erased the left side of his print, brushing gently across both the heel pad and the four-toe impression. There was no mistaking it for anything but male lion. It was easily too big for leopard and had the three lobes across the heel pad distinctive of all the cats, as opposed to the double lobes of both dogs and hyenas.

I had shown the shallow impression to my three clients, Ann, David, and Wayne, pointing out how close the beast had passed to me as I slept by the fire. Leon, my co-guide for this safari in Zimbabwe, had marveled properly when he saw it as well. Only our Ndebele tracker, Agrippa, whom Leon had hired, had not yet seen the paw print, but he was coming up to the fire on his way to breakfast.

"Agrippa!" I called as he walked by. "He came by pretty close last night." I gestured toward the print. He barely glanced at the track as he walked past without a word. Then when he reached the edge of the circled chairs he looked straight into my eyes and said simply, "Thet isa yuers."

Agrippa had seen right through the ruse without breaking stride. I had gotten down on my hands and knees, pursing my lips almost in the sand as I blew softly across the track I had made, matching the direction of the previous night's wind. Tricking my clients had been easy enough, but Leon is a top-flight guide in Zimbabwe. So my windblown paw print must have been fairly good. Not as good, however, as Agrippa's consummate knowledge of the bush. There is no substitute for time in the field, time gaining real intimacy with tracks.

I had not been all that impressed when my group had met the unassuming

Agrippa ten days before, but this was only because he felt no need to prove anything to anyone at anytime. Call it arrogance, call it self-assurance, but he just didn't care. His skills were supreme, and he knew it. Final proof of his talent was furnished by Leon, who had been employed by the Zimbabwe Wildlife Department or as a safari guide for more than twenty years, but who still never argued or even questioned Agrippa's interpretations of the evidence on the ground or his convictions regarding exactly when an animal had passed this way or even where it was headed. Leon also never questioned Agrippa's determination of the sex of an animal, because from its tracks the man simply knew and then informed us, simply, in Ndebele/English.

Agrippa always packed a pistol strapped crookedly, even awkwardly, to his hip, but not for show. This was a pure foot safari, for which you needed some firepower for protection. For seven days we had accomplished virtually everything on foot, never using the truck. At dawn we left camp in single file and at dusk we returned in the same formation. Occasionally we would use the truck to take us to a more remote part of the Chizarira National Park, basing the decision on what we knew about the vegetation, the water, the cover, and the wildlife, and then we'd disembark and march out on foot. Days had already passed thusly, without our seeing another vehicle or person, and fortunately there were still days to come.

Fortunately, also, I had the perfect group for such a safari. They had done the classic East Africa road-and-camping trip and wanted to experience more, even if this meant they might not get as close to the cats or see as many of them as they could in a vehicle. I prefer being on foot: one attains more intimate involvement with the land and the animals; it is unmitigated and to my mind, honest.

Ann was the first to reach the fire. She seemed terribly underdressed for the cold air, but I guess it was still a lot warmer than Chicago, her hometown. She squatted by the fire and slow-roasted her hands, turning them occasionally to make sure both sides were done evenly, greeting Leon and me with a soft and musical "Good morning." Dave and Wayne followed on her heels and adapted to the quiet mood.

Finally, Leon was forced to talk, explaining what we would be doing this morning and what the rules of engagement would be, which were the standard ones for all walks and stalks, with one particular admonition. "Never get in front of the rifle," Leon reiterated. Then he gave us ten minutes to get our day packs ready, and we did so. Leon strolled over, his rifle resting on his right shoulder. When Agrippa appeared he had on the same long pants he had worn since day one and the same pistol that he has probably worn since time began. He walked past our assembly and headed straight down onto the riverbed. Leon gave us a once-over like a mother eyeing her children before they sat down for Thanksgiving dinner. Apparently we passed inspection, and without a word Leon also started toward the Busi River as we quickly fell into a loose line behind him.

Agrippa was a couple of hundred yards down the riverbed when I saw him next, his head down and swinging from side to side as he perused the sand for telltale signs. To my now chastened eye, the crumbled grains were too large to allow any track to be distinctive and easily recognizable, but I searched hard as we walked, hoping, I suppose, to come up with a lion track before Agrippa found it. When I looked up, he was waiting for us by a small depression that had once held water but was packed smoother than the surrounding sand. He jutted his chin toward the tracks that ran along one side of the shallow and broad hole. Even I could see that this fresh and sharp-edged print was a lion's. Leon and I studied it together. A male had walked here last night, presumably one of the ones we had heard calling all evening long. Agrippa pointed to another set of muddled impressions farther back, in the rough sand. I could see the series of depressions, consistently spaced, but these could have been hyena or leopard tracks, for all I could honestly tell.

Leon translated Agrippa's low words.

"This is one of the three males that came by here last night, and these other tracks are one of the two females accompanying them."

Ann asked the logical question: "If he only sees two sets of tracks, how does he know that it's three males and two females?"

Leon answered evenly for his tracker. "We're in their territory, and we know them. They wouldn't allow any other adult lions into this area, so it has to be them."

We started walking again, Agrippa at the point a few hundred yards ahead of us. Every time I looked up his head seemed to be down, but I doubt he ever stumbled onto anything without first knowing it was there. Leon walked in an entirely different manner. With his .458 caliber resting on his shoulder, his large right hand tenderly wrapped around its oiled barrel, he moved with long and solid strides, so unlike Agrippa's broken and irregular small paces that he jigged and jogged in a dancelike way, searching for signs. Leon also kept his head up much more than Agrippa. It was a good division of labor and of responsibility. It wouldn't make much sense for the man with the rifle to be going along with his nose to his toes. He needed to see things as they came out of the bush and could never be caught by surprise, always mentally set and physically able to get between the game and the people following him. I decided to take the middle ground between the two. I wanted to see whatever was coming or going within our sight range, but I have always been enthralled, almost hypnotized, by tracks and hated the thought of missing one. I'd have to learn to look up and down, and still keep the pace and keep on my feet.

A peninsula of trees jabbed out into the Busi River sand. In the cleaner dirt that had collected around the trunks I found first one, then a second, and finally a third set of lion tracks. The lions had not stopped here but had weaved through the trees as they continued downstream. I called to Agrippa, and he came back from where he was waiting for us in the shade. I indicated the three sets of prints, and he nodded, grasped my shirtsleeve between his thumb and index finger, led me over to a fallen log a few yards away, and showed me the other two sets of tracks, bringing the total to the five Leon had assured us of earlier. Agrippa bent down, still holding onto my sleeve, and drew me closer and closer to the fallen log. In silence he pointed to a blond hair a little over an inch long, then to another. In stepping over the log the lions had lightly scraped their tummies across the wood, leaving behind a few snagged hairs as proof of their passage. I walked back to the rest of the group sitting in the shade of a tall acacia that now threw long and muted shadows across the sand as the sun gathered strength, though it was far from hot yet. Leon had been watching and asked me if I had found any lion hairs on the log. I nodded as he took his rifle by the barrel and swung it onto his right shoulder, the sign that we were off again. We rose, swung our packs into place, and again fell in line.

Agrippa walked hard for a few minutes and was soon out in front, comfortably ahead of anyone who might disturb virgin tracks and interfere with his hearing. He proceeded slowly, yet magically kept the same distance from us. It was still too early to merit a break, but after twenty minutes we found Agrippa waiting for us in a bowl of sand created when one of the huge acacias had fallen a long time ago, its roots tearing out a giant divot, the winds of years mostly refilling it with fine-blown sand. Leaves and small bits of wood and thorns had also been swept into the wind-sheltered depression, making it look like a pale brown saucer fifteen feet across. Agrippa spoke to Leon, and the two of them took a slow lap around the saucer's rim, pausing occasionally. Leon then reported that the lions had rested here, that they could be fairly close, and that we therefore had a very good chance of coming upon them. He wanted us to stay closer and quieter now, but this was a given for my clients.

With Agrippa now staying within thirty yards of us, I knew he meant business, and I marked this closeness down as a significant change. Leon and Agrippa would not be joking with each other now. The trust between them wouldn't allow it in these settings. I noticed that everyone kept stealing glances at Leon, trying to follow his searching eyes. I let my eyes wander the far tree shadows and clumps of bushes. If the lions were close everyone would see them, so it seemed better to work the far side of each view, rather than the near. Twenty or thirty minutes later, just as we were all loosening up, Agrippa suddenly crouched, Leon went down next, and the rest of us followed like dominoes. Agrippa neither looked at us nor made any hand signals. Leon waited, watching Agrippa as he finally extended an arm back toward us, palm down and fingers spread. We didn't have to be told twice, or even once, really. We stayed low, motionless and quiet, dying of curiosity.

An eternity later, Agrippa slowly turned his head toward us and silently mouthed the English word, "Lions." I desperately wanted to know how close they were, what they were doing, and especially if they were aware of us.

Leon worked his way forward, his rifle held low now, just inches above and parallel to the sandy ground. He reached Agrippa, raised his binoculars, and in a few seconds turned and beckoned me forward.

I felt privileged as I crawled up to join the two of them. They knew their business. Without using my lenses, I could see the lions out in the dry riverbed ahead of us, eighty yards away. In the midst of their circling bodies was a dead buffalo, looking from this distance still relatively whole and untouched. Leon put his mouth right to my left ear and whispered so softly that I had to concentrate on what he was saying, "We'll go back a hundred yards or so and then head away from the river, work on downstream until we are opposite the lions and then come back down toward them."

I nodded that I understood, and he instructed me to carefully go back and pass the word. If we were seen, he said, it would all be over in a heartbeat. The lions would abandon the kill and vanish. Crawling back lower than when I had come, I grabbed the nearest ear and relayed the whispered instructions. The two of us then bent to two more ears, and we were all party to the plan. We stayed put, however, until Leon had come back to lead the retreat.

Trying to withdraw unseen and unheard was surprisingly tense and tiring. Even with the soft sand muffling our steps, each footfall seemed to echo in the air. Finally Leon was only half crouched, and then in another twenty yards was standing upright as he walked away. One by one, as we reached the spot where he had come erect, we copied him and then hurried to keep him in sight as he walked hard into the thicker cover away from the riverbed.

Before we turned and started back downstream toward the lions, Leon pulled us together as Agrippa caught up and continued right on by. Leon told us that when we got to the kill, he would explain how he knew this was the lions' kill and not one they had poached from a hyena. He reminded us to stay very quiet and watch him for hand signals, and then we were off again. Suddenly we broke ninety degrees to the left, and we were headed directly back toward the feeding lions. We hoped. Not because it was necessary, but just because of what we knew was ahead, we instinctively stooped over again. The trees surrounding and shading us made no difference; it just felt better being lower. Finally we reached the point where Agrippa was down on the ground, Leon beside him and already waving us forward, then down, then forward again in a confusing blur of hand signals. I hung back, pulling Wayne into the line ahead of me, and nudging Ann forward with my other hand. Dave was already up by Leon, looking through his own binoculars. He turned back and gestured repeatedly in the direction of the riverbed. I don't think he was believing what was right there, not thirty yards before him.

I thought about photographing the tightly packed observers, heads jutting out at odd angles as everyone leaned to get an unobstructed view. The lions seemed far enough away, far beyond the distance the shutter click would carry, but if it did reach lion ears, the unnatural sound could ruin all we had. So I worked my way forward and crowded in. Questions and explanations were whispered back and forth, lips against ears. Leon's powerful grip suddenly clasped my forearm, startling me with its intensity and jerking my eyes back up to the lions. All five were staring directly at us from half-crouched positions. We waited, and they stared, making me, at least, terribly self-conscious. They could not possibly have heard us, but somehow they had picked up our presence and were trying to figure out exactly what we were.

Whatever answer they came up with they didn't like. First one male, then the other two suddenly turned and slunk rapidly away toward the trees beyond the far bank.

The females both stared a bit longer and then walked off, much more upright, to join the disappearing males. Seconds later there was just us on one side of the riverbed, a dead buffalo in the center, and the knowledge of five lions on the far side. Several minutes passed before we could accept their disappearance and allow ourselves to stand up and start talking.

"What gave us away?" David asked.

"We stayed down, we didn't make a sound," complained Wayne.

"Not much I can say," was the crumb that Leon offered. "None of you did anything wrong, so maybe one of them just picked us up as he glanced around."

It was possible. Lions, like cheetahs, continually swivel their heads even as they tear into their kill. These five could have defended their meat from virtually anything here, except a coincidental herd of elephants passing by, but it was still ingrained in them to stay vigilant and wary. Even five powerful lions will avoid conflict with the unknown. Elephants, hippos — all the big boys — would prefer to avoid an altercation with something unfamiliar to them.

Leon suggested that we walk down and examine the buffalo and turned to go, Ann right with him, the others soon following. I watched them as they crossed the rapidly heating sand and tried to imagine them on the streets of Dallas and Chicago. They all moved easily, crossing the open ground and drawing near the buffalo as if it were simply another exercise in another day's work. Leon's earlier comment about identifying the killer came back to me as I etched a slow circle around the huge dead beast, whose muzzle was torn and tattered and stripped of its lips and hide. It was obvious that whatever had killed it had done so by biting it right across the face, clamping its mouth shut and suffocating it that way. Hyenas, I told the group, would have killed it by disemboweling it and gradually eating it alive. This group had already seen the handiwork of lions two weeks earlier, in the Maasai Mara, where we had studied a wildebeest kill in detail, pacing off distances, measuring teeth marks and the depth of the claw cuts. Here, even Ann, a strict vegetarian, was astonished by the power and determination the lions had needed to kill this huge animal. We crouched in front of the upturned buffalo, looking down our lenses into his partially opened mouth, staring at the macabre smile of his torn face and exposed gums and teeth. While the rest of us examined the kill, Agrippa kept more than half an eye on the far trees. I couldn't imagine the lions coming back to reclaim their kill in our presence, but I was not nearly dumb enough to question him.

The lions did not return as we sat down around the dead buffalo and broke out our tea and biscuits, since it was still not quite hot enough to drive us into the shade for our break. The more we studied the buffalo the more we saw. Dave tried to move one of the buffalo's stiff legs and failed. He could not even start to imagine, he said, the strength required to pull it to a standstill and to knock it off its feet, which lent to uneasy thoughts about what a lion could do to one of us.

As we headed back to camp, I caught up with Agrippa as he bent over to inspect a log. "New wind," he said.

Two words were not much to go on. I kept staring, trying to see what was so obvious to him.

"New wind. Look at the grass tracks."

Then I understood. The dry and broken stems of the sun-cooked yellow grasses had created an arcing track in the sand, having been blown back and forth, always on the downwind side. One of my sandal tracks from the stalk toward the lions lay over a section of the arc, flattening the rainbow pattern in that area. Now the grasses were sticking out in the same arcing pattern, but on the opposite side of the clump of grass. Clustered, they had already begun cutting a new series of recordlike grooves in the fine sand, clearly showing that the wind had shifted since we had come by on our downstream walk. It was even obvious to me now.

Agrippa and I started walking again just as Ann and Wayne came up.

"What do you have?" asked Ann.

"Grass tracks."

"What did he say?" Wayne asked Ann. "It sounded like 'grass tracks.' What the hell is a grass track?"

Now that everyone was tired and full of tension from the stalking, we decided to stop for breakfast — a big and much needed decompression. Leon, however, carried on like we hadn't even started out yet. "Three down and two to go," he proclaimed, and we all knew what he meant. In the old days of hunting, clients wanted to shoot the Big Five — buffalo, lion, leopard, rhino, and elephant.

Leon and I kicked around what to do for the remainder of that day and the following morning. He suggested visiting a stunning little swimming hole that was tucked well up a narrow and deep box canyon. We would need only a hour or so of steady walking to get there, and the ancient gorge and clear water would be worth the hike regardless of whether we saw a single animal. Minutes later, bathing suits in hand, we were out of there, on our way for a swim and a poolside lunch.

The sun straight overhead depicted none of the shallow shadows of dawn that make prints stand out. Ten minutes before we reached the swimming hole the smell reached my nose, and it was good. Leon pulled us in close behind him and politely ordered us to pipe down. If we could already smell the water, imagine how far away an elephant could pick it up. He was absolutely certain the elephants that frequented this area knew about the water hole, and this would be the time of day when they would use it.

Just before we reached the water, Leon stopped us. The problem here, he explained, was that any animal already at the pool would have no choice, upon our arrival, but to come racing back down *through us* to get out of the box. This would be a confusing and unhealthy situation, particularly if we didn't know about it ahead of time, so he and Agrippa would go forward alone to check out the water hole.

Leon's bold voice echoed off the rocks a minute later, and then ricocheted down past us again. I couldn't hear what he was saying but also couldn't imagine his making any sound at all if wildlife had preempted our water rights, so we started walking forward. Agrippa was perched on a chunk of basalt that overlooked both the pool and the route by which we had come. It took me a few seconds to locate Leon, because he was underwater when we walked up, surfacing as we reached the pool's edge. I was so excited I dove in still wearing my sunglasses. Ann, David, and Wayne followed soon thereafter, stopping first to remove their sunglasses.

We swam, lazed around, and enjoyed a small melon Leon had brought, along with the coffee that is never in short supply in Africa. Then, astoundingly, we slept for almost two hours, propped against rocks in the shallow part of the pool. Finally the sun breaking through the skylights in the thick canopy gave notice of the declining of the day; our hike out would be far more comfortable than the trudge in had been. We packed up and changed from swimwear to bushwear. Agrippa, who had never moved from his lookout's perch, finally came down and ate one of the remaining slices of sweet melon and poured himself a plastic mug of presweetened coffee.

The sun was easily bearable when we stepped clear of the canyon and started across the more open sand headed for the Busi River. We no longer had to squint against it. The birds were starting to move, and the larger mammals would be getting active. For almost an hour we walked uneventfully, Leon with his rifle on his right shoulder as always and Agrippa ahead of us a hundred yards or more. Just before reaching the sandy drop-off that emptied onto the riverbed, we had to wind back and forth between a number of large termite mounds. Ironwood and ebony trees poked out and euclea bushes formed a circular crown around each one. Birds, snakes, rodents, and small dik-dik antelopes were drawn to these sheltering mounds. The hard, raised earth serves an important function as a complete and miniature world, but it also blocks the view. Since Agrippa had cut off the path and headed right to check out any action at the oxbow of the river, there was no one to warn us about the elephant.

A massive blast froze us solid, legs and hearts. Leon half-crouched and instantaneously cycled his rifle's action, chambering a heavy-grained bullet as he slammed the bolt forward and down. We had surprised the old bull elephant at least as much as he had surprised us. Forty feet away, he ran off for another fifteen or twenty feet before swinging around and trumpeting again, shaking his neck and slapping his huge ears against it. His trunk came up as he thrust his chin at us three times in quick succession.

"Back, you guys, back," I whispered hoarsely.

"Which way?" asked Ann.

"Just go," said David none too quietly. "Just get going."

Leon and I waited while the bull decided what he wanted to do about our presence. I knew there was no way Leon would shoot this elephant, but I didn't even want him to have to fire in the air to back it off. One rifle shot echoing down the Busi River might well push game out of the whole area for days, maybe weeks.

The stand-off didn't last long, as the huge bull swung violently away and headed off behind the next termite hill and was out of sight. Leon ran back past me and to the right to get into better position, just in case the elephant was only circling around for advantage. We waited, my pulse thudding in my ears. After a minute or so we called for everyone to come out of hiding. It was astounding, everyone agreed, that something that big, probably more than five tons, could move so quietly and remain unseen until we were that close to it.

We found his tracks and looked downriver whence he had come. No other elephants were in sight, which wasn't unusual. Old bulls frequently prefer to move alone, having only chance encounters with breeding herds during their long, meandering days and years. Agrippa appeared from behind another termite mound, giving us a momentary start. He looked at the tracks, at us, and never even asked a question or cracked a smile, for there was nothing to add to what he had heard and could see by the story in the sand. Back at camp, Agrippa agreed to walk our three guests down to whatever action there was at the oxbow of the river while Leon and I motored westward to check out an area for tomorrow's game walk.

We took the Antichrist, Leon's evil Land Cruiser that refused to start without being pushed, beaten, or jump-started by the supply truck. Grant's gazelles, impalas, and a harem of zebras passed us by in the cooling air through groves of ebony and stands of acacia — and then a rhinoceros came charging hard across our bow, tail curled and held high on her fat rump. Even over the sounds of the rushing air and the speeding Antichrist we could hear this female huffing and snorting in anger and surprise. Leon hit the brakes so hard we skidded as we ground to a halt to watch her go. We were right beside a now dry waterhole that was embroidered by a tremendous network of tracks left behind by visitors using the hole before it dried out. It was like a textbook, with duck-footed hyena tracks mixing with a set of a porcupine's shuffling footprints and a fine set of lines etched by the long-quilled tail sashaying behind. White-tailed mongooses, greater kudu, buffalo, Burchell's zebras and untold numbers of quasi-identifiable split hooves had all crowded down here at one time or another. But all the prints, except for the rhino's, were days and days old. No lions had even dropped by lately to check out who was still around. At the next salt lick I came across both fresh lion spoor and, even better, two sets of recent rhino tracks. They hadn't been laid down that day, but the rhinos might have been there the previous night, or maybe even at dawn. That cinched the decision for us. We'd be back here in the morning.

Leon had backed the Antichrist up a small slope just in case we needed to use the "gravity starter" to get it going again, but for the first time in months, Leon said, his truck started without outside inducement for a record second time in a row, and we bounced back toward camp, slowing before we got to the draw where the rhino had crossed ahead of us, but she was long gone. Only a pair of bateleur eagles turned their wide and owlish heads at our approach. Leon stopped, and we glassed the two birds for a minute before moving on again. Agrippa's group hadn't made it back from the oxbow yet, so the campfire was Leon's and mine. We poured cups of hot tea from the ever-present and eternally dented kettle and passed a tinful of rusks. Half an hour of human silence passed between us, and between us and the surrounding bush, before Agrippa and the group arrived to tell us about the bachelor group of greater kudu that had slowly tiptoed down to the bend of water above which the humans had hidden. The four bulls never saw or heard them. They hadn't even glanced up to where the four-some was sitting under the lee of a termite mound; for more than five minutes the handsome spiral-horned males had drunk from the still and dark water, frequently pausing to look up and around but never at the four people. Ann, Dave, and Wayne were thrilled even though they hadn't been able to take a single picture. You don't have to score the Big Five in order to have involved and in-depth experiences on foot safari. In light of all their excitement, Leon and I didn't mention the rhino, but we did tell them about the fresh tracks we had found at the second salt lick.

Our lions came very close again that night, walking downstream on our side of the river this time. In darkness I walked softly out of camp, my tape recorder over my shoulder, the shotgun mike in its case threaded on my belt. Five minutes out I stopped and readied the machine. When they started a series of roars they were so close I had to turn down the recording level to keep it from blasting the needle off the scale. I could hear the gravelly texture in their voices as they moaned long and low — territorial calls, definitely. A minute of silence passed, *total* silence, which is a rare emptiness during the early hours of darkness, and then the lions roared again, one starting by himself, with a second and third joining his lead. Then the deafening dark silence again. All of Africa was listening respectfully and fearfully to the massive males. I waited again, ready to record more, but the third set of roars, to my surprise, came quite a few minutes later from the *other* side of camp. Whether the lions had seen me or sensed me in the dark I do not know, but they had prowled right past me — at least three of them, and probably all five — without a sound, a motion, any clue at all.

The five faces illuminated by the fire turned as one as I stepped into the circle of light. They could tell I was happy. The recorder had cleanly picked up every little gasp and growling roll. Just knowing I had this on tape made the hair on my neck stand up. The lion's roar is a sound designed to take all the wind out of your sails; at close range it does so beautifully. My recording over, we listened to more declarations from the lions as they proceeded down the valley.

For what seemed like hours that night I lay awake visualizing the lions as they walked through the darkness, their bulging shoulders rolling with each stride, their heavy heads swinging as they took in everything around them. As I lay on my back in the bedroll, the fingers of the surrounding acacias reaching across the sky over me, I wondered how it all must look through the deep amber of the lions' eyes. From their lower perspective, coupled with their super-keen senses and predator's mentality, they must walk in a different *world,* even though it is the same place.

And then it was almost dawn and I could hear Agrippa and the cook, Collette, talking by the cook fire behind me. As usual, I waited until I decided the coffee was ready before rousting out into the cold air. I went straight to the scattered wood we had thrown beyond the fire, picked out a half dozen small pieces and walked back to place them selectively. The fire responded to the attention and gave back a grateful flame. We didn't tarry that morning; it was still just dark when we loaded into the vehicle. The air was so deeply chilled we pulled out the blankets that had been stashed under the wide bench seats, but Agrippa, sitting high up in the back, the most exposed to the wind, refused a proffered wrap and slowly swiveled his observing head as we drove along. What he hoped to find in the low light I had not a clue, but my eyes wandered, too; old habits die a slow death, if they die at all. Suddenly Leon braked on a dime and gave me a sideways wink before he said, "Agrippa, check out those rhino tracks, will you?" Leon had stopped where the animal had torn across the road yesterday evening. Agrippa vaulted down and found the tracks immediately. He squatted there for a minute and then headed off, following the faint line of cloverleaf prints as they headed away on the hard earth. We watched him as he reached the far side of the open dirt and walked along its perimeter. We followed his long and loose strides back to the truck. He vaulted cleanly back up on the roof with the same effortless dexterity he had demonstrated getting down.

"That female will be long gone. She came by yesterday afternoon," he said. "There won't be any point in trying to track her. We'd never catch up." And with those words he sat back and resumed scanning the landscape. Leon and I continued to stare at him until he finally asked, "What?"

End of conversation. Leon's eyes met mine, and he arched his eyebrows as if to say, "I told you he's good."

At the second salt lick, where we had found the fairly fresh rhino tracks the previous evening, we dismounted from the Antichrist and, for the first time, altered our accustomed line of march for the stalk. Leon posted me one hundred yards to his left, Agrippa one hundred yards to his right, with the three clients behind Leon. I walked quickly away, turning right when I reached a fair distance and started up the barely perceptible draw that was the valley, looking for fresh rhino tracks. It's tiring to walk fast and still try to search every bit of bare ground for signs of an animal's passing. I also had to keep half an eye on Leon and be careful to stay clear of the grabbing wait-a-bit thorns. I loved it though, as I always love this game. Who had come by? What had they been doing? Were they alone? Where were they headed and why? I saw assorted tracks and some animals, but no sign of rhinoceros. After half an hour I angled back over to Leon to report a set of leopard tracks paralleling our route. They looked like a male's from last night, I elaborated. Agrippa had come over when he saw me moving in and heard me mention the cat tracks.

He cut in softly, "It's that same male we saw in April. He came from over that ridge, and is probably headed to the same rocks as last time."

Leon turned back to me, reached out, and chucked me under the chin to close my gaping mouth. "Doesn't it just piss you off?" he asked. Yes, but I had been forced long before to accept that Agrippa is in a class by himself.

Not ten minutes later Leon gave his soft whistling call, drawing me over to the group. He and Agrippa were staring at two very fresh pairs of rhino tracks pointing up the draw. Leon asked Agrippa if they were worth going for and Agrippa nodded in return and started down the double line of thick-stemmed cloverleaf tracks, easily visible in the low light. The chase was on, and our pace quickened a full two notches. The rhinos had a head start but would be stopping to browse as they moved. We had two advantages: their tracks before us and the enthusiasm within us. We were firing on more cylinders than the Antichrist ever did.

The enthusiasm began to fade as the steps turned into miles and the minutes into hours. Still, we stayed together and kept moving without stopping for either water or rest. All of us had it easier than Agrippa, who had to keep cutting and turning as he followed the wandering tracks. We just followed him. Around noon, with the sun giving us all it had, the land changed from largely open woodland with sandy soil, easy for walking, to an increasingly dense, shrubby forest of low thorn trees. The ground lost much of its sand as it turned to eroded and dry dirt, but it wasn't what we walked *on* that concerned Leon and me, but what we walked *through*. We would probably not see the rhinos in this stuff until we were almost on top of them. With the animals' phenomenal hearing, they would have the drop on us as we approached.

We heard the oxpeckers long before we saw them. Agrippa, Leon, and I knew that these starlings employ warthogs, impalas, waterbuck, giraffes, buffalo, and other mammals as hosts. Also known as tickbirds, they pick insects from their hosts' ears, noses, bellies, and sores, and the hosts also get the advantage of the birds' remarkable ears and eyes. When anything at all approaches, they spiral into the sky, trilling and buzzing as they go. The red alert is sounded for every animal within earshot.

Rhinos may be the birds' favorite host. It's rare to meet rhinos without oxpeckers aboard. Agrippa and Leon froze. I reached back and stopped Wayne in midstride. Ann and Dave locked up on the spot as well. A few hundred yards dead ahead, the flock of fifteen or so sentinels spiraled above the low and densely packed trees. It wasn't too bad; at least the birds weren't twenty yards in front of us. On the other hand, there was no question that the rhinos now knew something out of the ordinary was in the vicinity; they would be keyed up and hyper-alert. Leon waved us to him like a coach at a time-out, and we crowded in for critical suggestions. Leon explained that the rhinos would know a threat was around, but not what or where, so we would wait a few minutes to let things simmer down. Then, if we wanted to see the rhino, we would have to move in, thick bush or not. As we got our cameras out of our packs, mounted the longer lenses, and reshouldered the day packs, Leon explained about the rhino's virtual blindness but mind-boggling hearing.

Side by side now, Agrippa and Leon stalked slowly forward, Leon's rifle now held comfortably low, stock to the right, instead of casually on top of the shoulder. For every step they took we probably took at least two and sometimes three, in our desperate effort to walk silently on the outside of our shoes as we picked our steps. Not once did my group's eyes meet mine. They were either looking down to select the next placement for a foot or were focused on Leon and Agrippa. When I'm not on safari I either play squash or run five to ten miles a day, and yet such excruciatingly careful stalking still strains the muscles in my legs. It must have been worse for the others, but they stayed close, as if tied on a tether. I seldom have to tell clients to keep up when we are finally getting near the big game we are after. No one wants to be left behind, for several reasons.

Agrippa stopped, went down on his knees, and all of us followed. Leon leaned in and sighted down Agrippa's outthrust arm and index finger. But he didn't seem to see the target, for he ducked and bobbed his head as if trying to get a view, or at least a clearer view, through the bush. He stole silently back to us and we pulled in again.

"Agrippa has just seen the rhino, but it ran on, so we'll have to just keep moving forward. Stay close behind me, and stay quiet." We didn't really need the instructions. Having worked as hard as we could in both regards, we desperately wanted a glimpse of the mythical beast.

Five minutes later, the sudden halt was repeated, though this time Leon reported that he had seen the rhino as well. Again we started slowly off, the trees gratefully opening up just a bit. Within a few paces, the whole area changed again, opening up wider than it had been in hours. Low and well-spaced bushes were ahead of us with very few large trees anywhere in sight. Agrippa and then Leon froze. I finally saw the rhino, well-hidden under a low and wide tree a hundred yards ahead. Leon grabbed Dave, and I pulled Wayne in close, pointing at the tree and the three-dimensional shadow underneath. It took forever for Wayne to pull the rhino out of the distant shadows, but he finally saw it. Ann had found it more or less on her own. He weighed probably three times as much as all of us put together. We had our fourth of the Big Five.

The hulking animal took a few tentative and timid steps out from under the tree, and then we saw two of them, the second having been hidden by the first one's broadside posture. The second rhino jolted forward a few steps, pushing the other one before it. Leon's rifle came up, and I got ready for the charge. Everything was in motion, and major motion. Agrippa ran back past Leon as Leon rose to a solid stance, the rifle at his shoulder and pointed high. Even now I remember how the sun cast a shiny line down the length of its barrel. Both rhinos chuffed and blew hard, sending clouds of mucus blasting from their nostrils as they hurtled toward us at twenty to twenty-five miles an hour, almost as fast as elephants. The ground shook, Leon shouted and swung the rifle barrel back and forth, but still they came on. There was no reason for silence now, so I fired a few frames. I saw with my right eye that two of the group broke and ran for the tree that Leon had pointed out before the final stalk.

Leon held, I kept taking pictures, and the rhinos kept charging. Agrippa was standing calmly beside us; waving and yelling just wasn't his style. Leon shouted again and that was all it took, this time anyway, to turn the pair. They tore past us on the right, shaking the ground under our feet, and then turned back in a wide circle aimed toward where they had started. They ran past that tree and plunged into the scattered trees at the far end of the open ground. Leon and I ran after them, with Ann joining us. Agrippa must have stayed back with the other two, though I didn't see any of them.

We reached the trees and kept right on running and almost plowed straight into the rhinos, who had pulled up surprisingly short, probably feeling safer with some cover around them, thin though it was. At the sound of our approach they started blowing again and came on a second time. When Leon shouted and waved his arms, so did Ann, and I barely had time to take two more shots before the rhinos turned tail and were gone. In a few seconds a dead tree some fifty yards ahead of us snapped with a crack and crashed to the ground. The rhinos must have brushed it in their hurry to depart. Leon looked at Ann, who was radiating that smile of hers, and we all clapped each other on the back and hugged one another, laughing.

Once we had settled a bit, Leon debriefed us on the rhinos, the oxpeckers, and the whole final stalk and run. Agrippa quietly broke open another melon he had been carrying in his pack and passed the chunks around. Tearing into that fruit was great fun, the juice flowing freely down our dusty faces. Within seconds the melon was nothing more than a scattering of bright green rinds tossed on the hot ground. We passed the water bottles between us and then packed up the cameras and started the long walk back to the Antichrist. The very long walk. Hour after hour. We hadn't realized how far we had come, though we did realize how hot it was and how hungry we were.

At four o'clock the truck still was not in sight, but we were back where the valley had a defined shape, so we knew we were close, and in another thirty minutes we spilled out of the trees onto the upper edge of the salt lick. Agrippa took a turn around the edge of the clearing as we cut straight across to the truck and the cooler in the back. Nobody felt like eating lunch, but the warm beer and bottles of water evaporated at a record rate. The Antichrist wouldn't start until we supplied the manpower and were off like a herd of turtles in a cloud of peanut butter, the air blowing across our red faces blessedly cool again. We slouched against one another, occasionally saying something about the rhino charge, but generally just smiling dumbly at nothing as we cruised along.

That night Leon broke out the port and recited Robert Service's "The Cremation of Sam McGee," and Wayne rattled off a few old camp songs, and the fire launched spiraling sparks into the blue-black sky. The next day got off to a predictably slow start but reached an early climax when we spotted our leopard — number Five — as he bolted from a series of rock bands exposed across a seasonal riverbed.

Five of us were instantly running, Leon and I forward, out of habit, and Ann, Wayne, and Dave back, out of habit. Agrippa stayed put, too naturally cool to run either way. The ground suddenly dropped away and I sailed off into the air, hit the sand below hard, pushed up, and was off again. When Leon hit bottom I heard the impact and knew he was right behind me. Our pursuit paid off, for as we rounded the blocking hill we caught a flash of light on its left flank, and there was the fleeing leopard. He was a huge specimen, had to be a male, and he was digging hard as he pulled up the hill and shot out of sight as he crested the top. Leon was slowed by his rifle and by his bulky frame as well, but I ran another thirty yards or so and caught sight of the leopard again as he loped down the far side of the hill, turned left, and was gone for good.

Under the rock band that we had catapulted over we discovered a half-eaten

Grant's gazelle that had been stashed under the cavelike lip. This explained how we had been able to get so close to the leopard in broad daylight before being busted. The other three finally joined us and examined the kill, which was classic leopard all the way, with a few deep claw marks on the shoulder and four deep, wet holes in the throat where the canines had held the victim in a strangling grip.

"Another amazing day in paradise," Ann marveled. There followed a pregnant pause. It was an interesting choice of words. Maybe the gazelle didn't agree.

And it wasn't long before I had reason to disagree. Like me, Leon prefers to sleep outside because it keeps you in touch with any wildlife that might be in the area, although Agrippa doesn't seem to need it. That night, for warmth and protection we slept close to one another, but Leon began to talk and toss in his sleep, even throwing an arm around me and pulling me close. I finally grew tired of his sleepy advances and dragged my sleeping bag away from the fire, but mostly away from Leon.

I was awakened some time later when I found myself bouncing unceremoniously across the ground at a good clip. I figured Leon was dragging off my sleeping bag as some kind of unwelcome prank, so I was more than shocked when my eyes finally focused not on his eyes but on the two hyenas who had the bag clamped in their jaws and were running off with me.

It took me a few seconds to register the situation and sound the alarm, shouting and waving my arms. The two hyenas dropped the bag with me inside it and turned to find out what had caused the noise. I yelled again and thrashed my arms in the air, putting them to flight.

I got out of the warm cocoon into the cold air and stumbled back to where I had started, tugging the canvas and blankets behind me. Leon had heard the yelling and asked from deep within his bag what was going on. I told him, and he laughed. I slid back inside my own bag, refolded my bush jacket as a pillow, and waited to settle back down and fall asleep, which I must have done, because my head suddenly thumped against the ground. This was annoying. Whatever Leon was up to now, it was too late in the night and I was too tired. I opened my eyes wearily, only to find myself nose to nose with one of the hyenas again. He had my bush jacket in his mouth and rocketed off when I yelled at him, but he didn't release the jacket.

My shorts and sandals were already gone. My knife was on the belt of my shorts, and that was the final straw. Forget the clothes. I wanted the knife back, and badly. I had carried that knife for more than a decade. It had ridden on my hip during a train wreck in the Ivory Coast, while I was going down in a plane, while I was swimming in the Indian Ocean after we had flipped a dhow, while we had stalked the rhino the day before. I wasn't going to lose it to some desperate, leather-eating hyena.

My boxer shorts had dropped out of my hiking shorts, so that was all I had to wear as I debated about what to do. Down the track that faded into the grasses I could still make out the two hyenas humping off into the bush. I had to use the Antichrist, I had no choice. When I threw open the front door, I found that the hyenas had taken the sheepskin seat covers as well. Inexplicably, the machine started up instantly, perhaps sensing the urgency of what was being asked of it. I just floored it, slammed it into second, and floored it again. I leaned forward, pressing unnecessarily close to the glass as I strained to see, and a few seconds later I could just make out the hyenas at the far end of the Antichrist's weak beams. I kept the coal to it and was gaining fast. I had no plan whatsoever, but just tried to run the two of them down. As hyenas always do, these tail-tucked predators sidled off the road at the last moment and headed across the plain, and I saw my shorts and belt dangling from one heavy jaw. I stayed with them, bouncing over the rougher ground. When I was just about on top of one, I honked the weak horn. The hyena dropped my clothes and jigged to the right. When I turned around and found the clothes, I raised them into the light, already knowing from the lack of weight that my knife was gone. It was somewhere in the hundreds of yards of grass between the camp and where I now stood dejectedly.

Back at the camp, Leon was still wrapped up by the fire, despite the commotion and his disappearing truck. The lights of the Antichrist held him briefly until darkness took over again. I got out and walked slowly back to my bag, barefoot and holding a pair of chewed shorts that looked like a rejected roadkill. Leon's muffled voice asked, "What was all that about then?"

I think Leon laughed again, but alone. I wanted my knife. With first light I set forth on foot, and less than three hundred yards from where I had been sleeping there it was, between the two sets of tire tracks. Amazing! Finding it so quickly was unlikely. My heart leaped as my fingers closed around the tooth-marked ebony handle. I turned back to the camp to wave at Leon or Agrippa, but they weren't following my progress.

When I got back to the fire, Agrippa walked past and asked what I had been doing.

"The hyenas stole my clothes and my knife last night. I just went looking for my knife and managed to get it back."

He barely paused in his passing. "You should sleep near the fire."

I looked at him and then at Leon, but he was back under the covers already, though not asleep because I could see the blankets shaking rhythmically. I walked over to the fire, where Collette had left my coffee mug, kicking the pile of blankets as I went past.

"I started out by the fire, but it got a little crowded there last night."

"You be more careful. Maybe next time they take your face, too."

A rare tranquil moment with a cheetah on the plains of northern Kenya. (*Photo by Birgit Freybe Bateman*)

Two male cheetahs take down a five-hundred-pound wildebeest. For the fragile, one-hundred-pound cats, this is a huge risk, as even minor injuries can render them unable to hunt. (*Photo by Mark C. Ross*)

A herd of Burchell's zebras wade through the red oat grass of the Maasai Mara; the Isiria escarpment is in the background. (*Photo courtesy of the DeWulf family*)

Two balanite trees frame a wildebeest at sunrise as he plods along a ridge in the Maasai Mara Reserve. (*Photo by Mark C. Ross*)

The stampede at Lewa Downs. When Cynthia fell down, I ran between her and the herd, diverting their charge and escaping unscathed, barely. (*Photo by Len Loudis*)

A female leopard lounging on the elevated end of a fallen acacia elatior. (*Photo by Mark C. Ross*)

A mother cheetah and two cubs, just displaced from their kill by the hyenas, reluctantly give ground. A wildebeest gazes on from the horizon. (*Photo courtesy of the DeWulf family*)

A herd of grazing Cape buffalo. Buffalo kill more tourists than do lions, elephants, and crocodiles combined. (*Photo courtesy of the DeWulf family*)

The camp crew posing with the DeWulf family at the end of their safari. (*Photo courtesy of the DeWulf family*)

The DeWulf family after sleeping outside their tents one night. (*Photo courtesy of the DeWulf family*)

A huge male lion spotted on the rim of the Ngorongoro Crater. (*Photo by Mark C. Ross*)

The wildebeest migration snakes for miles from the distant Musiara Swamp. (*Photo by Mark C. Ross*)

The Cessna 206, an ideal six-seater bush plane, on the sandy airstrip at Samburu. Wildlife constantly clog the park and farm runways of Kenya and Tanzania. (*Photo by Birgit Freybe Bateman*)

A female spotted hyena hunches over a yearling wildebeest in the shallow waters of Lake Magadi, on the floor of the Ngorongoro Crater. (*Photo by Mark C. Ross*)

The one photo that exists from our trek back from the Congo border. From left are me, Mitch Keifer, Gary Tappenden, Michael Baker, Masindi, and Dani Walther. Mark Avis took the photo with a tiny camera Dani had hidden in her trousers. (*Photo courtesy of Danja "Dani" Walther*)

7

Stalking on the Serengeti

More than twenty-five years after first seeing the Serengeti Plain, I still get an overwhelming and desperate urge to run out onto the immense flatness every time we come sliding down the highlands of Ngorongoro and cross the Olduvai Gorge. The first time I saw this sight I actually did rush from the Land Cruiser and fling myself childishly onto the ground. I can still feel how the uniform dimples of compressed ash that form this rich soil pushed up into my sweaty shirt like a cornhusk mattress. With my clients today, I do the more "mature" thing and ask the driver to stop and then get everyone out of the truck in order to just stand there, gaze west at the vast nothingness, and soak it in. Nowhere on earth can possibly be more suited to impressing upon us our own smallness within the world's great bounty. Olduvai is known among archeologists as the "cradle of mankind" because of the skeletal discoveries of Mary and Louis Leakey; the Serengeti is the very breast of life-giving Africa. I have never had a client who fails to sense this pulse.

These plains have the largest concentration of large mammals on the face of the earth, bar none. Nowhere else is even close. An area somewhat larger than Connecticut is home to almost two million wildebeests, over half a million zebras, a quarter million Thomson's gazelles, one hundred thirty thousand Grant's gazelles, and hundreds of thousands of various antelopes. There are three thousand lions and significant but uncounted numbers of cheetahs and leopards. During eight days in the Serengeti and three days in the adjacent and ecologically united Ngorongoro Crater, my clients on one recent safari saw 164 big cats, including 11 leopards.

The depth of the volcanic ash laid down by the explosion of Ngorongoro that created the Serengeti is amazingly uniform: twenty-nine inches, on average. Drive a yardstick into the ground and you will hit a hardpan of calcium carbonate — limestone cement, in effect — that is essentially impermeable. This is why the plain is a grasslands, not a deep-root forest. The sky here is always achingly blue, often packed with

Georgia O'Keeffe-clouds all the way to the western horizon, almost always punctuated by a cluster of circling, searching raptors and vultures. The wheels of the Land Cruiser roll effortlessly over these endless grasslands with a soft, lightly hissing "white noise" that I know I have heard before, but the precise identification tauntingly eludes me. But now I have it. This is remarkably like the sound of gentle waves washing ashore. I can easily picture us surfing on ocean swells of yellow-golden grass, far from the distant shores of Ngorongoro to the east, the cone of Lengai to the northeast, and the Gol Mountains to the north, with the forest patches painted in a sumi-e of pale blue ink and the west-facing drainages showing dark and angular as they widen and descend toward the plains. To the south are the tiny pyramids of Twin Peaks and the broken mosaic of woodlands at their base. Just to the west and much closer is another rise, Naabi Hill, its distinctive saddle shape identifiable from a great distance.

Anomalies appear in the gentle grasses, an occasional patch of rougher grass and short shrubs, all the cover a cheetah will need. Grazing antelopes are scattered in every direction, and we see the occasional crisp silhouette of a giraffe, sailing with its neck forward like a ship with an odd mast tilted into the wind. We all lean gently left or right in unison as the vehicle swings casually around a hyena den or aardvark hole. We feel a slight thump, a double thump, like crossing a set of unusually gentle railroad tracks. I don't have to look down to know what is. The wildebeests in their millions mindlessly thunder across these plains in tight single file, like obedient soldiers off to war, which is somewhat the case, because 10 to 15 percent will not be returning this way again. Each sharp hoof cuts the turf just a fraction, followed by another slice from the next in line, and so on and so forth down the line of perhaps ten thousand animals, forty thousand hooves. In a matter of minutes this incredibly durable sod is hacked inches down to bare soil. These pale brown streams etched by the wildebeests' passing are a scant four inches wide. They meander back and forth over one another to form a dendritic pattern like the tendrils of some monstrous tree whose trunk is long gone but whose roots remain. Still, there is a very definite direction to the pattern, south by southwest. (Ironically, the wildebeest population was way *down* in the fabled era of the big game hunts early in this century. Rinderpest, a viral disease of cattle and other ruminants, had been introduced to Africa by Italian cows in the horn of Africa in the 1890s, and in Kenya five years later. It proceeded to wipe out the ruminant herds of wildebeests, buffalo, giraffes, and others and therefore depleted the predatory species that accompany the prey species in the Serengeti. Zebras, who are not ruminants, were spared. Immunization for rinderpest was not completed in East Africa until the 1960s, and it took fifteen years for the wildebeest population to stabilize.)

A sharply defined outline of a solitary tree occasionally breaks the horizontal scene. I find myself wondering how they ever got started. The most dramatic of all the landmarks are the kopjes of the southern and central Serengeti. As far as we can see in any direction, these scattered outcroppings of upthrust metamorphic "basement" rock are the only shapes, besides the Land Cruiser, that really don't seem to meld into this landscape. They emerge so abruptly from such smooth greenery and rise so high — a couple of hundred of feet, in some cases — that it seems as if some architect of nature has crossed up the plans, arbitrarily scattering oversized rock formations across the even plains instead of setting them in some mountain range more suited to their scale. Each individual rock formation is massively out of place here.

With the kopjes, the winds of the Serengeti finally encountered something that even they could not conquer. The winds defeated themselves by shoving blown dirt and ancient volcanic ash between the rounded outcroppings, slowly building an accumulation to leeward and providing an opportunity for seed and root to gain purchase. The word "kopje" is Danish for "bald head," but these rocks are not bald at all. Water soaks into this soil, allowing indefatigable plants to cling to life. A chain is started. Wind gives rise to soil, then to water, hence to plants. Any branches brazen enough to venture beyond the protection of the rock will be punished by the wind. Like gnarled and aged hands, the trunks of the acacias curl around the Stonehenge stacks, creating bonsai forms of wind-scarred branches. Within certain kopjes, there is more than enough space between the higher rocks for full-sized umbrella acacias to propagate. These flawless trees make the arthritic dwarfed trees seem even older, tougher, and more stubborn. Agama lizards skitter across shelves of rock like smooth stones skipping across a glassy pond, and just as the kopjes seem out of place on these plains, so the blue bodies and orange heads of these lizards are an odd contrast to the subtly hued kopje.

Shade is a scarce and precious commodity in the Serengeti, and the kopjes provide most of it. The cats, therefore, use these islands of rock most heavily and in almost every way. They use the rocks as marking posts, lookouts, and cover from which to range out and hunt or to hide safely within. It would be a rare day indeed to spend a few hours driving from kopje to kopje, circling each in turn, and not come across some predator, probably feline, during the course of a morning. Every tree of any size will bear the scars of untold years of lions passing. The rocks themselves have yellow-orange patches scattered across their bases, pungent urinary testimony to the repeated territorial claims of many centuries, and many species.

Cheetahs need the kopjes. Shade is perhaps even more vital to them than it is to the lions. By force of evolution the cheetah's body has to operate within an incredibly narrow temperature range. They have a high body temperature to allow them to use their only weapon, their blinding speed, yet a scant rise in temperature of three degrees forces them to break off the chase. A lion living in the comfort of a pride has others to help with the hunting, but the solitary cheetah is on its own. An enthusiastic and uncoordinated young male cheetah, not knowing any better, may spend hours chasing Agama lizards around the base of a kopje as its mother sacks out in the shade. Avian predators abound here as well, ranging from pygmy falcons to Verreaux's eagles; all are capable killers, whether the prey be grasshoppers or gazelles.

On the plains of the vast Serengeti, death occurs around the clock, 365 days a year. My clients and I are in and out of the Serengeti and the Ngorongoro Crater during the first half of the year, when the wildebeest migration and the zebras and gazelles who move with them make this part of the world such a marvel. In July this parade of millions of prey animals passes into Kenya until October or November, when it heads back south into Tanzania yet again. The saga is never-ending for the migrating herds. The venue changes, but the birthing and the dying are continuous. By themselves, white-backed vultures consume more than sixty thousand pounds of meat here every single day, and these white-backs are but one of six species of vulture winging overhead. Then there are all the meat-eating raptors as well as the lions, the leopards, the cheetahs, the hyenas, the crocodiles, the jackals, and the African wild dogs (which are quite rare). There is much dying out there, and it exerts a powerful fascination on us. I have never had a client who was not gripped, positively or negatively, by the tableaus of predation acted out on the stage of the Serengeti.

People are torn: they want to see a "kill," but fascination can also give way to revulsion, depending on what is being killed and how. Telling the story later, people will testify that they've come on a kill "minutes" after it happened; often it's not minutes, but they want it to be. Often the death is quick and quiet, as with the lone golden jackal rapidly coursing the ground in the Serengeti. He is so intent on his work that the noisy and smelly approach of our diesel does not interrupt his search. This jackal is not moving in a straight path, head up, in that famous, single-footed dog-trot that can so easily eat up the miles. No, he means business right now, so I ask my driver, Olotu, to hold up a second. We will sit for a bit and see what happens. The jackal's course brings him steadily closer to us, nose still glued to the ground, eyes serving no function whatsoever. He passes only thirty feet in front of our bow, intent on something far more important than our mere presence, perhaps a Cape hare, a prey that's about the right size. But not a minute later a female Thomson's gazelle races in, intent on butting the jackal with her stubby, short horns. The jackal is forced to pay attention, dodging at the last flash of a second, still keeping to his course. The gazelle pursues, repeatedly dropping her head and trying to run into the motley yellow-brown jackal. The jackal must be on the scent of a newborn Thomson's, I realize. The gazelles are born with no odor, supposedly, but the afterbirth and the blood must have gotten this jackal's attention. He tacks steadily back and forth, back and forth, always downwind from the smell.

There is indeed a tiny gazelle, and it now makes its fatal mistake. Instead of lying motionless, ears flat, black lips on the ground, it vaults onto unsteady legs and bolts off in a crooked and jerking flight.

Lying still, *maybe* it would have eluded detection; bolting like this, not a chance. Like a fighter plane switching from missiles to guns, the jackal switches from nose to eyes and similarly locks onto the target. In spite of the mother's tremendous determination, the jackal rapidly narrows the distance between itself and the newborn. The mother repeatedly strikes the dog in the hindquarters during the pursuit, even knocking it off its feet on several contacts, but the gap between predator and prey closes and closes. Finally the jackal grabs the baby Tommie by the back of the neck, shakes it vigorously, tossing it to one side in the process. The mother gazelle is still defending her fawn, however, and charges again, and the jackal jinks and dodges and shoots in again to grab and shake the baby. A half dozen bites later, the baby lies still, with the jackal standing over it, tongue hanging out of the side of its mouth, panting heavily. The dead gazelle's mother stands still, appearing to study the situation, and then turns away and slowly high-steps off and rejoins the herd. A minute later she is grazing peacefully among the group, with nary a backward look.

Wildebeests and hartebeests look brain dead at the best of times, and, like the gazelles, thirty seconds after one of their own has been taken down the rest of the herd is grazing peacefully maybe only 150 yards away. For all they know now, it never happened. Africa is not at all a harsh mother, only a very matter-of-fact one. The killing between predator and prey is not born of anger or personal vendetta, and the rest of the herd shows no sign of bearing a grudge or malice, though they all struggle to live. Even with something as dramatic as three lionesses dragging down a wildebeest, there is no blood flying, no terrified voices screaming.

If you have not spent hours, or days, following a certain predator and are not keenly aware of its exact position, the target it seeks, and the time when it is doing so, you will seldom see the actual chase and kill take place, in spite of all the dying that is happening around you as you cruise the game parks. The plains *appear* to be, and mostly are, peaceful. Then suddenly the killer rockets out of cover in a golden explosion, followed by a ferocious flurry of running feet and hooves slamming into hard ground as both predator and prey seek desperately to live. Just as suddenly it's all over, and either the prey slows back to a walk after the predator has broken off the pursuit, or the killer is lying, panting and played out, over the life it has just claimed. It is a screenplay that builds slowly from the first steps of the stalk. These are strong and noble characters, with remarkable physical features and highly honed skills and they are capable of actions larger than life. The story has several acts, played in various settings, and with various motives. The final dramatic scene is often over in seconds, and it is worth all the time, knowledge, and effort that it takes to get the front-row seats.

I almost always root for the predators, because their role is so much harder than the prey's role, their numbers so relatively few. Sometimes, however, I find myself with mixed emotions. Not infrequently my clients and I want to retch from the vantage of our front-row seats. A slow, bloody, gruesome kill is often a necessity, but it's hard as hell to watch. The cats generally kill their prey before eating it, but hyenas and jackals don't. When a pack of either is dealing with an animal larger than a tiny Tommie, they eat the animal alive, tearing off strips of meat and scooping out gobs of guts, taking these helpings off to the side for consumption, then returning for more as the poor victim *stands* there, fighting if it can, numbly passive otherwise, until it dies. It's brutal to watch, and clients do turn away. I, too, have turned away.

Elephants are not a prey species per se, but they occasionally do get taken down. In Samburu, my group once watched seven lions bring down a six- or seven-year-old elephant that already had tusks. For hours they were on this elephant, which went down and got back up, went down and got back up, bleeding, crying, and bellowing, while the other elephants in its herd were running around, obviously traumatized. It took forever, and it was hard to watch, because we identify with elephants. The astonishing "lightness" and gentleness of their movements belie their massive size. In fact, the grace of their movements is the basic aesthetic model used by the women who perform the ancient dances of India.

The same clients had previously watched a young elephant play with a stick, picking it up, throwing it, going to get it, and starting all over again. What's the food value here, or the social value? It has to be play value. We watched little ones horsing around with each other, shoving their age-mates into the water, intentionally running with loose legs in order to splash as much water as possible. We had seen how newborn, hairy babies are nurtured and protected by the entire herd. Even when all seventy were running hard, the little ones were watched out for and never trampled. Female elephants are very tactile with babies, picking them up, pushing them over rocks, pulling them out of mud, while the baby almost never removes the tip of its trunk from the touch of its mother. It must be a wonderful sense of security to have a mother who weighs five tons, and aunts equally sized. We watched a baby "suck his thumb" by nursing on its own trunk. He didn't know what to do with his trunk. He tried to pick up a stick but couldn't quite do it. He couldn't surmount a log eight inches high. We spent close to four hours watching this herd, mostly focusing on the one baby. We could have spent the entire day.

Researchers used to refer to herds of elephants and prides of lions and families of gorillas as #1, #2, #3 and so on, and within these groupings were individuals 1A, 1B, 1C and so on. Everything was numerical and quantified and impersonal. Now the herds, prides, families, and individuals in research projects are given *names*, and by hard-nosed research scientists, not by soft-hearted tourists who have named two leopard cubs Dawn and Dusk and one particularly friendly elephant Gilbert. This naming betrays a belief, new in some quarters, that there is more going on with these animals than we might have formerly thought.

And then to watch seven lions take two hours to kill an adolescent elephant and to saunter away without even eating much of it? It's a cliché to state as much, but we bring our own morality to a "natural" world that has no morality, and we may therefore lie awake in our tents at night with roiling emotions. What kind of system is this?!

But a "system" it is, and a perfect one, honed over the millennia and now functioning as smoothly and flawlessly as some over-engineered German sedan. We stand in ignorant awe of the thing.

In Africa, one always seems to pause on the high ground to scan the scene below, to see what's being offered up, or just to use the opportunity to soak in the size of the country. In the Serengeti, I study the unending seas of gently rolling, blowing grasses for anything that seems to stand apart from this mesmerizing uniformity. Even I, a mere human who does not depend for life on my ability to pick up the unusual, can easily tell when something is going on out on the great openness. The slightest "deformity" is a cause for suspicion, alertness, and investigation. I may be tipped off by a squadron of vultures as they slide down the morning air, arrow-straight and wingtip to wingtip, closing the distance on some kill on the ground. I may notice that all the wildebeests or Thomson's gazelles are facing one direction, ears alertly forward, hooves planted directly underneath shoulders and hips in a stance too straight to signify anything other than a predator's presence. Perhaps something as simple as a "gap" in the great nothingness of the uniform grasslands informs us that a cheetah or some lions have recently passed through, and the prey species have not yet returned in the wake of their passing.

For their part, predators are looking for the unusual as well and are far superior at it. One reason they have better sensory systems and higher intelligence than the prey species is their need to look at an entire herd and evaluate which one has a slight flaw. I try to do the same thing for my clients, observing the same herd of antelopes that a cheetah, say, has its eyes on.

Which animal has a slight limp, or is too far ahead of the group, or too far behind, or too thin. In short, which are the young, the old, the infirm, and the weak? These individuals stand out to the predator, and prey does not want to be a standout individual. After just a few days my clients can often spot the animal a lion will go for: Look at the third wildebeest from the left in this group. He's a little stiff in the hip and walks differently. If we can see this, we know the predator can. When a lion charges into a herd of a dozen Cape buffalo, it is obvious which buffalo he is after: the one whose head and shoulders are moving up and down more vigorously as he favors one leg. Once locked on, the lion will not shift his target.

In a series of fascinating studies, researchers marked selected prey animals with white paint. These animals were as healthy as the others in the herd, but they now looked different, a bizarre difference that the predators had never seen before, presumably. But in both the predators' hard-wiring and in his experience, *different* in any way means *vulnerable*. Almost without fail, these painted animals were selected as prey.

But there can be extenuating circumstances. Most notably, perhaps, cheetahs will often go for an adult male Tommie in perfect shape. Why? Because this male, though healthy, is often solitary, because he has lost his harem to another male and has yet to join a bachelor herd. This solitary male is on its own in terms of threat detection, and a cheetah may be able to get much closer to him than to a whole herd, many of whom are always on the alert and have every direction of approach covered. In terms of evolution, this is the whole idea for organizing into a herd in the first place. And sometimes predators behave in ways that defy all logic.

It was morning in the Serengeti, north of Lake Ndutu, and I didn't see anything special at 6:15 a.m. that required me to ask the driver, Chambulo, to stop the vehicle for a minute, so it must be an embedded habit that had us grinding to a halt on the flat overlook. With the sun not yet up, the dawn was still so soft it felt as if we could gently push our fingers into it and leave a smoothly rounded depression in the air when we pulled our fingers back. The sun had risen just above the left shoulder of Mount Lemegrut, and the smooth, dulled turquoise of the lake stretched out before us. I swept my eyes over the smooth surface before reaching for my binoculars. The pink wash at the west end was flamingos, I knew, but at this distance I couldn't make out the individual birds, just the rosy brush-strokes. I swung my elbows up on the rim of the roof hatch and braced them there to allow me a steadier view through the strong glasses. I started my scan on the left end of the valley that led down to the lake, stopping after glassing only the first three hundred yards because my warm face and eyes had fogged up the cold lenses. I wiped them with my shirt and then began working up the left side of the valley, across the open slope, straining my eyes between the acacia trees, hoping for a hint of dull yellow-brown standing out against the sparsely grassed hillside. Reaching the top of the valley, I continued working across the flats, staying in the trees, ignoring the tempting open plains behind them. As I rolled the binoculars westward the low light from behind sneaked around the edges of my eye cups. I pulled the binoculars firmer into my cheekbones and continued working my eyes over the landscape, over the dead jumble of logs, above the bare soil where we had watched the young hyenas only last night, and down the gradual decline leading into the next shallow drainage.

I froze and very slowly backed up my view, making sure my lenses didn't shift up or down but retraced the last area perfectly. Again it was there, a flickering movement of lighter color. My clients sitting in the seats below me were anxious to get out onto the Serengeti Plain where the action was. I could feel it, but I hung in there a bit longer and so did they. No doubt about it now. Something, no, *two* somethings were working the slope on the west edge of the lake, moving parallel across its face, angling south. I was finally confident enough to tell my group that I thought we had some cats. This announcement proved to be a mistake, as everyone scrambled excitedly through the roof hatches, asking for directions and shaking the dickens out of the car. "Freeze, please, you guys, or I'm going to lose them." These cats, if that's what they were, were two, maybe two and a half, miles away, and any motion of the truck sent my elbow-propped binoculars whipping wildly across that far landscape. The truck stabilized. Again, the images became clearer out of the wet-air dawn, two dull-yellow animals, coursing slowly, side by side. I saw no large manes, so these had to be lionesses.

"Niko na paka wawili," I told Chambulo. I've got two cats.

"Wako wapi?" Where are they?

He had already started the vehicle, called Salim on the radio in the second truck, and had us rolling before I could respond. It's great that Chambulo always gets as excited about this work as I do, as my clients do. The whole safari is much more fun when everyone's involved. Chambulo reversed our original direction and headed west out of camp, driving hard, with the people on top ducking branches continually. One bit of inattention and an acacia thorn will draw serious blood from your scalp or face. But the air, so chilled that it made our eyes water, felt heavenly and added to the anticipation. My cat-obsessed crowd ignored the pairs of little dik-diks that we whistled by, which stayed frozen, only their awkwardly long noses showing any sign of life, quivering continually as they gathered the news. We slip-slided headfirst down a twenty-foot embankment, our tires gaining poor purchase on the broken clumps of caliche rock, and shot out onto the smooth, dry shore of this alkaline lake. We were racing, with a very definite and mobile target in mind, but I couldn't help looking down at the volcanic sand shore flats, which had welcomed quite a group of visitors last night. Wildebeest tracks were everywhere, of course, making a Jackson Pollock mosaic of fractals driven into the sand. I looked down at the chaos and shook my head with a resigned smile. Those wildebeests were wild ones, seemingly unorganized, stupid even, but they were here, and in huge numbers, so the powers that be must have something figured out.

We slowed as we reached the slope where I had seen the lionesses. All we had to do was traverse parallel below the slope, and with the dawn light behind us we should be able to spot them easily. However, in the twenty minutes it had taken us to drive here they seemed to have evaporated, and I was about to ask Chambulo to turn back and start a second sweep when, way up ahead, I glimpsed an ochre back and rolling shoulders disappearing into a small *korongo,* or gully. I let Chambulo know that I had them, that he needed to swing left, stay on the flats for about another two hundred yards, then turn uphill into the broken acacia woodland. As we drove ahead I pointed out the felines to everyone and was startled to realize that our ladies were not lionesses but a pair of cheetahs, large-framed, full-grown males at that.

"*Chambulo, hawa ni duma, si simba; pole mzee,*" I informed Chambulo. This was the first surprise of the day. Cheetahs are solitary animals, classically aterritorial, with a home range they frequent but do not defend. (Mating is therefore a chance encounter, which explains why the female is in estrus more than two-thirds of the time, a much higher percentage than that of the other big cats.) Occasionally, however, and for a temporary period, male cheetahs will drastically alter behavior and take on a partner, perhaps even two, and become ferociously territorial. I had just finished Tim Caro's book on cheetah behavior and now saw before me one of the very coalitions of adult males that he researched. This was a rare treat.

"*Hakuna matatizo. Paka ni paka,*" Chambulo replied. No problem, cats are cats. Yes, from the clients' point of view.

The cheetahs seemed not exactly jumpy but a little nervous, certainly aware of our presence, so we stayed well off, serving as a flank escort about two hundred yards below them and to the left. Quickly enough they ignored us and got their eye sweeps going again, working rhythmically left and right with their small heads, eyes hidden well below the shelf of brow. Each twenty degrees of swing matches a stride: right leg, left leg, shoulders rolling, head low and extended, tail held stiffly out and angled down. Ten minutes later the two cats pulled up in the shade of a large acacia nilotica, gathered their thin haunches underneath them, and, bracing themselves on stovepipe-straight forelegs, paused to search. Every so often one or the other would extend his head forward, eyes locked on some distant evidence of life. With my binoculars I tried to make out what they saw, but always with frustration. I knew they'd detected something, but I just couldn't pick up a clue. Or were they just playing with me, aware that I was watching them so intently with my jealous vision? I would love, for just one minute, to be able to look through eyes with such incredible magnification and resolution.

While we waited for the pair to move on, I took the opportunity to sketch out the tail ring patterns. The black dots on the yellow-gold backs of cheetahs extend down their tails, eventually joining together to form rings. These rings are irregular in width, in shape, and in number — a fingerprint for a cheetah. I had my guests draw each tail pattern as well, so they would have a reference for the next five days while we camped there. We would undoubtedly see these two cheetahs again, and the tails would be proof positive.

They rose up, stretched with their rumps high in the air, front legs extended low and far forward, yawned in perfect synchronization, and commenced walking again. The land in front of them dipped slowly away toward a wide, shallow draw. The little creek in the bottom ran brackish red, bordered by green salt grass, and shadows from acacia trees reached across the open sand for the red water. A small, widely scattered herd of Grant's gazelles resided in this little valley, but surely they would see the cheetahs the moment the cats stepped out of the thinly spaced trees and emerged onto the short grass and sand of the valley floor.

Indeed, they did. A short series of sneezelike sounds, repeated again and again, confirmed that the Grant's had visual contact. Their verbal warning seemed to sweep the length of the valley, being picked up and passed along by more Grant's, by Thomson's gazelles, by Coke's hartebeests, all employing their own version of the snorted warning. It was beneath the dignity of the stately giraffes to snort, but they would slowly pendulum their heads around, in wide-sweeping arcs, to peer in the same direction as the other ungulates.

The cheetahs pretended to ignore all this nasal congestion, tried to rise above it, and purposefully stepped out onto the valley floor. They paused at the red water, put nose tips to the surface, but didn't drink — unsurprisingly, because they get most of their water from blood. Perhaps they were, Narcissus-like, temporarily caught by the reflections of their own angular heads, each cheek cut with a teardrop line of black extending from eye to jaw. If so, the fascination was short-lived for the pair moved on, not jumping the small stream but turning right, away from the gazelles, heading up-valley. The wide grass alleys on either side of the water course narrowed, with the tree line closing in as well. At a narrow point the pair turned again to the right, this time daintily stepping up through a rocky patch to settle in the shade once more. As they laid down, a Cape hare sprang from beneath a fallen log, startling the wired cats, but not enough to elicit a chase — the effort wouldn't be worth the paltry reward. With ears straight up, the mottled brown hare jumped away and froze under a clump of heliotrope flowers, the ears going flat down on its back the instant it stopped.

The cheetahs ceased their vigilance and flopped over on their sides, dappled cats in dappled shade, oblivious to the world. Neither the growling calls of the mourning doves, nor the staccato, metallic chink of the blacksmith plover seemed to register. Cheetahs don't eat birds. Lulled by the low massive drone of the insects, they were soon asleep. We decided to go eat breakfast and then return. Two hundred yards away, I asked Chambulo to stop and then told the clients to look back and find the cheetahs, knowing this would be impossible. They'd been swallowed by the very Africa that spawned them.

At breakfast we discussed cheetah coalitions, their advantages and drawbacks. Contrary to what my group thought, the advantages are not obvious. They should have greater hunting success and lower individual risk, but the amount of food taken, per individual, will remain the same. The energy expended per calorie per cat is no different, whether he is solo or in a partnership. (Lions team up because they have less mobility and seek larger prey.) Caro's research suggests that the advantage lies in the cheetah pairs' being able to hold smaller territories that are more frequented by females, with whom they then share access. It comes down to the old story of being better able to pass along genes. But my group was not convinced, and maybe they were right. Wildlife biology is not just mathematics.

At any rate, here the rare behavior was, and it was nice to have a little mystery right in front of us when we returned, loaded now with slower film, to find this pair. They seemed to have left without a trace; however, down by the creek they had left a calling card. Two sets of distinct tracks reached the river, turned right, and headed farther up-valley, away from the lake. Cheetah tracks show the telltale three-lobed heel pad of all cats, but only with cheetahs do the claw prints show, and the outside lobes of the heel extend well past the middle lobe. There was no mistaking that the sun was well up, the humid air long since burned off and replaced by still heat, with a hint of much more to come.

Following the tracks upstream, with a bit of science and a lot of luck, within ten minutes we saw our two fellows striding purposefully ahead, and we fell in line some three hundred yards behind. Dust filtering through the flat-topped acacias ahead of us signified the coming of yet another wildebeest herd, and this pair changed direction slightly and worked toward the incoming herd. I advised my group not to get too excited, because wildebeests are too big and powerful for these slightly built cats. In fact, I'd never seen cheetahs take an adult wildebeest, and seldom even seen them take young ones.

The adult wildebeest weighs 500 or more pounds, a big male cheetah 120 pounds. Cheetahs are too fragile of frame, slim of legs, and small of teeth to behave in any brutish fashion. Moreover, they prefer wide open spaces where they can use their only weapon, speed, unimpeded by trees and bushes. There was plenty of such space within a short distance and plenty of lighter prey around for them to try for, and with much lower risk, so we'd just be patient and, maybe, get our just reward somewhere down the road.

But these cheetahs had apparently decided to throw the book completely out the window. They appeared to be considering this herd of wildebeests in an open woodlands quite seriously, stalking forward in a beautiful, classic approach. This behavior *was* textbook, with heads held low and forward, eyes never, ever, leaving the herd, scanning for that one *different* animal. The cheetahs' entire bodies were now suspended low, compact and tight, yet fluidly moving forward in small, controlled paces. At a distance of 150 yards from the wildebeests the two cats got down behind an old fallen acacia. This partially rotted wood provided the males with all the shading they needed, but at too great a distance from their potential prey. Sixty to 70 meters, undetected, is the maximum strike distance for cheetahs, and these two were well beyond that range at the moment. (Other cats have to be much closer before they attack, lions no more than 50 meters, and leopards no more than *five* meters.) In pursuit, cheetahs can hang in for 400 meters on average, and I've measured a chase of more than 600 meters. That was a long, long chase on a relatively cool day. Lions will pursue maybe 250 meters; leopards, no more than 15 before breaking off. Among the predatory cats, there's a direct correlation between the energy expended on a single attack and the overall success ratio. The more the animal puts in, the higher its success ratio *has to be*. Cheetahs invest a lot of energy, but only a small number of times, because they have a 70 percent success ratio. If cheetahs go hard, they're going to get their prey. Lions put out much less energy and consequently have a much lower success ratio: 10 percent for a single lioness, 15 percent for a group. Leopards invest little and almost always fail — 95 percent of the time, in fact. They don't give a hoot; they'll get one eventually. And they're usually in thicker vegetation, where pursuit is necessarily limited anyway.

It all makes wonderful sense, once it is figured out. And what about hyenas and African wild dogs? They are at the other extreme from leopards. Dogs will start their chase from something less than half a kilometer, occasionally almost a kilometer, and chase for eight kilometers (I measured this in one instance) at thirty-five miles an hour all the way. They ended up getting the wildebeest. Phenomenal. Hyenas will start from half a kilometer away and pursue for five kilometers.

With the cheetahs, we had watched the entire stalk through our binoculars and knew exactly where they went down beside the acacia, yet we could no longer see them. Finally, dark yellow ears with black patches on the back slowly rose up, melding almost perfectly with the height and color of the grass tops. I scanned through the wildebeest herd time and again but saw no youngsters there. I just couldn't see this happening, I told the group with regret. But the stalk was phenomenal and the herd was moving slowly closer, at a tangent to the cheetahs, so we decided to wait it out. Time slowed. We all had gotten our cameras out, resting on the tops of the vehicles, nestled in various sweaters or bean bags, and the anxiety was killing us. My heart is always with the hunter, though I am not one myself, and I would have loved for my clients to have the opportunity to witness an actual kill sequence. In more than twenty years, I have seen about one hundred cheetah chases and kills, dozens with lions, and exactly three with leopards.

The clock now ground to a complete standstill for me. The air was dead calm and hotter; all sound had died out. I couldn't hear any doves, though surely they could not know about the hunt in progress. Even the crickets and grasshoppers had somehow lapsed into silence. Now the male farther from the herd coiled up, and I passed a warning to everyone to get ready. This cheetah must have seen something that I had overlooked, for all I picked up were adult male wildebeests.

The other cheetah actually rose up slightly, turning his head to look quizzically back at his partner instead of watching the prey.

Suddenly the first cheetah was up and running — hard. The second cheetah vaulted fully up as if sprung from a jack-in-the-box, but then only casually loped after his hard-sprinting brother in arms. Little clusters of brown-yellow dust were shoved into the air, behind the rapidly disappearing cheetahs. Instantly, the wildebeest herd broke from relaxed formation into total confusion, half disappearing in a rising tide of flying dirt, the other half bursting into the clear space beside us. Into this cloud the two cheetahs raced, swallowed from our view. A single adult wildebeest emerged, cut left around a double-trunked acacia where the herd had broken right. This decision brought him into an open circle of ground perhaps one hundred yards across, which was all the room the cheetahs needed. At full speed, around sixty to sixty-five miles per hour, these cats were covering seventy-five feet each second, taking four long strides in that amount of time. It is hard to believe, but when they run that hard they can't see where they will come down at the end of each racing stride. And unbelievably, they were definitely after this big adult wilde-beest. I had never seen or heard of something like this.

The second cheetah reached the animal first. With no hesitation, but also with no finesse, the cheetah crashed bodily into the wildebeest's hindquarters, knocking him off stride but not off his feet. The cheetah sank his stubby canines into the rump of the still stumbling wildebeest and cupped his front paws around the front of the prey's rear legs. His stride thus shortened, the wildebeest slowed down, and the cheetah dropped onto his haunches, while maintaining his tooth hold and paw grip. The pair slid to a halt, trailing a river of dust in their wake. The other cheetah, who had originated the chase, arrived on the scene still going Mach 1 and, to the total surprise of both the wildebeest and myself, tore straight in and, with great risk, launched himself right between the horns of the now stationary prey, which had time only to duck his head and aim his horns at the flying blur of spots diving in at him. But the cheetah's aim was fortunate and he passed between the sharp points with only inches of clearance on either side. Our two Land Cruisers came crashing in as well now, plowing right over small trees and bushes in our rush to reposition our vehicles in the clearing. We threw the trucks sideways to the struggle unfolding before us, spraying up roostertails of dirt.

We were now close enough to hear the panting breaths of the wildebeest and the wheezing from the cheetah that had bitten into the hip. The one that had leaped between the horns was getting tossed into the air as the wildebeest attempted to dislodge him. With front legs wrapped around the wildebeest's neck, the cheetah was thrown skywards again and again, always slamming back down between the horns. The wildebeest fought for survival, while the two cheetahs were hanging on for dear life. The risk that those cats had taken was astounding. Surely one or the other of the fragile killers was going to suffer for such a brazen attack on so large a prey. Finally, the cheetah on the wildebeest's neck reached under and attained a grip on the lower lip of the thrashing animal. With claws splayed wide he pulled back with incredible strength, toppling the wildebeest by his lip, and sprang for a new grip. But the ungulate was up too quickly, and the front cheetah had to resume his purchase on the back of the neck, his body still stretched vulnerably between the horns.

Four times the pair brought the 500-pounder off his feet, and four times he struggled back up, raising with him the 120 pounds of muscled cat on his neck and the other 120 pounds hanging from his hip. Finally, the fifth time, the wildebeest no longer had the strength to get back up, and the front cheetah managed to switch his bite from the back of the neck to the all-important throat grip. The wildebeest resigned; his kicking diminished, then ceased. The rear cheetah did not lessen his grip in the slightest, while the front cheetah remained draped bodily over the neck and shoulders of the now dying animal.

We observers were out of breath too, and I, for one, was almost shaking from watching this gut-level struggle for life. The power and the efficient savageness had left me panting; the riskiness of the attack had me awed. I looked around at my guests. They were transfixed and glistening with perspiration.

Eventually, after fully five minutes ticked by, both cheetahs released their grips and, as a team, immediately began to drag the carcass into the shade. The pair were certainly exhausted, possibly injured, but by sheer force of will — tooth grip, power, and willpower — they pulled the wildebeest against a stubby acacia and out of sight of prying, preying eyes. It was another eight minutes, by the watch, before either cheetah had regained his breath enough to start the next tiring process, tearing open the kill. But they had to do it, because they are too fragile to defend their kill as lions would, and unable to drag it up a tree like leopards, and they are usually alone as well. The only way these cheetahs could carry their prey was in their stomachs, so they had to start eating as quickly as they could. Now a second kind of speed was of the essence.

Both of their faces were soon fully red, as one cat tore into the lower stomach and the other ripped into the body through a foreleg. We kept filming, but the sounds of crunching bones, panting predators, and tearing flesh was too much to be ignored. Our gasps and exclamations mixed with the sounds of eating. The whole picture of blooded cats and lifeless, misshapen wildebeest was almost overwhelming, but death is essential for life in this system; in any system. Nor could anyone deny that these cheetahs had earned their kill. This doesn't mean that it was pleasant to witness, but in context we should be happy for the life of these two cheetahs.

My group was exhausted. I heard sighs and heavy exhaling as my people slowly finished shooting frames and dropped down onto the seats to watch the final minutes of the feast from the lower vantage of the windows, instead of remaining standing through the roof hatches. There was little conversation other than the occasional remark of admiration for both the predators and the prey. The wildebeest never quit until the death bite on his throat stole his air, his will. And what about the luck involved? The cheetah in front could easily have been gored and gutted.

The following dawn we drove by the kill and found only the wildebeest's tail and a dark wash on the ground, surrounded by a flurry of predatory tracks. Where is the plaque or other tribute to commemorate the courage and power of the cast of players? But it is as it should be, I suppose, that a battle that occurs hundreds of times a day across this vastness should be marked only with blood-stained and trampled grass.

8

Killing in the Crater

Compared with the balletic athleticism of the cheetahs, lions are thuggish pool-hall brawlers. They stalk with finesse, it is true, but only to get close enough — to within fifty meters at least — to use their killing weapons of weight and strength. A lioness doesn't tactfully slap down an impala and then turn it over, carefully avoiding the horns, in order to sink her teeth into the antelope's throat and slowly suffocate it. Depending on the size of the prey, a lioness will just swat the animal hard enough to break its neck and then disembowel it, or perhaps she will take the entire head in her mouth and crush it with a overpowering clamp of her huge teeth. It may not be pretty, but it is effective.

Of all the choices a lion may have for a kill, Cape buffalo are perhaps the toughest. The males weigh three quarters of a ton, have literally bulletproof horns, and are immensely powerful and very fast, even in the swampy highlands of the Aberdare Mountains or on the rim of Ngorongoro Crater. A buffalo has to be considered carefully by a lion, or usually a group of lions, before the decision is made to try and take it down. The size of the reward, meat for a week, say, must be weighed against the lethal risks involved. The lion must consider the buffalo the way the cheetah must consider the wildebeest: the disparity of size and strength in the two match-ups is somewhat similar. It often takes a desperate lion to attempt a buffalo kill, and probably most of the dead buffalo on which we find lions feeding were actually killed by a pack of hyenas, who were then driven off by the poaching cats.

This is not always the case, however. Just as those cheetahs at Lake Ndutu chose a wildebeest when there was plenty of smaller game around, for years and years there were four huge, exceptionally heavy male lions who made a good living on the southwest rim of Ngorongoro Crater by killing buffalo and virtually nothing else. I first encountered them during an evening run after a long and dusty-hot day in the crater floor. The return to the cool and green of the rim was a welcome relief after the oven heat of the alkali dust and bleached landscape of the crater floor. I had run many times along the crater road and had not infrequently come across buffalo and elephants. Leopards would hear me, see me, or smell me coming and therefore evaporate into the surrounding dense greenery. Elephants would probably smell me but, being elephants, would refuse to move away for a reason as puny as a single human. But I would most likely see them if I could manage to keep my head up and not fall into the trancelike state of the long-distance runner. That left only buffalo, which had jumped me on a number of occasions in this habitat, usually just before dark, when the bulls felt it was safe to come out onto the drainage ditches that were spaced along the often-wet road. They would graze quietly on the short grass that got the extra runoff water until I ran up on them, unseen and unheard because of the ditch they were in. This surprise usually resulted in a charge, but I was well warmed up and a properly inspired sprint for a hundred yards or less would do the trick. Ideally, I would avoid them by running so as to be back before dusk settled, along with the heavy dew, on the crater's heights.

One day I had a distance runner, Mike, with me. For me, running is a chance to be alone, which is so rare during a safari, and also the opportunity to *not* be responsible for someone else's life. But Mike needed to burn some energy, so he came along. It was an unusual streak of bad luck, this run. Between the lodge and the main road we ran into a herd of elephants, complete with females and young. We waited patiently, Mike very at ease, until a passing vehicle came by and we hopped on its bumper to get a lift through the herd. Before we started off again, however, I ran over the drill with Mike. Buffalo: run for a tree. Elephants: wait for my command. Lions: never, *never* run, but slowly give ground, facing them the entire time, and do not trip as you retreat, for falling down would almost certainly bring a charge down on us, even if one hadn't been intended originally.

The road along the crater rim is a terrible running course. It winds steeply up then suddenly down and is speckled throughout with holes, puddles, and stretches of washboard. It sits at just under eight thousand feet in elevation. Mike and I weren't talking much. We were about two miles out when I glanced up on the inside embankment, fifteen feet above the road bed, and thought I saw something. With air at a premium, I reached out and arrested Mike by his left arm. He pulled up short, looked at me, and then followed my gaze up the embankment. Four lions were crouched there, all adult males with impressively dark manes, lined up in a row, eight huge paws hanging over the edge, eight inquisitive eyes casually looking at us.

"Lions," I stated rather unnecessarily. "Slowly start backing up, and just keep facing them. They don't look angry, more just curious about us. Just keep slowly moving and don't stumble on anything behind you."

I was talking to myself, however, for Mike was long gone. I craned my head away from the lions as far as I dared, expecting to find him crouched in the ditch on the opposite side. I located him instead at least one hundred yards down the road, running hard, and showing no signs of slowing, in spite of the altitude. I kept backpedaling slowly and the lions gradually raised their heads higher and higher to keep me in sight as I got farther and farther away. Finally they all stood up to watch my departure, not one of them making even the slightest move in my direction. When I was at least seventy-five yards away, I finally turned to trot off, but I kept looking back every third or fourth stride, just in case any of them had a change of heart.

When I caught up with Mike, he was bent over at the waist, his palms on his knees as he gulped in the rarified air. Fortunately the foursome wasn't coming our way, as it seemed that Mike had spent his last nickel. A miffed tone may have sneaked into my voice when I said, "Let's keep walking, just in case their curiosity gets the better of them."

A mile short of the turn-off to our lodge a buffalo came thundering out of one of the many drainages we had passed. This was surprisingly early in the evening for him to be in there. "Run!" I yelled, and Mike didn't even bother turning to see why, but dug in once again, sending little spurts of dirt flying back from his shoes. I pulled in behind him and ran hard, too. No one I know has ever seen a bluffing buffalo, and this one didn't bluff either, but he did veer to the left and, with an alacrity surprising for his size, clambered up the embankment and into the hagenia forest. "All right," I said to Mike as I tapped him on the shoulder, which only made him speed up more.

"He's waved off," I said. "You can stop running now."

"Jesus fucking Christ," he blurted. "Is it always like this when you run around here?"

"No," I answered in innocent truthfulness. "It's just one of those days, I guess."

He gave me a rueful look, and started walking on. At the lodge we told the rest of the group to get their cameras, as there were some lions just down the road. Ten minutes later we were approaching them again, this time from the safety of the truck. They had barely budged. The group was awed by these exceptionally maned creatures, at least three quarters of a ton of lion. From Mike's and my vantage on the ground they had looked gargantuan; from the Land Cruiser they looked merely huge. On foot, Mike and I had intrigued them a great deal; in the Land Cruiser we were worth a quick once-over before they flopped back down, all four exhaling heavily as their ribs pushed flat into the thick grass.

For the next four months I was up and down the road from the crater to the Serengeti, often driving the crater rim at dusk. Sure enough, I started to find these four lions quite consistently, in a locale they had inventively chosen that was perfect for stalking buffalo. Once we even came upon them while they were in the process of dragging a dead buffalo up and out of a ditch. Imagine the power it takes to tug something that heavy, while it is lying on its side, up a steep slope for thirty feet and then into the safe cover of the forest. Two of the lions, working together, gripping the bull's buttocks with their teeth, powering backward with their massive shoulders bulging under the strain, finally reached the edge of the trees. They rested for fully ten minutes while their cohorts tore into the buffalo's belly, which belched warm steam into the cool mountain air.

Five weeks after that run, I had four pediatricians with me in the truck as we ascended the road from the hamlet of Karatu, heading toward the lip of the crater. July and August are typically misty here, and so it was on this day. Heavy as it was, this mist forced my guests into the relative dryness of the vehicle. I remained on the roof, more out of stubbornness than out of expectancy. The cold moisture felt very clean after the dusty drive up from

Lake Manyara. Our world had shrunk to perhaps twenty feet in each direction, so it was not surprising that we were well past the lions before their presence registered with me. I told Stephen, our driver, to stop the vehicle, rapidly told the group about the four males, adding that I had seen only one, now behind us, walking along the top of the embankment on the uphill side of the road. The pediatricians scrambled for cameras and film as we slowly and steadily backed up, worried more about another truck rear-ending us in the thick mist than about the remote possibility of the lion's taking umbrage at our use of the reverse gear.

It was amazing. First one lion, then another, and then a third appeared right beside us on the bank as if conjured up by smoke and magic. We could actually see the gray tatters of clouds swirling around them as they marched purposefully along in the wet and clinging grass. The fourth lion was not in sight. Had he caught the point of a buffalo's horn during an attack? I was too busy trying to get the other three apparitions on film to dwell on the possibility. As the lions came, so they went, first one, then the second, then the third turning away and disappearing almost instantly in the miasma of cloud-thickened, moss-covered trunks of the bordering forest. As if posing, the last of the three stopped just before he was cloud-swallowed and turned back over his shoulder to grace us with a royal glance. My camera was already focused, and as I squeezed down with my index finger he hesitated just a second. By the time I had lowered the lens to look at him with my bare eye there was only the swirling moisture before me. He did as I would have done.

Ten days into another safari and I was already out of tricks. We had seen everything, usually twice. In February and March, the Serengeti Plain is so packed with fauna that you can end up almost overloaded. Seeing five to ten cheetahs and thirty to fifty lions in *one* day is not all that unusual. You can overdose on predators, or become complacent and jaded. *"Pole, Pole, ndio mwendo."* This is a favorite phrase used all the time in Kenya and Tanzania: "Slowly, slowly is the way to go." It is certainly true when it comes to wildlife, and a strong start in Tanzania leaves us free to do a lot of tracking, to analyze the microworld of the termitaria, to spend a whole morning looking just at the differences between moths and butterflies, or at the differences between beetles and true bugs. Birdcalls now merit the time required to learn them. And — surprise! — not all acacia trees are the same when you look a little closer. Anyway, this very large group told me at dinner on the night we moved from the Serengeti to the cool heights of Ngorongoro that they would have all gone home happy if the safari ended right then. Everything else was going to be gravy, they said. As it turned out, I think they were duly impressed by the gravy.

We left the lodge perched on the crater at 6:30 a.m. In my truck I had four of the older women from the group, late fifties and up, "blue hairs," as they called themselves, who had asked if they could be in my car that day, which was fine by me. I knew they would be in no rush for anything, which would make the day so much better. I'd be allowed to stop and photograph a good clean animal track, key out a new flower, or stop to just shoot "scenics" with nothing in them but mood. This was a game group, an attitude that helps at Ngorongoro, because the one-lane road that winds two thousand feet from the crater rim down to the flatness below is an exciting experience in itself. Four-wheel drive is mandatory, not because of the mud but because of the loose rock and massive holes on the steep and narrow pitch. It's all a 4 x 4 can do to maintain a grip. More than one truck has accidentally taken a shortcut to the bottom, going over the edge and arriving earlier than expected, an accordion of crushed metal. My ladies were not put off by the road; in fact, they insisted on standing up so they could peer over at the incredible land spread out below them like a vast pale-green dinner plate, with patches of forest here, a swamp there, and dry places looking like servings of various vegetables. Their excitement far surpassed their fear, and this cinched it for me. With the blue hairs in charge we were in for a good day.

With Sosta at the wheel, we crept steadily down, down, down, the vehicle's transfer case grinding all the while in protest. Candelabra trees rose majestically above us like scarecrows with upraised arms as they clung to the nearly vertical crater wall. As we descended lower, red hibiscus and the occasional huge purple one welcomed us as if we were cruising along some country lane to some great estate. (You would swear they were planted for the purpose, but they were not, believe me.) By seven o'clock we were on the crater floor, which was still surprisingly cool in spite of our elevation loss of two thousand feet. The crater is enormous, and from the end of the road, over a vast misty plain the fever trees of the Lerai forest were visible, about a half mile away, and beyond them lay the still and reflective surface of the lake.

The buffalo sitting on the flat plains chewing their cud rhythmically launched twin shots of steam from their nostrils with each exhalation. When they shifted position, steam radiated off their bellies and the insides of their legs as warm skin was exposed to chilled and damp air. The only predators we could see in our wide scope of vision were two golden jackals single-footing across the short grass. But this was all deceptively serene: the 110 square miles of the Ngorongoro Crater has the highest density of lions anywhere on earth. The same is true for the hyena population.

We elected to motor straight to the near shore of the alkaline lake, being careful to stay back from the water's edge so we wouldn't end up trapped in the soft black mud just beneath the shellac of the brittle alkali. We would work on our shorebirds, including all the Eurasian migrants down in Tanzania this month. Flamingos also dotted the lake and formed a tight cluster of pink in the northeast corner, where a small freshwater stream dumped in. These round-bodied birds that look skewered on their own spindly legs gather there to bathe and drink, preferring the fresher water to the stagnant alkali. A line of greenish black rushes on both sides of the stream drops straight down from the north, aiming those who need the assistance directly at the flamingos concentrated there. In another month those rushes would become dry and brittle, breaking off in the relentless, salty winds that run daily circles inside the crater. The dry season had yet to peak, however, so the rushes stood strong and green, shoulder to shoulder, standing guard over the valuable fresh water. My four ladies thumbed through the pages of their field guides and added notes to the plates, sorting out the little stints from the Temmink's stints, the curlew sandpipers from the wood sandpipers, and the ruffs from the stilts. Out of habit, I ran my binoculars up the stream. Thirty feet away, not even trying particularly hard to hide between the clusters of rushes, sat three lionesses.

Then I got my guests onto the cats, which they picked up instantly even though only lion faces peeked out from the dark green. We drove forward, making no attempt to be subtle, and shut down beside the lionesses and photographed their heavily panting faces, tongues lolling over their six lower incisors. All three golden heads suddenly elevated a few inches as their ears perked up and bent forward. Their instinctive reaction was followed immediately by our instinctive reaction as we turned as one to look behind us. A small herd of wildebeests approached the stream just where it emptied into the lake.

I had the driver, Sosta, immediately pull away, go upstream, and cross over to the other side. As we bounced through the creek, grateful that its bottom was hard where we had risked the crossing, we picked a point seventy-five yards or so out on the alkali flats from where we could watch the action, if there was any, without affecting the outcome. The wildebeests were leery of the tall rushes and only drank for a few seconds before jamming their front legs hard into the crusty soil and launching themselves backward, though nothing was in pursuit. The jumpiest may drink the least but may well live the longest.

The lionesses, when we looked across to them, had let their heads sink back down, their eyes almost shut against the harsh light and intense heat. Two heads sank down to rest on huge paws, but one lioness staying marginally awake and watchful. I reminded my group that lions do 86 percent of their hunting at night.

By nine o'clock, having settled in for the duration, we had been driven down from the roof hatches by the unrelenting sun and had taken our seats, caught up in watching the raptors always soaring somewhere overhead in the crater. Bateleur eagles, four species of harriers, two types of falcons, and two species of vultures were all sorted out before the heat drove us to quietness and near somnolence. When I glanced up, a herd of about thirty wildebeests, with a half dozen zebras mixed in, was walking dejectedly toward the water. Of course, "dejectedly" is an inexcusably anthropomorphic adverb. They weren't dejected. I don't imagine they can be dejected. That's simply how wildebeests look to us as they plod along with their heads down, tail to rump. This is actually an efficient way to walk, and the single-file formation guarantees that only the lead animal will be exposed to any predator hidden directly ahead.

The lions had slipped down and out of sight, I pointed out, which meant they could mean business. These wildebeests seemed much more blasé than the previous group. Forty yards from the stream, they were still slow-marching forward with their heads down, eyes to the ground. Thirty yards and closing. Twenty. No golden heads poked out of the grass, but I didn't expect to see them until they were charging ahead full speed. The ladies were all eyes now. The zebras passed the file of wildebeests and reached the water's edge first, fanning out side by side. The wildebeests, well mannered and orderly, spread out on either side of the striped cluster and started drinking without even a glance. I knew these three lions were *right there*. The potential prey was paying no attention. Could the lions be this *lazy?* The herd continued to drink in peace. The water shimmered as rippling rings radiated out from their muzzles.

"What's up with those lionesses?" someone finally asked. Minutes passed. Had the lions left the scene earlier, unknown to us? Maybe they weren't even in those high grasses now. We could only remain ready and be patient. The wildebeests and zebras now raised their heads, their thirsts slaked, the water dripping from their noses, forming a sheet that seemed to connect one animal to the next. As one, they then turned and plodded back in our direction, their rumps toward the hidden lions. I kept telling myself to relax my pressure on the shutter as my eye stayed glued to the viewfinder, waiting for the blurred explosion of charging lionesses.

It didn't happen. But the lions had moved. They were now a lot closer to the junction of the lake and the creek than we had thought; and there was a lot more open space between the lions and the water than we had thought. The wildebeests had not been as close or as tempting to the lions as it had seemed; our long lenses had compressed the distance. We returned to our observation post on the flats, out of the way. On the wide whiteness of the far shore of the lake, columns of dust rose vertically and spun with the wind, each anchored to a cloud of salt. Every tree had its inverted twin in the mirage that spread like a mirror in the foreground between the water and us, floating on an island of cooked and brittle grass, with no horizon to define heaven and earth.

Two white Land Rovers painted with the

crater's grayish brown dust drove up, and the passengers inside asked why we had been parked here so long. They had noticed us from across the broad flats and figured we must either be stuck or have something unusual near the vehicle that they couldn't see from their distance. One of our blue hairs, Samantha, spoke up brightly, saying we were waiting for the three lionesses, which made everyone in the other vehicles spin around rather smartly, as if the cats might be sneaking up behind them even as we spoke. When this reaction didn't produce the expected results, their eyes swept an arc around the immediate area. Finally, risking humiliation, a man in the front of one truck asked us exactly what lions we were expecting, to which Samantha gave a chirpy response. Everyone now looked at the sparse line of the distant rushes, and then looked back at Samantha. She continued to explain what had just happened and why we were still here.

One of their drivers spoke next, saying we were wasting our time, that the lions were just there for the shade and wouldn't hunt until that night. They always hunt at night, he declared, and with that he spoke briefly to the driver of the other truck and they roared off, encircling us in a net of dust.

Well, *almost* always at night. So the gauntlet had been thrown down, it seemed, and the women took up the challenge with relish. "We'll just wait and see," said Eleanor. "Does that sound good, girls?" A general assent confirmed that we were here for the duration.

Soon enough the sun was coming straight down through the roof hatches. There was no shade anywhere in the world now. Noon on the equator makes for a very short shadow, and on this crater it made for blistering heat. It crushed all animation out of us. We slouched and sweated in silence.

After twenty minutes, Kathy spoke. "Did you hear about the three men from Wyoming whose car broke down, forcing them to spend the night at a farmer's house?" I couldn't figure out where she was headed with this remark or what it had to do with anything. No one else could either, apparently, because no one answered. But Kathy continued. "Well, it seems that this farmer had quite a nice daughter, who had never yet been with a man. The three men had all gone to sleep in the hay barn and the daughter decided to go out and . . ."

We weren't sleepy anymore. We even sat up a bit and turned around to look at her, sitting in the back seat. She carried right on as if telling dirty jokes at this time and in this place, dying of heat prostration while waiting for the outside possibility of three lionesses making a kill in the bottom of Ngorongoro Crater, was the most natural thing in the world. It turned out all four of these women felt this way. They had an inexhaustible supply of off-color material. The next hour flew by as they traded joke for joke, all new to me and mostly funny. I couldn't imagine what Sosta was thinking, but I knew he was listening carefully in spite of his expression of disinterest. His English was plenty good enough.

Another herd of wildebeests, this time with an equal number of gazelles accompanying them, marched across the heat-reflecting ground toward the creek. The gazelles let the wildebeests lead the way to the water, and the wildebeests obliged them. The lions did not oblige us, however, and in a few minutes this group, like the previous two, moved out of the area. I didn't see the lions, but they hadn't moved through the bare patch in the middle of the rushes, so they still had to be in there, hidden somewhere.

"So anyhow," Eleanor continued, "this

blonde had never owned a dog before, so of course she . . ."

At 1:30, yet another herd of wildebeests came around, this one larger than the others and with a scattering of yearlings. These youths were almost eleven months old and would have no problem moving like the wind, the same as their mothers, when the situation called for it. Still, they might be more tempting to the lions. Without a word from me the group got into position, but Eleanor didn't miss a beat with the joke of the moment. Suddenly a pair of snipe rocketed out the rushes, startling not the wildebeests but me, because I was sweeping the line again and had the two birds right in my binocular view, but unnoticed, when they exploded. *Something* made those birds fly, I knew, and I began scanning again.

Ten feet to the right, I finally had a lioness in my lenses. I got the ladies on to her, using an isolated clump of rushes as a starting point for their search. All of us were locked on her back as she slipped quietly forward. Now the jokes stopped. Follow the lioness, I reminded them. Following the prey risked following the *wrong* prey, but if you stayed on the predator and just waited for the intended prey to come into your frame, there was little chance of missing the shot. Of course, I added, there was also little chance of the lioness charging, despite the movement forward. But no one responded.

With sixty to seventy wildebeest eyes facing their direction, and six sets of binoculars in our truck, all waiting and watching for the smallest of motions, somehow the two other cats just appeared on either side of the lioness we had seen first. I couldn't conceive how they had managed to move as far as they did undetected. One of the other two had even crawled slightly past the first one. Then all three disappeared again. Lions never cease to amaze me.

"Get ready," I said. "This could well be it. All three are down and must be moving." I didn't dare lower my lens, but I also had to find the moving lions, for without them in my sights ahead of time there was little chance of picking them up after they rushed forward. Sosta, who was not shooting pictures, finally found a brown head with its black-backed ears showing above the rushes. They had moved another thirty yards left and now had the herd virtually pinned between themselves and the water of the lake. But still the cats waited, now standing behind the wall of rushes that hid them from the wildebeests' view. The wildebeests were oblivious. This was excruciating to watch, and it was nerve-racking to stay so ready with the camera, finger on the trigger.

The cats suddenly sank, leaving us a view of only dark vegetation and dark animals behind it. "Get ready!" I said. "Get ready! This has got to be it."

All three lions launched out of the rushes and began running hard back to the left, trying to cut off the wildebeests instantaneously fleeing in panicked retreat. A portion of the herd tore out into the shallow water of the lake, scattering the previously peaceful flamingos that had been standing one-legged in the still water. I picked up one lion in the lens and had no choice but to stay with her. She did not even change her stride as she hit the water, but splashed out with the same determination with which she had started her run. Now, it was water instead of dust flying everywhere. She was going so fast that by the time the splashes rose and fell, she was well beyond them. She closed the distance on a young wildebeest and swung at its hip. A huge fountain burst up as the yearling slammed down onto the surface of the lake. The depth charge-like explosion was

357

so great and so widespread that the lioness came to a complete stop and looked around, searching the roiling water for the prey she knew she had hit. When the wildebeest appeared above the waves, she took two bounds and was on it. The other two cats had apparently not done as well as the one I had followed, because now they came trotting out into the water toward the female who was already returning toward dry ground, her kill clamped between her massive jaws, its legs and lower body dragging in the water.

This yearling was small enough that the lioness could lift it and run when the other two members of her pride approached. She had no intention of sharing the efforts of her work and ran hard through the shallow water, the wildebeest swinging so wildly that neither of the other two cats could latch on to it. But as soon as their successful pride mate gained the beach, they jumped her again. She swung the wildebeest like a rag, trying to keep it clear of the other two, but without a kill to carry they were agile, and soon all three had canines sunk into wildebeest flesh. They pulled against one another, with the calf stretched tight between their back-peddling bodies.

Sosta quickly drove us closer, knowing that at this point we would not, could not, easily disturb the intensity of the lions. We stopped twenty feet away and could hear the death-deep growls as the cats fought for position and possession, no one willing to loosen her grip enough to gain a new purchase. They sank to the ground, each trying to twist away from the other two, but all the grips were too well secured. The calf got gradually longer and noticeably thinner. With a god-awful tearing sound, a leg and shoulder came loose from the kill, and in a flash one lioness was up and running, holding her prize high in the air above the dust. The other two took no notice and stayed crouched and locked on, growling ominously in one long, nonstop rumble. Then the smaller of the two tried a sudden change of tactics and spun around, throwing her entire body over the torn wildebeest. The growling and the gnashing rose to a level that was frightening even to us within the safety of the truck. The larger lioness flipped around, landing directly on top of both the other lioness and their shared kill. The bottom cat, like a house cat on the defensive, turned turtle and began to rake the belly and chest of the lioness above her. I know my camera was firing rapidly, though I did select each exposure, not trusting to the luck of the motor drive. I'm sure my blue hairs were equally enthralled, aghast, and amazed at the intensity of the battle, but I couldn't hear a thing over the sounds of snarling and yowling.

Finally, the wildebeest was pulled exactly in half, the vertebrae separating part way down the spinal column. The suddenness of the tear caught both combatants by surprise, launching one into the air and spinning the other more than half a circle as the carcass tore apart. Each lioness ran from the other and dropped to the ground twenty feet away, coveting its share of the kill. This meat was engulfed, not chewed but gulped, with bones crushed, hide ripped into chunks. Within minutes there was no trace of a wildebeest calf, but each lioness stalked a circle or two, looking for scraps. They kept a more than respectable distance from one another until the ardor of the kill that had flamed such a fight had died back to the ever-present embers that a predator must have.

"Unreal," someone in the truck exclaimed. "Terrifying," blurted someone else. The superlatives didn't even seem to do justice to what we had seen and what we had felt. Now the two cats approached one another, not in greeting, but more out of curiosity, I think. They were caked with dirt and blood, mangy-looking and weather-beaten. They avoided each other by yards, studying one another like rivals about to brawl in a bar. Each surveyed the spot where the other had consumed its share. Finding it empty, each circled back to the neutral ground between them.

Then it was over, just like that, as they swung into stride, side by side, and started off in the direction of the third lioness. When they reached the tall rushes they lay down and slipped from sight. I looked at my group and they looked at me, red-lipsticked mouths still agape. Finally Kathy spoke up in a singsong monotone, "Eighty-six percent of all lion kills occur at night. Single lionesses only have a ten percent success ratio." There was a malicious gleam in her eyes. "Even groups of lionesses succeed only fifteen percent of the time, so we may well be wasting our time."

She cracked us up as she mimicked my habit of absentmindedly blowing on my binocular lenses as I speak. "Come on, my blue-haired harem," I finally said, almost drowned out by their laughter, "let's go say good-bye to our cats and head on up the hill."

Our lionesses, all kissed and made up, were lying in a loose pile, backs touching, tails flopping randomly, each studiously cleaning off the mud and the blood. A touching sight, the way they curved their massive muffs sharply at the wrists so they could wipe their dirty faces. The lioness who had made away with the meat early in the battle was now spotless, but we could tell which she was. The other two didn't seem any the worse for wear, however, despite the ferocity we had just witnessed. I glassed each one from nose to tail and couldn't find even a blood-filled scratch, much less a wound of any depth.

Peace had returned to this corner of the crater. The flamingos had come back to the shoreline that had been so rudely disrupted by the rampaging lionesses. We passed a calm hour with proven killers before finally rolling off for the coolness of the crater rim. When we were two hundred yards across the pungent-smelling alkali flat, I asked Sosta to stop for just a second and then suggested that the ladies look back. Even knowing *exactly* where the lions were at that moment, we couldn't see them. The crusty layer of the lake bed was torn and beaten where the fight had occurred, but even this was hard to discern, as the winds of the last hour had already redusted it, blending it in. There was no dark ground where the calf had been torn and engulfed.

"So," Kathy asked as we started the ascent, "did you hear about the doctor and the veterinarian who were playing a round of golf?"

9

Crossing the Grumeti

June 1998 found me hidden in the tall grass on the south bank of the Grumeti River with Susan Miller and Rob Haubner, who were already repeat clients of mine, and avid students of the wildlife and the people of Africa. For more than a year, my old friend and coworker Willy Chambulo and I had planned our camp on the Grumeti — the killing field in East Africa that eclipses all others in ferocity.

About all you have to do is rendezvous with the wildebeest herds when they are forced to cross the Mara River during their migration into and then out of Kenya. The Mara flows west through the African vastness to Lake Victoria, the inland sea. Similarly, on their way north out of Tanzania, the incredible mass of almost two million wildebeests plus half a million zebras must somehow get to the other side of the Grumeti River, which flows east to the lake.

Fortunately for Rob, Susan, Willy, and me, this season the wildebeests had cooperated in terms of timing and location. In some years I have had to change my plans at the last moment, but the logistics worked out perfectly this time. Rob and I had endlessly discussed via e-mail what lenses he and Susan should bring, what film would be best and how much would be needed. We had debated the appropriately camouflaged colors of clothing and the correct times of day, all in an effort to make sure we could maximize the window of opportunity. And so the house lights dimmed, and the curtain was about to go up. Our select audience of four grew silent, and the actors that had been milling about backstage for months took their places, because this was one show that evolution says really must go on. These actors must get to the other side; the supporting cast awaits.

We and the wildebeests were not the only ones in attendance that day. The predators whose very lives depend on killing are even more tuned in to this opportunity than are we, who are merely awed by the spectacle. Hyenas will travel for long days, even leaving their territories, to take advantage of the abundance offered by the river crossings. At different times, I have walked right into both lions and leopards as they were waiting for the exhausted animals to clamber up the banks, soaked and beaten by the strong currents and nearly trampled by the mass hysteria. For hours, clients and I have waited in the shade of an olive tree, keeping an eye on a cheetah hidden by the rise of a termite mound, who is in turn keeping an eye on the herds as they emerge from the river.

Even more than zebras and Thomson's gazelles, wildebeests hate the water. They must drink from it continually, must cross it twice yearly, and still they work themselves into a state as they approach the river. A lark or francolin bursting out from under a clump of lantana while the wildebeests have their noses in the murky water will invariably cause them to explode into pure panic, stampeding into one another in their desperate flight, only to return to the water thirty seconds later. Instinct, not logic, is coursing through the muscular bodies of the grazers, and instinct rightly tells them that these next few minutes are among the most dangerous of their lives. It is instinct as well that keeps the crocodiles waiting motionlessly in the water, with only their wide noses and narrow eyes protruding above the surface of the black pools.

I told Rob and Susan that it was imperative to remain out of sight from the keen eyes of the zebras who would accompany the wildebeests and probably be leading the way. Zebras have excellent vision and they, too, are hypervigilant the nearer they get to the river. The wildebeests key off the zebras, relying on the superior senses of the horselike migrants to detect and divulge the presence of any waiting killers. Once the crossing started and was in full swing, we kibitzers would be free to reposition at will during the chaos that ensued. We would be the least of the prey's problems and would be completely ignored.

Willy and I scanned the riverbank on our side. In an effort to sneak up to a good position from which to watch the crossing, I had, on three occasions, accidentally come up on a cat hidden and waiting, too. It was a heart-stopping surprise for both parties, and all involved retreated rapidly. I don't need any surprises like that when I have people with me, or even when I'm alone. Though I saw nothing, I kept occasionally running my eyes carefully among the trees and thick bush, since the situation could change in a moment.

Willy Chambulo put a palm on Susan's head. He also removed the hat whose brim was flapping in the dung-smelling wind. We watched, tense and expectant, as the zebras moved forward on stiff legs with measured steps, their ears pricked forward and their eyes sweeping up and down the vegetation that forms a thick border on both banks of the Grumeti. They moved forward another five feet and stopped again to look, then came ahead eight more feet before pulling up again. The wildebeests, heads down, crowded the zebras from behind, occasionally causing a zebra to kick violently as if to say, *"Stop shoving."* The wildebeests paused only briefly and then crowded right back in again. In all, it took over an hour for the zebras to timidly work their way down the narrow gullies that empty out onto the flat and packed dirt that gave them easy access to the water itself. The wildebeests choked the narrow gaps behind them. As the first animals finally reached the wide beach, the zebras moved forward and drank, keeping their legs as far back from the water as they could, many dropping onto their finely striped knees in a further effort to keep their distance. The wildebeests filed down to the water between the striped clusters of zebras and, unwisely, waded directly out into the shallow water, lowering their heads and casually touching their lips to their lips' reflections.

Susan, Rob, Willy, and I were looking at a solid sea of wildebeest. There was no ground showing through the solid phalanx of legs. The animals were so tightly crammed into this area that a sheep dog could easily have stepped from one back to the next for a half mile or more. The suspense was killing me. It always does at the river. The pressure builds and builds, then the herd backs up for some reason as inane as a flock of guinea fowl walking by. It's frustrating to sit through it all, anticipating the astounding but having to put up with the totally brainless. Willy was anxious, too, as he kept moving slightly left or right to get an improved view. I asked Susan and Rob to follow me and crawled around a fallen acacia and repositioned behind a scraggly fig tree. From there we had a clear sight down the river for more than one hundred yards. We could also see more than a dozen crocodiles, some ready and waiting, others already moving forward with the gentlest of tail movement.

I took one last look at my camera, making sure I had everything set as desired: metering system on "matrix," winder selected for "high speed," aperture 4.5, film counter at "1." Bring it on, bring it on! When Rob saw me going over my camera he checked his own equipment, and I reminded him not to use the autofocus, as this sometimes worthwhile feature would, in this instance, waste invaluable time searching unsuccessfully across the water's shiny surface. A pair of hadada ibis flew up the narrow gap between the trees, directly over the clustered herds. Predictably, the animals backpedaled in terror. The zebras returned to the shore, the wildebeests obediently trailing behind their broad buttocks.

As the wildebeests returned to drinking, a lone zebra mare waded in to the tops of her cannon bones, with all the other zebras watching her. She paused, staring intently ahead to the far shore while a crocodile slipped out from under an overhanging tree. His body sank slightly lower into the murk, leaving only two predatory eyes, separated by seven inches of water, exposed to the probing eyes of the potential prey. Our group was anxious as hell, but I reminded everyone to stay back. Without full forward momentum, the herd could still break back from the river. We kept our cameras up, but I heard no shutters or motor drives cycling as the crocodile shortened the distance to the zebra still standing in the shallow water.

"Jesus," Susan whispered. "What is she waiting for? Surely she must know that every second out there she is risking it!"

I had no answer. It did seem unwise to delay at this point, that it would be better to charge on in rather than wait at that depth, a perfect target for the crocs. But there must have been some reason for the holding pattern, because the zebras almost always start it this way, with overall success for millions of years. We wanted this zebra to live, but we were also keyed up and ready to see if a crocodile took her under.

"What the hell is she waiting for?" Susan was exasperated. "Get going! Get going!" And as if hearing Susan's imploring voice, the mare waded farther in, almost up to her chest, and now she finally lunged forward and began swimming steadily toward the far shore forty five yards away. On cue, crocodiles upstream and downstream dispensed with deceit and powered strongly forward, pushing out white, bubbling bow waves as they moved in.

"Get ready! This is it! You're going to see it!" A crocodile from the far shore now slipped in directly ahead of the swimming mare's head. "Get ready, get ready. He's going to take her."

The massive jaws opened, showing the broad, white mouth and ivory teeth. Water poured into the gape, dumping out of the corners of the mouth as the croc gained speed and momentum. The zebra finally saw it and turned slightly downstream and tucked her ear as the croc closed the final meter with a sweep of its tail so powerful that it launched the reptile from the water in an explosion of foam. He flung his head sideways as his jaws slammed shut, inhaling the zebra's entire head and upper neck. The zebra weighed 600 pounds, the eleven-foot crocodile 1,500 pounds. This was not a fair fight. In an instant, the mammal was gone, the water suddenly smooth and quiet. I kept one eye in the viewfinder and watched the remaining zebras, still standing frozen on the wide shore.

Like iron filings pulled by a hidden magnet, crocs now came pouring from all directions in their frenzied effort to get to the drowned or drowning zebra somewhere in the dark below. The water erupted, calmed, and erupted again and again in a profusion and confusion of black and white, green and yellow, as the zebra and the crocodiles rolled over, with less of the zebra remaining every time. The water gushed red and bubbly white as an entire front leg and shoulder were pulled free by a corkscrewing crocodile's jaws. Another croc slammed into the zebra's flank, paused to regrip, and then spun over and over, disemboweling the mare. With its snout tightly wrapped with entrails, this croc broke free and set sail downstream in an effort to keep its prize.

Susan, Rob, and I were wrapped up in our photography, but it's hard not to make judgments as well. We were only ten yards away. I heard groans and gasps of horror. Over my left shoulder, Willy exhaled heavily as two crocs surfaced while fighting over the zebra's head. The crunch of bones as the jaw was ripped from the skull reached us over the splashing and surging water. The current dragged the raging crocodiles and their carcass steadily downstream from our position. We lowered our cameras and faced one another, forming our own tight circle. Our eyes were wide, our mouths open, our heads shaking in disbelief. It had all taken ten minutes.

Rob said, "Did you see that? Can you believe how they did that? I had no idea the power and brutality these guys had. You couldn't pay me enough to get any closer to the water than we are now."

"Awesome! Simply awesome!" was all that Susan could come up with, but this pretty much said it all. Willy and I had witnessed many such kills, but it always leaves us physically shaking.

"And look at these guys," Willy said, indicating the remaining zebras still standing on the bank. "They just stand there and watch it all, and wait for their chance to go, knowing that the crocodiles are in there and waiting."

It defies all logic, or at least all human logic, which is so often based on the individual and not on the species. Our reason is no match for their instinct. We go wrong trying to apply our logic to these animals.

"Jesus, what a show," Rob concluded, as he rocked back in his seat and slowly shook his head.

"It's far from over," I said. "Now's the time to check your film, reload, change your lenses if you want, and get all that taken care of. And you'd better do it quickly. These other zebras are ready to go, and there're still all the wildebeests behind them."

I asked Willy what he thought of our position, and he suggested that, once the wildebeests started in, we should slide over the edge and get right down onto the ground at their water-side level. Willy knew that one of the axioms of wildlife photography for this part of the world is that you can never get too close or too low. Long lenses are more than handy, but they limit the width of your frame and the depth of field. A wildebeest, when photographed from the height of the truck's roof, looks smaller. Furthermore, from up there you do not see Africa as the wildebeest sees it. The high perspective weakens the photograph and distorts the world the wildebeest inhabits. You don't want to get so close as to disturb the natural behavior of the animals, but there was little chance, if any, of disrupting the barely organized confusion of the crossing. Even if we had positioned ourselves right alongside one of the paths, the wildebeests, once they were stampeding, would not alter their course.

Rob and Susan wanted to know if going down to the water would be safe. Yes, because Willy would watch out for us.

"If you say so," Rob said. Susan gave him a hard look, and then looked at me in turn. She pouted and looked back down at her camera. We silently urged the zebras to come into the muddy waves quietly lapping the shore, but they slowly retreated instead, winding single file through the mute wildebeests. The whole mass of animals ebbed steadily back to the higher ground away from the narrow cut of the river. It turned out that it was all over at this particular crossing until the afternoon or evening of the following day.

Back at our truck, we sipped coffee, compared more mental notes, and contemplated the zebras and wildebeests now grazing as if their own lives had not been mortally threatened, and would not be mortally threatened again, and soon. Willy heated the glow plugs and brought the diesel to life and drove us parallel to the river, downstream. At the far side of the next small plain, we emerged from a band of acacia trees and had an encouraging view of the much vaster field before us, completely covered with an intertwined and seething mass of animals moving slowly but steadily in the direction of the river.

No one said a word. We knew what this meant. It only remained for us to find a location, low and hidden, close but not close enough to disturb, from which we could see the chaos and the carnage of a crossing. Willy swung back to the right, keeping us in the trees of a small trough, perhaps thirty feet wide, that drains into the Grumeti. This low draw had a very good chance of ending up exactly where we needed to be on the river. And so it turned out. Willy parked, wedging out of sight between two acacia nilotica trees, and joined the rest of us on the roof watching the procession.

Dozens of animal trails cut deeply through the thin sod, proof of other crossings here. The herd funneled unconsciously onto these narrow paths as it drew nearer to the river. Characteristically, the heads of the wildebeests remained low and "dejected" while the zebras' heads were high and alert. They did not feed at all. Their donkeylike calls filled the air, along with dust. Our excitement built right along with the zebras' wariness. They couldn't see the river from their low vantage point, but undoubtedly their black nostrils, flaring open constantly, had detected the water and keyed the brain as to the dangers ahead.

The bank on this side of the river was a smooth approach, but the far bank was almost a vertical cliff. It looked to me like a trap. Will the zebras see this as well? Willy pointed out that the spiderweb pattern of tracks would tell the zebras that their brethren had been this way before. Those tracks beneath them might trigger their instincts more than the sight of the cliff on the other side. I decided we'd make our stand here and had better get in position now. Be sure you have plenty of film, I advised. We won't be back for a while.

At the water's edge, an ideal position presented itself not twenty-five feet downstream. A sizable tree had toppled, probably during the last rains, and its trunk extended sixty or seventy feet upstream. Susan, Rob, Willy, and I crouched in a row behind the trunk. From our knees, the viewfinders were precisely at eye level. What a setup. Now if the wildebeests and zebras would just cooperate; the crocs we could depend on.

Across the river was a large, slowly circling whirlpool full of wood, bark, leaves, and grass, detritus that had probably washed downstream with the recent attempted crossing. A black sandbar protruded at an angle from the bottom end of the basin. With a bit of a shock I realized that the sandbar was completely covered by rows and rows of scales — the backs of a pod of crocodiles. The beasts laid lined up across the bar, some heads facing upstream, some down, all lolling heavily on the sand, catching the tree-filtered sun-light. The bulk of the bodies was hidden below the waterline, but, judging by the head sizes, there were two exceptionally large ones lying there, four or five others that were fairly big, and only two smaller ones who had managed to stake out a bit of the sandbar.

I pointed out the sandbar, but no one at first discerned the scaly leather hiding there. I didn't say a word. When Rob finally separated sandbar from crocodile, he gasped, briefly frozen, and then pulled Susan by the shoulder so she could sight down his arm. I watched her eyes working the area.

"Oh God, I don't like the looks of this." She wasn't sure that she could watch this time, she said. If it became too much, she would just turn away and we should go right on shooting. But we still needed a bit of luck. The wildebeests hadn't come down to the water yet.

With our backs against the fallen trunk, we could see two hundred yards up the Grumeti, with two twists and turns along the way. Croton, grewia, and fig trees fought for waterfront property on both shores. Overhead, narrow beams of sun-light punched through the arboretum, each holding a cloud of dust. On two smaller trees that stretched far out from the bank over the river yet retained their purchase in the soil, a small cluster of turtles had gathered, shining dull and wet like paving stones not yet properly set in place. The only sounds were the chips and chirps of the dark shapes flitting erratically among the boughs. The *brrrip, brrrip* of a paradise flycatcher was distinct, along with the descending, steady notes of the emerald-spotted wood doves. A pair of yellow-billed ducks burst from downstream, their grating duck calls rudely breaking the peace. They had to bank hard left and right in order to negotiate the many branches in their flight path. I rose up over the log and turned downstream to follow them and found that hundreds of wildebeests had moved right up to the water with uncharacteristic stealth. I was shocked that they had sneaked in without our noticing. I poked Rob's thigh.

"They're already here. They tiptoed right in behind us."

Everyone turned to study the scene. "It's show time," I said to myself out of habit while pulling the cap off the 300-mm telephoto. Susan and Rob took their cue. The waiting game began again, though the mass of the instinct-driven herd was much closer to the threatening water than last time. Free of the photographer's responsibilities, Willy dozed. Suddenly, Rob, Susan, and I heard a splash, followed almost immediately by a second and then a third echoing crash. We looked and listened, trying to find the source of the sound. I finally figured it out. "The wildebeests must be jumping into the river farther downstream, around the bend." Rob asked if we should head down there. "Actually, no. We've invested a lot of time getting here, and we're sitting pretty. If we do go down there we may arrive too late, and we'll destroy the possibilities here the moment we head for the truck."

Susan agreed. "Let's wait it out. We're already here, and these are just about to go for it, it looks like."

Willy had awakened, listened, and now agreed. The wildebeests sixty yards away were not drinking anymore, but standing right at the shoreline, looking vacuously at the far shore as if waiting for someone to wave them over. No one did, but one yearling with stubby horns pointing straight up started moving forward. I once believed that crocodiles are alerted by the reverberations in the ground caused by the stampeding herds. But now that I have been stalked a few times by crocodiles and been defeated in my attempts at stalking them, I realize that they have extremely good eyes. As the yearling waded in, a solitary crocodile pushed himself silently back from the sand bar and sank ominously under the surface, like a silent and scaly torpedo. The wildebeest did not take a sudden lunging leap into deeper water, but gradually switched from walking to swimming as he moved progressively deeper. The crocodile did not go directly toward him, but angled for the river ahead of him.

"Stick on the wildebeest," I advised. "Stay on him and don't worry about the croc. He'll come into sight. Just be ready 'cause it's going to be quick."

Sure enough, the crocodile pulled into a holding pattern and treaded water, waiting, and the wildebeest swam almost into the blunt snout of the predator. Open — shut — *splash,* and then the water was calm again. I had been waiting, my finger exerting a slight pressure on the shutter release, and still I missed it. I fired one picture when the splash startled me, but I missed the takedown. It was so simple, subtle, and quick.

"Where'd he go?! Where'd he go?!"

Susan asked in rush.

"Down," Rob replied. "Just down. Gone!"

"Don't worry if you missed it," Willy said. "The rest are heading in now."

It began with barely a ripple and no sound at all. The whole teeming mass that was packed on the bank and backed up onto the plains behind burst forward frantically. The urge to cross spread from animal to animal quickly; they moved almost as if afflicted. When I turned to find out how the crocodiles were reacting, the sandbar was empty. That was my answer. I couldn't see them in the water, but I knew they were there, cruising below periscope depth, showing neither eyes nor wakes as they closed in.

"This is it guys. Just follow the front ones in each line. I can't find any crocs, but the sandbar is empty."

"Empty?" Rob asked, unwilling to lower his camera to check for himself.

"Empty."

All of a sudden croc heads appeared everywhere, on both sides of the swimming lines of wildebeests, and it was too late for the wildebeests to turn back now. The crocs had waited that long before surfacing. They came on hard from both sides, pushing the water to white in front of them.

"Check the right line," Willy almost yelled in my ear. All was noise and chaotic motion now.

I pivoted the lens on the beanbag just in time to refocus as a crocodile broadsided a big adult. The croc rose so high and with such power from its tail that I saw its light-green belly scales as it smashed into the ribs of the prey. It viciously swung its head in a tight circle, pulling the entire wildebeest with it. A second crocodile then bit into the white-eyed and terrorized animal. Like the lions in the Ngorongoro Crater contesting their kill, these two crocs spun and twisted in their effort to get this one away from all competitors. The wildebeest split in two, and each crocodile powered strongly off through the water with its half.

"My God, did you see that?" I asked no one in particular. "They just tore that wildebeest into two pieces, just like that."

No one answered. Rob and Susan were focused downriver, their noses squashed against the backs of their cameras in an effort to hold them tight and steady. In front of them, one entire section of water just below the main body of swimming wildebeests was a boiling caldron — black, white, green, and red. Six or more crocodiles had a grip on two wildebeests, and all the crocs, in an effort to make off with a section, had pulled their legs back flush with their bodies and were using their immensely powerful tails to twist themselves over and over, spinning like sharks, their greenish white bellies flashing in the light. A red splash showered out as another piece of wildebeest was ripped free. It was almost impossible to frame an individual picture.

Evolution and migration are not sloppy systems and have been refined by millions of years of trial and error. Dozens and dozens of wildebeests made it across the channel while the crocodiles were thus occupied with the victims. But when the lucky ones reached the base of the mud cliff there was nowhere to go, as we had noticed from the beginning. They packed in tighter and tighter, hundreds strong now, clambering over one another in pure panic in their efforts to climb out. Chest deep in the water, they charged first downstream and then back upstream, but they couldn't see far enough to locate a way out. They were left with one option: they had to return across the river.

En masse, the tide of mammals turned

and surged back toward our shore, swimming with their noses just above the surface, their eyes rolled up white in their heads. The crocs that had not made off with a big enough piece of meat from the early victims would now have a second shot at this particular herd. The second string waited patiently. Moments later they, too, had their fill.

Amazingly, we didn't hear a single wildebeest bawling. As the system would have it again, most of them made it back across, staggered from the water, and without a glance behind plodded deliberately up the gentle slope and onto the plain from where they had come.

Suddenly, right in the water beside us, a massive crocodile climbed onto the mud with most of one wildebeest in its jaws. I ran a short way upstream and dropped onto my stomach. As the croc moved toward me, I fired an entire roll, eye to eye. These are the best shots I've ever taken to demonstrate the fearsome power and size of these creatures. This one waddled slowly past me without so much as a glance and slid into the deeper water.

Rob ran his fingers through his thin hair. Susan sat with her camera in her lap, her left hand over her mouth in shock. She didn't speak for several minutes. Then she said softly, "I don't think I've ever seen anything so frightening in all my life."

10

Strangers in a Strange Land

"Tea at ten?" Bill Cooper asked. "We'll meet Nancy at the office and go down to the trattoria and have a cappuccino."

This innocuous question led to my introduction to the bloody history of Uganda. It was July 1985, about a year before I began guiding in Kenya full-time. My teaching contract in central Kenya had wound up a few weeks earlier, and I was still waiting for some paperwork from the States that would corroborate my qualifications to substitute teach at the International School of Kenya in Nairobi, one of the main prep schools in the country. My long-term plan was to work toward a full-time job there while still guiding on the side, as I had been doing for five years. (As it turned out, at the end of that year I was offered the job of head of the biology department at the school. Meeting with the headmaster, I had every intention of saying yes, but the word "no" came out instead. One month later I started The Ross Company.)

For the moment, however, I was jobless, frustrated, and with way too much time on my hands. Bill Cooper worked for Olivetti. His wife, Nancy, worked for *The New York Times*, more or less running the Nairobi office. The newspaper shared floor space with *Time* magazine, and as friends of the Coopers I would hang around those offices on occasion. After living in the countryside, I found the charged atmosphere of big-time international media an invigorating change of pace. Their office in the IPS building on Kimathi Street downtown was a great place to sit and have a cup of tea and keep a finger on the pulse of world events. Through the Coopers, I met the *Times* correspondent Sheila Rule, the *Time* photographer William Campbell, and his appropriately named bureau chief, James Wilde. James was a flamboyant character. They were all a tightly knit group, sharing offices, often working on the same story in extreme situations, such as drought and fighting in Somalia and the rapidly escalating tension and killings in Uganda. The president of Uganda, Milton Obote, had turned out to be just as brutal and bloodthirsty as Idi Amin, just less public about it. But the truth was being discovered, and tensions were escalating. To relieve the sadness and — as I would soon learn — the fear that can go with such assignments, my friends partied as hard as they worked. From just the brief time I spent as a fly on the wall, I could see that the work of the foreign correspondent could become a dangerous addiction.

The office was predictably chaotic when I walked in that afternoon. William was yelling on the phone, Sheila and Nancy were on the phone and soon yelling also. I took a chair opposite their twin desks and we all exchanged nods as I scooped up the local paper and flipped through it half-heartedly while waiting for Bill and a cappuccino. William strode into James Wilde's office and I heard still more yelling from behind that door, but James *always* yelled. A minute later the door was flung open so hard I was surprised it remained on its hinges as it bashed against the wall, and James marched out of his office, with William matching his stride and intensity and yelling, "He can take the pictures, and he knows the language as well."

James, wearing a dramatic, flowing white robe from Ethiopia, froze in mid-stride and stared at me as if he wanted to fight. I sat there, wide-eyed, still wondering who they were talking about and why James was canted forward, hands jammed jauntily on his hips, while he stared at me and waited.

"Well?!" he demanded. "Can you?"

"Can I what?"

"Can you shoot, caption and wire a photo, and do you speak Kiswahili?"

Years before I had been out of work in North Dakota, where I had hitchhiked to a ranch and bluffed my way into a job by answering "yes" to the rancher's every question. The lesson was not lost on me now. I was out of money and out of work. I owned nothing but my BMW motorcycle, two bags of clothes, and time, too much time.

"Yes!" I said, with all the firmness and confidence I could fake.

"We'll pay you one hundred eighty-five dollars every eight hours that you work, plus cover all your expenses, but any and all photos are ours."

I nodded and struggled at being cool. He was offering me a small fortune.

"Fine," James almost yelled as he walked out of the office. "You're hired."

I turned to William. "What was that all about?" I asked.

"You, my friend, just got hired to take a few correspondents into the war in Uganda, take a few pictures, and mostly keep everyone alive. You're also the driver and interpreter." He told me to get a few blocks of black-and-white film and he'd show me everything I needed to know about wiring photographs. I was out of there and back in fifteen minutes with the film I had bought on credit from my friend Mo. William, bless him, lined me out on the technicalities, which did seem within my capabilities, and I got straight with everyone else on my duties. I would be a shared stringer for *Time*, *The New York Times*, and *The London Times*, whose correspondent was on a plane from London at that very moment.

The problem was going to be getting into Uganda. The Uganda High Commission in Nairobi was part of Milton Obote's government, but early reports from the three-sided civil war seemed to indicate that he was on the run, and perhaps had even fled the country, so the UHC might not be of much value. William knew the old minister of communications, who had always been helpful in the past. Even though the bureaucrat might now be dead, William telexed his office in Kampala. Or tried to, without success.

In East Africa, perhaps throughout the entire Third World, you learn to think laterally if you just have to get things done. I suggested that we use *The New York Times* machine to telex the *Time* magazine machine in the name of the friendly minister of communications, saying that we had his approval to enter Uganda. We would take a small liberty, but so what? Apparently this war was by invitation only; we had to have someone's approval. A problem would obviously arise if we were using the name and authority of someone who had been killed, and this we wouldn't find out until we reached the border the following day. But no one in the office had a better idea, so we composed and sent the telex from one machine to the other down the hall. I tore it off, made three copies, and stuck them into my passport. All other issues we would just have to solve when we got to Busia, the border checkpoint between Kenya and Uganda. My cappuccino with Bill and Nancy would have to wait.

We left Nairobi at ten that night, with me behind the wheel of the official *New York Times* Peugeot station wagon, heading northwest up the Rift Valley toward the war. In addition to Sheila, I was working with Nick Comfort, the perfectly named *London Times* writer who was asleep in the backseat. In the front seat, Sheila tried to close her eyes. The first ten or so lorries barreling along on the narrow, dark, and shoulderless road had been enough for her. She preferred not to look, she said. For a change, I had no trouble staying awake. This was not just new work for me. It would be a radically new experience. I was a *wildlife* photographer, not a war photographer. I'd seen the shots coming out of drought- and war-stricken Somalia almost daily, gruesome and brutally real. Were these the kinds of scenes I would have to photograph in Uganda? I knew I could handle the job technically, but could I handle a war zone emotionally? And could I get us past the border and, if so, then around the country?

A long line of parked trucks signified that the border was ahead. It was 4:00 a.m. For miles I weaved in and out of dozens and dozens of lorries waiting to enter the war zone, most, I presumed, coming from Mombasa on the Kenyan coast, which serves as the port for landlocked Uganda. Finally my progress was halted by a large crowd of truck drivers, so I pulled over and told Nick and Sheila to wait in the car while I tried my luck — our luck — at the border station. I tried to sidle up to the crossing discreetly, but as the only white person in the huge milling crowd, this proved an impossibility. I wasn't hassled or jostled, just . . . noticed. I was amazed, in fact, that so huge a crowd was somber. The door to the guard building swung open just as I reached it, and I called *"hodi"* and entered. Not one of the weapons-bearing soldiers rose or even moved, so I stepped well into the post and let my eyes go from soldier to soldier. They weren't going to make this easy for me.

"Ninahitaji kuongea na nani kuingia tafadhali?" I inquired. Who do I need to talk to to enter, please?

Everyone remained silent, so I had no choice but to wait and become exasperated and feel helpless. I suppose that was the whole point of the quiet treatment. When it eventually became obvious that I could wait as long as they could, a soldier behind me spoke up. *"Huwezi kupita saa hii. Utahitaji kusubiri mpaka ashubuhi."* You can't pass through now. You'll have to wait until the morning.

So the civil war, invitations required, also kept hours, which struck me as ludicrous, but I asked simply, *"Utafungua saa ngapi?"* What time will you open?

"Saa sita, na si mapena," was the clipped reply. Six o'clock and not earlier. A war on a schedule, and a precise one at that. No single other event in East Africa runs that tightly. Utterly amazing, but there was nothing to do, so I trudged back to give my report to Sheila and Nick, who weren't bothered in the least and only settled farther down in the seats. Real veterans. I reached across and locked the doors and slouched down to snooze as well.

I woke up with the early light, but not quite early enough. It was already 6:20 by the time I had slipped quietly out of the car and reached the border post yet again. Inside, the same men were on duty. This time, however, they waved me in with hands and smiles, which left me flabbergasted. Where were our visas for Uganda? I could tell by his tone of voice that the man who asked knew no such thing was obtainable at the moment. I explained that we had been to the Uganda High Commission but those offices were shut indefinitely. We did, however, have an invitation and a clearance from the minister of communications, which I showed him. After several minutes of study by almost everyone in the office, the spokesman said we still needed visas.

I was stumped, but then tried a lateral tactic and suggested that we all just sign and stamp the telex itself and use it for our visa. The minister of communications would certainly accept the credential, since it was his, and obviously the minister of communications had rank on the men at the guard post. This latter point I tried to imply rather than state bluntly. They talked among themselves and then produced an old and battered inkpad and wooden stamp. Every single person in the cramped building signed it. I signed it. I even walked back and got Nick and Sheila to sign it.

Who knew what this piece of paper would be worth two miles inside the country? With all the stamped blue circles and all the signatures, there was no way to even read the telex now. But it was a good start, and, documents in hand, I inched the station wagon to the white barrier dropped across the road and patiently waited for the very same soldiers to ever so gradually stand up, walk the fifteen feet to the barricade, and ever so slowly raise it. They didn't even look at us as we drove through, though I said *"Asante"* in passing. Thanks.

Immediately after we were under the gate, it was dropped shut again and padlocked, locking the scores of trucks out of the war zone, but locking us in it. To my surprise, there were no weapons-laden soldiers on the Uganda side of the border. In fact, we didn't see anyone else at all, which gave me a false sense of security. I sped up, glad to put some distance between that border crowd and ourselves. Too many machine guns, too small a space, too little discipline and authority: a recipe for disaster.

Twenty minutes from the border, however, we encountered the first of dozens of blockades that would bar our way to the capital, Kampala. This was more what I expected. The soldiers at this first stop had dragged a felled eucalyptus tree across the road and were lounging in the sunshine twenty yards back from the road. At first I didn't see them. Only when I slowed to see if I could get around the tree did I notice the soldiers walking quickly toward us, obviously surprised to see a vehicle so early in the morning, and one full of well-dressed white people, at that. Our trio waited as these men walked a slow circle around the Peugeot. Then one thrust his head through my window, uncomfortably and unnaturally close and with a gun barrel just below it. I stared straight ahead and was careful to not move my hands from the wheel they were gripping too tightly. A surprisingly young voice demanded to know where we were going, and I politely explained who we were. My studied Kiswahili took him aback, as often happens in Africa. A bit flustered, he said we had no visas. He couldn't know if we did or didn't, but of course he was right. But we did have the telex from the minister of communications, and I slowly reached across to the glove box and gently pulled it out and handed it to him.

A half dozen men had gathered by this time and they pressed in tightly, their machine guns jammed haphazardly in the windows as they craned forward to study the paper. I told them that they could plainly see the stamps and signatures indicating that this was our visa. Doubting that these guys could read the document, counting on it in fact, I pointed to the line stating that this was our visa. The line said nothing of the kind, but he flipped the telex back through the window, and it fluttered to the dirty floor between my feet. For the first time, I turned to look at the soldier and was sadly shocked to see the ancient face of war etched into the once youthful and smooth face of a child —

barely a boy, much less a man. He briefly met my stare and then turned and half-sauntered, half-strutted, back to the edge of the road, jumped across the ditch, and headed toward the trees.

Nick and Sheila had stayed absolutely quiet during the exchange, and even as I started up and got us moving they didn't speak. A few minutes down the road I finally breathed out and translated the exchange, explaining about my lie regarding the already dirty, absolutely vital, completely bogus telex. The next roadblock, a few miles farther on, was merely a set of jerry cans lined up irregularly across the road. I could see quite a cluster of men on either side of the road waiting for us. I slowed gradually, giving all of them time to see who we were and who we weren't. This scene played out like the previous one, although all but one of these soldiers were boys. The exception was a cocky adolescent in sunglasses who did all the talking and most of the posing. Eighteen years old, no more. He held the telex upside down while confirming all that I told him. I asked him if there were more roadblocks between the border and Kampala. *"Mingi, mingi, mingi,"* he said — many, many, many — because of the war we are fighting. The word "war" struck me. Except for the boys and the roadblocks, everything we had seen was peaceful and seemed relatively normal. Perhaps there were fewer people walking around, but that was all. The whole land, thus far, had a deceptively peaceful "Sunday morning" feeling to it.

But there was no end to that exception of the boys and the roadblocks. The rest of the morning was stop and go, stop and go, even though we were the only vehicle on the move. I don't think we went more than fifteen or twenty minutes without having to stop for yet another bunch of kids and whatever they had dragged across the road. It became exasperating and very tiring. I wanted to take some shots but left my camera in its bag. We didn't even know which "army" was manning all these silly checkpoints. Finally, and without any really serious incident, we saw the hills and buildings of Kampala. The city looked calm and even beautiful, the structures smooth and clean on the majestic hills overlooking the lush green terrain. I slowed down, giving anyone we passed plenty of opportunity to see that we were not, by definition of our whiteness, combatants in the civil war. This was probably an unnecessary precaution, but it seemed prudent, and Sheila and Nick agreed.

Our initial impression of peace and calm was contradicted at the first roundabout, where two batteries of anti-aircraft guns were positioned on opposite sides, their barrels pointed expectantly skyward, two groups of uniformed soldiers lazing around them. I stopped adjacent to the first battery we passed and paused a few seconds before calling out to the men. I asked them where the Nile Mansions hotel was, saying that we had been told to go there. This wasn't true, but we had been told the Nile Mansions was one of the few hotels still semi-functioning. We hoped we could base out of there for the next week or so while probing the war zone around the capital. One soldier examined us for an uncomfortably long few seconds and then, with surprising politeness and in yet another startlingly youthful voice, gave me fairly explicit directions to our destination. The hotel was only minutes away. We weren't sure how to take this information. Would these artillery batteries protect us or *attract* incoming fire? We thanked the youth and drove on at the pace of a funeral procession, but not because of the traffic, because there simply wasn't any.

The words "Nile Mansions" were painted

in faded letters below the second-story windows of the tall, run-down, bullet-pockmarked building, located exactly where I had been told. A large number of soldiers were scattered around the grounds and even at the entrance. Rather than a bell captain and porters scurrying to our assistance, a pack of strutting youths playing soldier for the day, or week, or war, came forward when we pulled up. I was worn down by this point, and my mood was getting testy as I shoved open my door as the kids closed in. I pushed hard, forcing the door against first one, then a second, then a third soldier, and dismissed them and pushed through the double doors of the hotel, as if I either knew someone inside or was expected. Actually, I was only following William Campbell's last piece of advice before we left Nairobi: "In case of doubt, walk confidently." I now walked confidently right into a group of one hundred or so heavily armed soldiers. Four men, not boys, were seated behind a portable table, which seemed like as good a place as any to start. I went directly up to them, stood almost at attention for a few seconds, and then interrupted to announce that we needed three rooms, please, for a number of days.

The four stopped talking, all eyes on me. I repeated my request, and still no one spoke. Then they looked at one another and, like contestants in a quiz show, conferred in low tones before one of them stood up and walked away from the table. I stood back and glanced out at Sheila and Nick in the car, now so densely surrounded by soldiers dressed in green, with gun barrels poking out in every direction, that my first thought was of a porcupine. The soldier returned and told me to go with a second man now accompanying him, who took me outside, past the Peugeot, and across the driveway to a set of stairs that climbed to a long balcony that ran in front of the second-floor rooms. Halfway down the row, he pointed at three doors in turn and then turned on his heels and marched back along the balcony and down the stairs. Back at the car, I explained happily that we had rooms, but advised Sheila and Nick not to get too excited about their quality. We were scrutinized by all eyes as we unloaded and carted our meager baggage up the stairs.

I was keen to get a look around the immediate area and to get to the job assigned, and it struck me as a good idea to let everyone in the area know that we were there and had nothing to hide. So I decided to go for a walk. I told Nick and Sheila what I was up to, strung a camera around my neck, and headed for the street after taking the time to park the Peugeot between an army Land Rover and a personnel carrier. At the street, knowing that all the soldiers behind me were watching closely, I turned briskly right as though I knew where I was going. I made it somewhat less than two hundred yards before a Land Rover cut inches in front of me and skidded to a stop with a screech of tires and a dramatic cloud of blue smoke. The canvas flaps that covered the back were flung open and a dozen soldiers poured out, guns at the ready, and jabbed me with gun butts as I was herded toward the truck with admonitions, in English, "Go! Go!"

I was forced into the truck, afraid for the first time since crossing into Uganda. The soldiers jumped in around me, forcing themselves right up against me, one of them roughly pulling at my camera strap. I pulled back, he pulled harder, and I just tightened my grip until he quit. So many soldiers and their weapons were crammed in the truck that some had to stand hunched over between the two bench seats that ran down either side, machine guns swinging crazily as we sped off. I looked from face to face, though almost no eyes met my inquiring stare until I came to a young man with a broad, aggravating smile stretched across his smooth skin. His laughing eyes had no trouble meeting mine. "You are now captured," he proudly announced. "I have captured you myself."

His was a face begging to be slapped. The man's idiotic words and asinine popinjay's attitude had turned my fear to anger, but there was little chance of doing anything about it, so I sat quietly and boiled. But then he, too, tried to claim my camera. We pulled back and forth briefly until I yanked it stoutly back and said, more than sternly, "*We!*," which translates as "you" and is pronounced "way." Even with his AK-47 strapped across his chest, he gave up. The truck swerved hard to the right, causing us to lurch across and brace, and then we screeched to a stop, throwing everyone forward. I clambered back to my feet and hung onto my camera as I climbed down to the pavement, where I was jabbed with gun butts and driven toward a low building. The compound was surrounded by a high iron fence and protected on each side by a machine-gun emplacement. Within the parking lot were three anti-aircraft batteries, all tilted acutely toward the cloudless sky, just like the others at the roundabout had been.

This place actually had a distinct air of purpose about it. Soldiers walked briskly in and out of the sentry-guarded double doors. Inside was a hive of activity. As I was marched through the milling mass, the soldiers magically parted, almost dumb-struck, and stared at me in passing. I was forced a short distance down a narrow hallway and then yanked to a stop by someone grabbing my neck from behind. I was shoved in the back with enough force to propel me into the room, and the door slammed shut. I heard no turning key or clicking lock but decided against testing the door anyway. There were three chairs against the far wall and, surprisingly, an-other door as well. I put my ear to that door and to the one I'd been shoved through. Silence. They had not forgotten about me, of that I was sure, so I figured they were going to just let me sit there for a good long time to soften me up. I re-solved to stick by my guns, whatever those guns turned out to be. To my surprise I still had my camera with me, so I pre-tended to take a series of shots of my in-carceration room, in the off chance that anyone was watching through some hole or hidden camera. I wanted to appear relaxed, unintimidated, even indifferent. I told myself I was just being inconvenienced, nothing more.

A couple of hours later, I was beginning to wonder. I didn't know all the details about this war, but I knew that Idi Amin had overthrown Milton Obote and that Obote had then regained the crown from Amin and that both were ruthless killers. All the stories of mass murder, child killing, even cannibalism flashed through my mind. Millions had already been killed during ten years of more or less nonstop fighting in this otherwise beautiful land, and now General Okello had joined the struggle for power. Why the hell would the well-being of Sheila and Nick and I matter to these men? I easily envisioned some soldier walking through the door and simply saying, "Sorry old chap, but we've a war going on. Corporal, take him out back and shoot him, I'm late for a meeting." I was softening up beautifully, if this was indeed what they were doing — whoever "they" were.

Then "they" finally got around to dealing with me. With a startling racket, a cluster of soldiers suddenly jammed through the door into the room. They fanned out, ignoring me, and turned back toward the door through which they had just entered, chests forward, feet together, arms holding their weapons stiffly across their chests. I sat on my chair and observed this little parade with astonishment. Next through the door was an older, slightly heavyset soldier in a flawlessly pressed uniform, its chest speckled with ribbons. He walked briskly and was halfway across the room before he seemed to notice me for the first time, held stride for a moment, and cocked his head in my direction. I instantly came to my feet, bowed low, and greeted him with the old and traditional Swahili greeting, "*Shikamoo.*" At this he turned to face me and inclined his head more in my direction as he responded, "*Maharaba.*" I slowly raised up and met his eyes. Boldly he walked up to me until he was just an intentional fraction too close for my comfort.

"*Unafanya nini hapa,*" he asked. What are you doing here?

Here I was forced to take sides regarding which army had captured me. "I've come as a photographer to prove that it is not General Okello who has been committing the atrocities," I replied. This was not a wild guess, because I had learned in Nairobi that the other armies were days outside Kampala. I explained to this officer that I was on assignment for *The New York Times*, that I was walking down the main street, taking no photographs and talking to no one, when a truckload of men captured me and brought me to this compound. He asked me what I had heard of the war, and what atrocities had been reported. I explained as delicately as possible that we in the West knew that two different freedom armies were fighting to overthrow Obote. Rumors had reached Kenya and the Western press that General Okello's troops had been massacring civilians as well as Obote soldiers who were fleeing. *The New York Times* thought it more likely that those atrocities were being committed by a deposed and panicked Obote, who was taking revenge as he fled. We had come to write and photograph the correct story and set the record straight.

"How many of you have come?"

"Just three of us."

He turned and spoke to a tall man behind him, in a language I did not understand, and walked toward the door, which was opened by a young soldier who had been waiting there the whole time, his hand on the doorknob. "Follow me," the tall man then said, as he turned on his heels and went back through the door and down the hallway to the left. I didn't need to be told twice. I was far from sure that I had made the right guess. The senior officer had given me no clue. The tall man ignored my questions as I followed with my escort of four or five soldiers. Just before we reached the end of the hall the tall man stopped and waited for me to catch up. He then pointed to a chair and started back down the long, dark hall, eventually entering another door at the very far end. The soldiers guarding me would not meet my eyes, which made me sick to my stomach with fear. I was too scared to run, and besides, where the hell was there to go? So I just sat there, feeling the weakness in my legs and the weariness in my arms. What a helpless, worthless, and anonymous way to go, I thought.

What was happening with Sheila and Nick? I had no idea, and I hoped they were fine at the hotel. A hard and insistent clacking caused me to turn my head and look back down the hall. The same tall man was returning, and my heart sped up with every closing step. He barely stopped when he reached me and thrust a piece of paper into my hand. I took it but kept looking at him, searching his face for any clue, but he kept his military bearing and spoke curtly, in English. "Be here tomorrow morning, and bring the other two with you so that they may obtain their passes from General Okello." I was not just relieved, but overjoyed. We were "in," and could now get our story easily.

He left me there, staring first after him, and then at the half sheet of paper I held loosely in my hand. The writing was neither English nor Kiswahili, though I could make out General Okello's scrawled signature at the bottom. I was unwilling to believe in the deliverance I was holding and kept trying to construe the unfamiliar words on the page into something I could understand. I finally stood up and took a few tentative steps toward the door, waiting for someone to slam me back into the chair or haul me back down the hall to my silent room, but I reached the door to the outside unopposed. My confidence soared as I approached the soldiers at the gate. In brusque terms I told them to open up and advised them that I held in my hand General Okello's personal carte blanche. I flashed the paper and warned them never to bother me again, that I would be coming and going frequently, beginning tomorrow morning, and if anyone hassled me I would take them straight to the general. I had an attitude, which I mark down, in retrospect, to the explosive power of fear released and freedom gained, not wisdom under pressure.

Three or four hours after I had walked out of the Nile Mansions I walked back in, and Nick and Sheila were waiting for me. They hadn't raised any alarms about my absence because I had told them I was heading out into the city. They hadn't thought it was a great idea, but since I insisted, fine. Now they debriefed me, and Nick, who had covered over twenty wars and coups in his career, pointed out where he thought I might have gone wrong, where I was right, and where I had just been lucky. Anger, he warned, is almost always going to be the *wrong* reaction, no matter how scared you are. On the other hand, showing doubts and fear could easily be your own death warrant as well. War was new to me, and this was only my second coup (the first had been in Liberia, on the other side of the continent), so I listened intently as Nick evaluated my actions step by step. I could learn from him.

The curfew kicked in at 6:30, so we stayed inside the hotel and dined on rice and potatoes. In fact, this was pretty much our standard fare for the next ten days, but it didn't matter. Nick and Sheila were too seasoned to be bothered by something as trivial as the bill of fare, and on that night, at least, I was exhausted and starving, so anything at all sounded heavenly to me. Kampala was dark, so the meal was an unromantic but candlelit affair. Sheila and I were fairly quiet, but Nick carried on as I imagined he might have on a big night out in London. This civil war was just one more assignment for him.

We agreed that Sheila would get the middle of our three rooms, in case things came unglued during the night. Sometime around midnight, maybe a little later, deafening, shrieking automatic weapons fire erupted from the balcony outside our rooms. The Nile Mansions overlooked the heavily treed city park. If the men in the hotel were firing into that park, it stood to reason that opposing soldiers in the park were firing in our direction. I dove for the floor and yelled through the wall, during a pause in the shooting, for Sheila to get on the floor, but she had made the same analysis and was already down and prone. I dragged the pillow and the blankets off the bed and stretched out, far from relaxed but feeling relatively safe. The firefight raged for a solid twenty minutes, the casings clanging and jingling as they were spat onto the cement deck. Sheila and I yelled back and forth several times to confirm our safety. Sheila made no report about Nick in his room on the other side of hers, but I wasn't too worried. No mortars, rockets, or grenades had been lobbed in our direction. We should all be fine.

After the firefight finally died down we could still hear the occasional isolated shot or quick burst of automatic fire echoing from elsewhere in the city. From the floor I stared at the dark, glassless window, waiting for it to turn the least bit gray with the approach of dawn. When it did, I waited a further fifteen minutes and then couldn't stay put any longer and ventured outside, where I almost fell flat on my face due to the hundreds of slippery casings that littered the balcony. I shuffled to Sheila's door and knocked. A second later an obviously exhausted and strained face was before me. I didn't have it in me to make a joke and just asked if she was all right. "Done in," she said, but otherwise she was fine. "A little firing is exhausting, even if it didn't directly involve us and probably couldn't have reached us."

I waved at the veranda behind me, indicating all the spent cartridges, and said that it hadn't just been a "little" shooting. She leaned out and gasped when she saw the twenty yards of brass scattered there.

We were ready for breakfast, or at least coffee, so we went to Nick's door to roust him to join us. Our first knocks drew no response, so I knocked harder; when that also went unanswered, I opened the unlocked door to find that he was actually sleeping on his bed. I shook the bed, and he slowly rolled over and opened his eyes, removing earplugs as he looked at me.

"Quite a night," I said.

"How's that?"

"The shooting. I mean all the shooting, that's what. What did you think I meant?"

He blinked at me. "Shooting, huh? I thought I heard something."

Now I thought he was having me on for sure, playing the seasoned war-zone reporter, but the more I looked at him the more I realized that his innocence was also honest. He had remained oblivious to the din. He glanced at the dawn light skimming through the leaves in the park and then caught sight of the brass casings glinting on the veranda. "I thought I heard something last night. I figured it was a party and wished whoever it was would either quiet down or invite me along."

Sheila muttered, "Christ," and turned back to her room. A few minutes later the three of us kicked through the casings and descended the brass-scattered stairs for a breakfast of coffee, rice, and potatoes. We learned from the soldier acting as our waiter what perhaps we should have realized all along: the Nile Mansions was not really a hotel anymore, but had been commandeered weeks before as a barracks for General Okello's troops. That explained last night's firefight. If any opposition were trying to capture or recapture the city, the first place they would attack would be the barracks. Wonderful.

Our first stop that morning was the general's headquarters. Even with his blessings we would probably still get arrested and hassled on a daily basis, but without it we would be locked up at best. We weren't happy about the prospect of cruising the city streets, but we had to take the chance, and we did have the half page of Okello's interim approval. Kampala was a ghost town. No one manned the anti-aircraft turrets, walked the streets, or even patrolled them with personnel carriers. Nothing was stirring but us, which had to mean that all eyes, tucked inside doorways and behind windows, were focused on us as we crept down the wide and empty streets.

Not surprisingly, we arrived at the command post before Okello himself, though it was impossible to find out whether he really was actually present in the building. I stepped out of the white car and talked sternly with the soldiers who manned the gate. I handed them the sheet of paper, pointing out their general's signature, and told them to open the gate right away. We did not want to be exposed on the vacant street any longer than we needed to be. With intentional lethargy they swung open the iron barriers, and we eased inside to park next to a tank. I suggested to Nick and Sheila that it would probably be safer to wait inside, so we proceeded through the doors I had gone through the day before and found three empty chairs in which to kill time until the general showed up. A good hour passed before a small convoy whipped into the parking lot and came smartly to an official halt in the middle of it. I didn't need to point out to Sheila and Nick which uniformed soldier was the general. When Okello walked through the door, Nick and I came to our feet but Sheila remained seated, casually writing in her small notepad. A big, barrel-chested man with a childlike face unbefitting a general, Okello nodded at me and walked straight up to Sheila, who closed her pad. She has a beautiful face and smile and used them both now. It dawned on me that the general had assumed that the reporters from the West were all men.

"Good morning," he said to her.

"Good morning, General Okello."

"And how may I be of service to you?" he asked as he extended his hand. Sheila rose as she shook hands, and the two of them walked down the hall, the general's head inclined graciously toward his new friend and confidante. The attending circle of hangers-on closed in around Sheila and the general and funneled after them through a doorway. Nick and I looked at each other and sat back down. This was the best of all possible scenarios. Barely five minutes later Sheila reappeared in the hallway, the general bowing forward, shaking her hand with both of his. She walked past us, Nick and I falling in behind her like waiting servants, no one speaking. Once the doors to the Peugeot were shut she filled us in, her eyebrows hopping up

419

and down. "We, my fine gentlemen, are set for the duration. Not only has he written out another pass for us, but he will radio ahead to any place that we want to go, letting them know we are coming, and make sure that all the roadblocks know it as well."

"Fantastic," Nick exclaimed. "Just fantastic. Where shall we go first?"

"I took advantage of the opportunity and asked him if we could start by going to the house of Milton Obote. It must have been one of the first places that Okello's men went, and there's bound to be a story or a lead there."

I stopped at the opening gate and asked one of the guards where Obote's house was. He looked shocked at the question, didn't answer, and turned to speak to the guard behind him, who came up and rattled off a series of left turns and right turns, never using a street name. We drove slowly through the littered streets, Sheila and Nick pointing out all the usual signs of civil war. Burned-out vehicles were scattered along both edges of the road; any building more than two stories high was pockmarked and window-shattered. The city looked as if it had been abandoned years previously.

When we cruised past a human body lying inert against the curb, we lapsed into silence. From the burned and shredded clothing it was obvious that the person was long dead, and no one had bothered or dared to do anything about it. I drove past before I got up my courage and pulled over. I wanted to do my job. I put on the short telephoto and crouched low, sighting down the line of the curb to the abandoned body. The day before I had been frightened when I was captured. This was also frightening, but in a different, far deeper way. Then my concern had been for myself. Looking at this sight, taking this picture, I suppose my concern was for the people of Uganda, for all mankind.

I had to stop only twice to check on the directions to the former president's residence, an average house surrounded by a few acres of grounds, not at all what I pictured as the residence of any country's president. Guards were posted, but General Okello had been true to his word. The gates swung wide when I announced that we were the reporters who had the general's permission to investigate the home.

It was so normal; ransacked, obviously, but otherwise suburban. The broken dishes on the kitchen floor were cheap. I opened a few drawers and cabinets and found all the same items I had in my own kitchen in Nairobi. As I walked upstairs toward the ex-president's bedroom I noticed the occasional bullet hole dug deep into the plaster as well as the cheap art hanging at odd angles, local African paintings next to Western-style acrylics and reproductions.

The master bedroom reinforced even further the sense that Obote, good or evil, had been a regular human being as well. Lying broken on the bedside table was a small portrait of him and his wife, a posed black and white in a cheap metal frame. Inexpensive blankets lay crumpled on the king-size bed, as if the occupants had risen in an untidy hurry. A large cardboard box lay on its side against one wall, red T-shirts spilling out. I picked one up. It read "Re-elect President Obote." A great memento, I thought, but also a death sentence if it were discovered during a roadside search. I unnecessarily refolded the cloth and dropped it back in the box.

As Sheila and Nick circulated through the house, I followed along and fired frames of whatever they were writing about in their notepads. We were strangely, almost reverently, quiet as we moved from room to room. I'm sure we were all picturing the daily lives that had filled this house only days before. After ten or fifteen minutes we were back outside in the bright light, beneath the green trees of the modest garden. A number of men, some armed, some not, had gathered in the yard and seemed to be waiting quietly for our return. As I led the way back to the car a somber and soft-spoken young man approached me.

"Over there," he said, indicating a steel shipping container, "is where they were shot."

"Where who were shot?"

"All of them. All the people that worked here, that worked for Obote."

Then I saw the multitude of holes that had made a sieve of the container's steel side. I told Nick and Sheila what the man had said and reluctantly walked toward the forty-foot box as if drawn by some magnet of despair.

A homemade door had been fashioned in the side, indicating that the container had been in use for a long time. I wasn't surprised. In Nairobi, similar boxes were bought and sold routinely for all manner of domestic use. I paused before pushing through the opened door and let my eyes run along the weather-stained steel of the container's side. Bullet holes studded the entire surface, often only inches apart, from a height of approximately seven feet all the way to the reinforced floor only inches off the ground. I couldn't really understand what I was looking at or what had occurred here, so I naïvely stepped over the threshold into the darkness within, where the change in light forced me to stand still and let my pupils dilate. Hundreds of narrow shafts of light from the multitude of holes pierced the darkness. I could see how inescapably close these darting arrows of light were spaced. Anything larger than a small dinner plate would have been intercepted by one or more of the light beams. They were spaced that tightly.

I moved forward and felt my feet squishing through the mud and grunge that had gathered inside the container over the years of seafaring duty. My fingers probed the jagged, knife-sharp edges of the holes made by the incoming bullets, but the import of what I was seeing and touching still eluded me. The light in the container dimmed briefly as someone entered the chamber behind me, and I turned to face the silhouette. The man flicked on a flashlight, holding it low in front of him, as I tried to make out his face. He stood quite still and said nothing, the light of the torch angled at the floor between us. I said hello.

"Look at the blood," he replied after a few seconds. "Look at how much blood there is."

I froze and gasped, then retched as I realized where I was, what had happened here, and what I was mired in. This was not mud and oil and dirt I was sloshing through. It was coagulated blood, inches deep. Soldiers had rounded up all of Obote's personal house and garden staff, guards, and who knew who else, and forced them into this container. Once the captive targets were locked inside, the rebels had set up machine guns on tripods, while others stood with their handheld AK-47s. Then they had simply opened up on the humanity trapped within, filling the air with shrieking bullets and shrieking steel that must have drowned out the shrieking humans inside.

I couldn't flee. The footing was too slippery. I was forced to walk slowly and gingerly back to the door, lest I fall into this bloodbath. I pushed past the man still standing there, stepped over the threshold, and wretched again and again as I dragged my shoes across the lawn in a desperate attempt to clean them of the gore. My face must have been contorted in horror and anger and revulsion as I swiped the shoes desperately from side to side. As I looked up I saw Sheila reaching the door of the container and shouted emphatically at her not to go in there. She froze briefly and then peered into the darkness, and I yelled again at her to stay outside, but her head remained within.

I continued to drag my feet as I walked across the short, dry grass of the lawn toward the silky oak trees near its edge. I had never been hit so quickly by fever and headache as I was at that moment. I waited a few minutes before returning to stand where the murderers must have stood, and I took a dozen photographs of the hole-punched steel wall. Sheila was waiting in the car for me when I walked slowly over, and Nick arrived a few seconds later. In silence we circled around and drove back out through the gate and onto the open road. I had to think for a second before remembering that the Nile Mansions was to our right.

We stopped on the way back into town

and black-marketed some U.S. dollars for a briefcase full of Ugandan shillings that were losing value by the hour. The store-front banker and I argued briefly about the rate over his handmade wooden table; normally both of us would have enjoyed the exchange, bantering back and forth about the rate, the news, perhaps even about the war. But nothing was funny or fun now. I was suddenly too worn out to push a bargain hard and agreed too quickly on his price. Without taking his eyes off me, he reached under the table to a hidden drawer and removed stack after stack of dirty notes. He didn't have to count the rubber-banded bundles. I started to leaf through one packet but then just shoved the dollars across the table and scooped the debased currency into my camera case. We drove back to our army barracks hotel so that Sheila and Nick could write up the morning and decide on the afternoon. All the lines were down, so I couldn't wire my photographs.

I was still lying down when Sheila knocked on my door to report that she and Nick had decided we should go down to Entebbe, on the shores of Lake Victoria. The international airport was there, of course, with the buildings destroyed in the famous Israeli "raid on Entebbe" still standing alongside the runway. Sheila and Nick thought the juxtaposition of that world-famous episode and the current troubles in the country could be enlightening. So I rolled over, reached for my camera, grabbed more film and a couple of bundles of shillings, and headed for the exit. This was the job I had signed up to do. Once more I asked for directions at the gate, and then we were on the road heading south toward Lake Victoria.

Even though I knew we had the general's permission, I was wired and hyper-alert, but except for the usual roadblocks we moved unhampered. I was just beginning to relax when I heard shouting and screaming behind me. My eyes flicked up to the rearview mirror and saw the reflection of rebels pouring onto the road, guns pointed in our direction as they screamed and gesticulated. There was no outrunning a hail of gunfire, so I slammed on the brakes and pulled a bit to the side of the road, ducking instinctively.

The rebels ran up and surrounded us, making a show of leveling all their guns directly at our heads. I released my hands from the wheel and held them loosely in front of me. Sheila in the front seat and

Nick in back sat frozen. One of the soldiers yelled something in broken English, and only when I addressed him in Kiswahili, asking urgently what was wrong, did he settle down just enough so that I could understand his words. We had run his roadblock, he said, and now he was arresting us. "What roadblock?" I asked. I hadn't seen anything dragged onto the road for that purpose. He raved on, demanding to know whether I had seen the baby carriage on the side of the road.

I had seen it, I admitted. What of it? That was the roadblock. Why had I run his roadblock? My explanation that I didn't know it *was* a roadblock was ineffective. Sheila, who had finally reached her limit for the day, whipped out her note from General Okello, and demanded to know the name and rank of this soldier. He paused, probably startled by any woman addressing him so directly, and Sheila demanded her answers again. Befuddled, he read the note while I softly explained its contents and who we were and where we were headed. After a minute he threw the paper back in through my window and stalked off down the road, but Sheila wasn't through. She opened the door, stood in the road, and yelled after him, demanding once more his name and rank. He ignored her and proceeded on his way and Sheila finally sat back down and we tentatively started off, my gaze fixed on the rearview mirror. Her out-of-character outburst frightened me almost as much as the soldiers had. I was not alone in my sad weariness, after all.

Entebbe proved anticlimatic and a waste of time. The fighting in Kampala and elsewhere had not come from that direction. It had never even reached Entebbe. The airport was heavily guarded, naturally, but it was peaceful and showed no signs of war at all, nor any air traffic. We stayed only a half hour before starting back up the road toward Kampala, dreading having to go past the baby carriage again.

The pram was still there, and I slowed long before reaching it, coming to a gradual stop ahead of it. The same soldiers were all still there, but no one made the slightest move toward us — in fact, many of them never even got up from their seated positions in the ditch. We waited in the sweltering car, all of us muttering under our breaths, until finally I started the engine again and pulled alongside the group. I leaned across the seat and told them it was just us again, that we were going back to Kampala. Maybe one or two bothered to look at us. Certainly no one spoke. I paused a few polite seconds and then gently drove on, again holding my breath as we eased away. "Assholes," Nick muttered uncharacteristically as I shifted into second gear.

Nick had somehow found out about a little expatriate-run restaurant on the other side of the park from the esteemed Nile Mansions barracks. He had no solid intelligence on the food, but the place had wine and that was good enough for us. Moreover, it turned out, the potatoes and rice were spiced, and there were even some carrots and spinach on the side. In spite of the curfew we opted to try it. We ate fairly silently, the owners sitting at another table, never asking but probably knowing why three white people had come to the war. I felt ludicrously silly as I peeled off twenty-three thousand in Ugandan shillings, plus a five-thousand-shilling tip. Wasn't I the last of the big spenders?

We made it back to the hotel just before the shooting began. Unfazed, we discussed Sheila's plan for the following day over cups of instant coffee in the lounge. She had learned in Entebbe that some intense fighting was underway 150 miles north of

Kampala at a town named Gulu. She had also located an aircraft that could fly us up there. It seemed very unwise to me to travel slowly through the air in a little plane while the troops from both sides — make that three sides — who were hunkered on the land below us wouldn't know who we were but could be certain we were not on their side. My reasoning fell on deaf ears.

The following morning I drove us to the airstrip. I love to fly, and small planes are always more fun than the larger ones, but I was not at all up for this trip. Our pilot was also worried but was still willing to do it. He said the Okello rebels would almost certainly be occupying the field at Gulu, and that we would have to approach cautiously or risk getting shot. How, exactly, would we "approach cautiously," since we could neither talk with nor signal whoever controlled the airstrip? But I nodded just the same.

I felt very exposed and slow as we flew north at 140 miles an hour. This was much worse than driving in the Peugeot. Anything, even a handgun's bullet, could catch up with us and punch a vital hole in our soft aluminum. But the air was smooth and remained bullet-free, and an hour later I could see the tan field at Gulu through my binoculars. We flew a few circles ten miles south of town while I scanned the airstrip and outbuildings. Nothing seemed amiss. I couldn't see a soul, so we almost reluctantly turned on final.

That approach and landing were incredibly tense and blissfully uneventful. Even as we taxied to the buildings at the end of the field, no one came charging out to intercept us. When we stopped, I noticed a Toyota Land Cruiser and a few men in the shade of some evergreen trees. Leaving my camera, binoculars, and money in the plane, I strolled across the exposed ground and went over to them. They were rebels, and they were guarding the airstrip. They had not known about our coming but could tell we weren't a military threat. Besides, they said, we had stayed out of range, and then when we came into range they could tell we were going to land, so they could always shoot us after we landed, if it seemed like the best thing to do. I couldn't fault the ironclad logic.

The Toyota, it turned out, did not belong to the rebels but to a friend sitting by another tree. The rebels called him over, and we instantly agreed on a price to hire his truck for a few hours. This deal bailed us out of a tight spot and would earn him more money in those few hours that he normally would make in a month. This fellow was from Gulu, and he turned out to be a font of information. There were still many soldiers in that area, but there had not been any fighting for three days. Yes, he had been present during the fighting, and, yes, he did know where it had taken place, and, yes, he could take us there. Ground zero for the battle had been, ironically, the provincial hospital.

Everywhere I have traveled in Africa, and that covers a fairly wide swath, you find people walking. The only possible exception to that generalization is South Africa. Even on the most remote roads in northern Kenya you will eventually meet up with somebody walking steadily somewhere. Therefore the absence of people anywhere in Gulu was a glaring anomaly, and this wasn't just a "Sunday morning" feeling. Something basic was deeply amiss. Trash blew down the wide and vacant streets like tumbleweeds in a cheap Western movie. The bad guys had come to Gulu, and the bad guys looked to have won as well. The stalls and little shops were not peppered with bullet holes like the buildings in Kampala, but wooden

434

shutters and doors were left swinging in the wind, and looted goods were left scattered where they had fallen. The hospital was also vacant, and it, too, had been looted and vandalized. I photographed the empty wards and the looted pharmacy, with scattered plastic bottles of drugs and half-opened packets of bandages. Laboratory equipment that was too heavy to haul and too complicated to operate had been dragged out onto the bare red dirt that served as the hospital gardens.

On the broad entrance steps lay a young woman in civilian clothing. A man stood nearby, holding a homemade crutch of two heavy sticks fastened with a strip of inner tube. I asked him what he had seen and where he had come from, and he replied that he and his wife had arrived at the hospital the afternoon that the fighting had begun. She was due to deliver their first child; they had walked the whole day to reach the hospital but had been there only a few hours when the shooting started. In complete panic and chaos, the hospital had been abandoned.

His wife had been shot twice in the hip during the firefight. He walked over to her and gently lifted her blue smock. Each of the two red holes was ringed by a swollen ring of green pus. The woman seemed un-aware of these deep tunnels driven vio-lently into her hip and lay quietly, looking at no one. She was unable to walk, and there was nowhere to walk anyway. Per-haps some doctors, knowing the fighting must have left casualties, would return, or perhaps they had been forced to head for Kampala, or had chosen to cross the border. We will wait, the man told me, and thanked us for the bottles of water we left them. We were helpless, all of us — but Sheila and Nick and myself, only for the time being. We could leave, and when we did, what could we say? "Stay well"? "Good luck"? "Nice to meet you"? "Have a great war"?

As we left, I photographed and stopped to talk with three men who were still around. These sources weren't sure who had been fighting whom, where those fighting had come from, or where they were now. Quietly Sheila and I bid them good-bye. We drove to our plane and loaded up in silence. Only the roar of the engine and propeller broke the quiet that blanketed us as we lifted clear of the red ground and into the flawless sky.

So it went for the following week: strut-ting men-children at their pathetic roadblocks, their guns almost as long as they were, victims as well as victimizers who created more victims, I finally realized; scenes of horror and fear, but not much anger that we could find, the people were too weary; a rifle shot that came pretty close as I returned through the park to the Nile Mansions too late one evening. Leaving Uganda, we three reporters must have looked substantially different than we had coming in, because the rebels who blocked our progress never held us long. I think they saw a fraction of their war on our faces, and maybe this gave them pause. In any event, they waved us on. At the border crossing into Kenya, which we reached mid-afternoon, there were now trucks stacked up on both sides. The rebels wanted to make sure that neither Obote's soldiers nor any of his personnel made a safe escape out of the country. The Kenyans did not want these people either, or the rebels of any of the armies. For the moment, at least, this was not Kenya's war and the Kenyans were trying hard to stay clear of it.

The Ugandans let us slide through "customs" quickly, looking briefly at the dirty printout signed by General Okello. We were never even asked for a passport.

Kenya, however, was a different story. At that time it was illegal for Kenyan citizens or residents to have possession of U.S. dollars, but we had to have U.S. dollars in order to buy our visas into the country. I had tried for years to explain the absurdity of this catch-22 to the immigrations people, who said it wasn't their problem, while the bank people said that I should take it up with the immigrations people. This time we sidestepped the problem by stating that we had been able to purchase the dollars in Uganda, so we were legal all the way around. The border guys were understanding anyway, partially because they understood the dilemma faced by travelers, and partly because we looked so dirty and tired from our experiences of the preceding eleven days.

Only after the Kenyans had taken our money, stamped our passports, and opened the gate did I feel a final sense of relief, even safety. I don't think Nick much cared one way or the other, but Sheila, I know, felt as I did when the gate dropped back into its position. First, an infinitely heavy weight was lifted when we were locked out of that war. Second, it was great to be home.

The following day in Nairobi I had to

get busy developing my rolls, then making contact sheets and developing the best of them. I was glad I'd been working in black and white. The starkness and contrast provided by that medium were much more powerful for the scenes I had photographed than color would have been. I spent long hours working on enlargements of the container box at the presidential homestead, a few from the outside of the box, a couple from within its walls. As it sits in the yard in these pictures, the steel box looks much like a massively oversized coffin, which it was, although the hundreds, maybe thousands, of bullet holes are not really noticeable from any distance. Even close up they show smooth and round and *could* be something else. Inside in the close darkness there is no escaping the feeling. The needles of light and the partially open door don't really illuminate the scene, but they push back the darkness just enough to allow you to see and almost feel the jagged edges on which you could cut yourself, and thus add a bit more blood to the gelled pool on the floor, to see and almost feel the viscous depth of the gore. To understand the horror, you have to step inside.

11

The Impenetrable Forest

March 1, 1999, 6:35 a.m.

I stood before the man wielding a machine gun and hoped that Rob Haubner and Susan Miller had followed my instructions to find cover, and that Bob McLaurin and Susan Studd would somehow know to hide.

The man moved to the side and indicated that I should continue on the path that led to the main part of the camp. As I walked past him, he slammed me in the back of the head, maybe with the gun, maybe with something else. I swayed, my knees buckling. The blow was a jarring shock, but not that painful. I was able to keep walking on the slippery path. He crowded me tightly from behind as we walked, his gun in my back, then he reached out to strip off my watch and dig into my pocket for money, all the while roughly shoving me forward. This had to be armed robbery, I thought, although there had never been one in a Ugandan tourist camp.

The path opened onto the camp's central lawn. I saw Linda Adams, the California tourist in her fifties who had joined us on our gorilla trek the day before, sitting on the path surrounded by a group of ten men, all of them armed, wearing ragtag clothes, and none of them appearing to be the obvious leader. Linda looked up at me, white-faced and terrified. I stopped beside her and put a hand on her shoulder. "Linda, just be cool and keep quiet," I said in a low voice, the man with the machine gun directly behind me.

"Mark, what's going on?" she asked in a shaky voice.

I repeated my warning, my head throbbing, and stood so she could feel my hand on her shoulder and my legs against her back.

Someone grabbed me and ripped off my belt, my knife case, and knife with it. I had carried that thirty-dollar knife everywhere for fifteen years. I had chased those hyenas in Zimbabwe just to find it, and now I was losing it to this gang of thugs. I had just been shot at, but this moment with the knife, strangely enough, left me feeling angry, violated, heartbroken, even robbed of my personal history; that knife and I had been through a lot of history and hard times. Linda was stricken with fear.

"Sit down!" cried one of the gunmen in English.

I sank onto the path next to Linda. The thugs stared at us fiercely as we sat mute and stunned, waiting to see what would happen next.

For a while Linda and I were the sole focus of our attackers' attentions, but then I looked up to see Rob Haubner and Susan Miller being led in, surrounded by another half dozen armed men. My friends' faces were ashen, and they were somber and frightened. The gunmen shoved them toward Linda and me and they hunkered down behind us. Susan was gasping for air. I touched them gently, nodded a few times. "Be very quiet," I told them softly. "Don't do anything sudden. Just sit tight." They looked at me, too scared to speak. Rob rubbed Susan's shoulder and pulled her to him so she could rest her head on his shoulder — the same kind of gestures I had seen between this couple so often when we were in the Serengeti. I was glad they could take some strength from each other. "They're probably just going to leave us after they clean us out," I muttered.

Where were Bob McLaurin and Susan Studd?

A Frenchwoman we had briefly met the night before was brought down next, together with a girl I assumed to be her daughter, and shoved down beside us. Children in the Frenchwoman's care were herded into the circle, still in their nightclothes, crying and confused. I thought it was possible that the girls had been raped. The Frenchwoman consoled them — too loudly, too ostentatiously, I thought, gritting my teeth. I saw her begin talking in French with a few of the armed men; it seemed almost as if she were laughing. She stood up a few times and walked off with them at one point. Acting as if she had not the slightest clue how serious our situation was, she must have been behaving out of some curious combination of stupidity and true terror. She kept mouthing off as the children kept crying softly, and I resisted the urge to shake some sense into her. Instead, I focused on the path above me, looking for Bob McLaurin and Susan Studd.

"How many in your group?" one of the gunmen demanded.

"This is it. Just three of us," I said quickly, gesturing at Rob and Susan. "The other ones left yesterday," I added, as one group really had.

"How many are you!" he demanded again.

I repeated that the other whites and their guides had driven out the previous morning. I was afraid that I would hear two shots ring out when they found Bob and Susan. The Frenchwoman jumped up again and began badgering the group's apparent leader. I began to wonder why these people didn't just rob us and leave. There were too many of them to be a team of bandits, so it was possible they were guerilla fighters of some kind.

"Sit back down!" the gunman commanded the Frenchwoman, but she wouldn't listen; she kept jumping up and stomping around, as if she were unconcerned or unaware of what the hell was happening, as if she had some kind of diplomatic immunity from machine guns.

The woman sat but then immediately scrambled up, gesticulating, carrying on. When I heard one of the men say in Kiswahili that he was tired of listening to her, that she had no manners, no respect, I decided she was risking all of our lives. But there was no way I could intervene without inciting unpredictable reactions from our captors or from the woman herself. I felt doubly hostage.

More and more gunmen came up the path from the road below, carrying one of their own on a stretcher, which they laid on the grass about thirty feet from our group. The wounded man didn't move, but I couldn't see signs that he was bleeding heavily. He must have been shot when somebody at the camp resisted the attackers.

More tourists were marched into our camp, presumably from one or more of the other camps that ring this portion of the Impenetrable Forest. There were about twenty college-age kids I had never seen before and who were probably traveling around East Africa on one of the overland trucks that are often at Bwindi — an inexpensive and popular way to see Africa. Dazed, some still in their nightclothes, they were asked their nationalities. One of them who sat near Rob, Susan, and me was a French-speaking woman in her mid-twenties who said she was Swiss, not French. Her name was Dani. The lawn was now crowded with at least forty of our captors and thirty or so tourists.

The gunmen were well-armed, and, ominously, they were asking all of us our nationalities. They would take with them the growing cache of luggage, cameras, clothing, radios, and the like that I saw being hauled onto the lawn at a steady pace. I was stunned to recognize clothes belonging to Susan and Bob, along with their packs and cameras — even their computer. I hadn't heard any shots from the direction of their tent, and I was convinced they had been beaten to death. I blanched at the thought.

I was well acquainted with the existence of rebel armies in various parts of East and Central Africa. The Lord's Resistance Army (LRA) operated to the north of Bwindi. Five years earlier, nearly a million Rwandans had been murdered in just three months. Responsible for the slaughter were the notorious Interahamwe — an extremist group of Hutus that had a faction in western Uganda. *"Interahamwe,"* translated from the Kinyarwanda, means "those who strike together," and the group's members were known for their expertise with machetes. Virtually none of the almost one million victims of the Rwandan genocide were shot; they were systematically hacked to death. The Interahamwe would often disable their enemies by severing their hamstrings or Achilles tendons. They would leave their victims to suffer, then return to kill them hours later.

But southwest Uganda, the region of the Impenetrable Forest, is the territory of gentle families of gorillas, not the LRA or the Interahamwe. During the past five years, I had taken clients to the Bwindi Impenetrable Forest about a dozen times. Last year, I had advised these same four clients *not* to come to Uganda, because of my doubts about the still-roiling, warlike situation in neighboring Rwanda. This year, however, I had already led safarigoers into Uganda five times, while keeping in close touch with the Abercrombie & Kent camp's main office in Nairobi. I wanted to make certain that things were still fine, that no robberies or other activity had occurred anywhere in the region. There had been absolutely no warnings that anything like this could happen here. For me, this rebel assault was more astonishing than a volcanic eruption.

No shots had been fired for five minutes. "Where from?" the rebels kept demanding, standing uncomfortably close, their faces almost touching ours, their weapons bumping our bodies. The captives answered in scared, reluctant voices: "America." "Australia." "Canada." "France." Yet we were not separated into different groups based on our nationalities, perhaps a portent of some greater plan.

"Where from?" asked a rebel, looming over me.

"I am an American living in Kenya," I said in Kiswahili, noting the shock on the rebel's face when he heard me speak his language. "I teach science in a small village in Kenya," I said — something I had, in fact, done, but many years earlier. By telling them this lie, I wanted to establish myself as the leader, the local; I knew I needed to be the go-between so that I could control the questions and answers and keep us alive. Right answers and we might live; wrong answers and we would die.

The Kenyan camp manager was brought in, his arms tied behind his back. He sat down, not too close to us, but keeping an intentional, premeditated distance, to improve his chances of staying alive. "I am not a Ugandan. I am not a tourist," he said to the rebels in Kiswahili, his voice quivering, pleading. "I am an African like you, a Kenyan." He was trying to save himself by ignoring his clients, and that angered me. They disregarded his explanation that he was the camp manager; they appeared much more interested in the white people's nationalities. That left me convinced that there was some larger, unknown motive at work.

As the barrage of questions continued, other rebels emerged from surrounding tents loaded down with loot: radios, cartons of food, clothes, a computer — anything they could carry. They looked like people fleeing a house fire. Baskets of food and sodas were hauled up from the kitchen. The rebels seemed to take great pride in opening the bottles of soda with their teeth, guzzling them in one go, and slamming the empty bottles down on the sidewalks near us. One rebel brought out a beer bottle and put it to his teeth, but another grabbed it from him and smashed it on the sidewalk, then yelled at the beer drinker in a language I didn't recognize but decided was probably Kinyarwanda, and slapped him violently across the face three times. The man never raised a hand in self-defense, never even turned or lowered his head, emphasizing that incredible brutality had become a normal way of life for them. But it also suggested some chain of command.

One rebel walked by wearing Rob's dark blue jacket. Another had a familiar tan backpack slung over his shoulder. It was Bob McLaurin's. There was still no sign of Bob or his wife.

Throughout more than two decades living in Africa, I had experienced a lot of adventures and close calls: dodging rampaging elephants, losing my Cessna's engine over Mount Kilimanjaro. I had been frightened out of my wits several times. But what I was witnessing that morning in Uganda was a different order of fear and terror entirely. Sitting on the lawn, surrounded by rampaging human beings and knowing that any instant any one of us could be shot in the back of the head, I was losing feeling in my body. My sense of touch was almost numb, my hearing was muted, and all my motion was slowed down. I was even losing color vision and seeing only shades of gray. I was drifting off, gradually fading away.

I realized I was rapidly sinking into a dangerous state of shock. I looked vaguely across at the others. Linda had already gone somewhere else mentally. Rob was holding Susan by the shoulder and Susan was slumped into him, eyes shut. All around me, people were falling into paralysis. They were no longer reacting to the rebels' yells, the smashing bottles, or the total chaos happening all around us, right beside us. What had some of these other captives already experienced? Had they been eyewitnesses to the gunshots I had only heard?

Individuals as physically able and emotionally stable as Rob Haubner and Susan Miller were checking out right in front of my eyes. If I succumbed, if I didn't struggle out from under the blanket of fear, I would not live to see the following day. Neither would any of the rest of us. I had to make myself focus in order to stay alive. I had to. From that moment, I knew I had to stay present to live and keep others alive as well.

"No more jumping or blinking," I told myself with conviction. "Don't give these bastards the satisfaction." In an effort to stay present, I started taking note of as many details as possible. I cataloged clothing and weapons — all automatic with two old G3-type Enfields. Anytime I saw a rifle I checked for a grass plug in the barrel. The plug keeps out dirt and other foreign matter; it also indicates whether the weapon has been recently fired. A sizable percentage of these weapons were still plugged, though an uncomfortable number of the rebels casually strolled around with their fingers inside the trigger housing, more than ready to shoot on the spot.

These men were not the child soldiers I had encountered during the civil war in Uganda in 1985. All appeared to be in their twenties, or older. And virtually all of them were carrying machetes. Were they the Interahamwe? I knew that this pathologically violent and sadistic Hutu group, notorious for its prowess with machetes, was responsible for the brunt of the massacre in Rwanda in 1994. The group was not known to be in southwest Uganda, but if they were . . .

If these were the Interahamwe . . . I fought the fear.

Even as I saw dawn take command of the sky, I knew we were about to enter deepest night.

"Stand!"

Suddenly all of us on the ground were forced to our feet. We were pushed forward, past the last group of captives, who were being brought in at the same time.

"What's going on?" Linda asked me in a quavering voice.

"I think they might use us to cover their

escape back to the border of the Congo," I said under my breath. Linda looked wide-eyed, perplexed, stunned. I knew the Ugandan army was stationed twenty miles farther down this same valley; they must have heard the shooting in the tourist camp. Even as we were being rounded up, they would have started coming toward the sound of the firing, just to investigate if nothing else. The rainforest was ideal cover for a rebel movement, since the jungle is so thick you can't see people until you are a few feet from them. To further ensure their safe passage out of the area, the best thing the rebels could do would be to take tourists along as escape cover, hostages for the day, thus preventing any possible firefight between themselves and the Ugandan army.

They made the tourists form a line, and began marching us out of camp. I was near the front of the line, and I turned to make sure Rob and Susan were with me. They swayed against each other as we moved forward, and I noticed with a stab of painful sympathy that they had to walk barefoot; the rebels had taken their shoes, as well as those of many of the other tourists, and wore them tied together over their shoulders. The rebels all were booted; they just wanted to keep their captives from running. I saw the young Swiss woman, Dani, but I didn't see the French group. I was afraid they were going to be killed because the Frenchwoman had pushed things much too hard, obviously unaware of the irritation she was causing.

Linda Adams was in no better shape than Rob and Susan. "I think I'm going to lose it," she told me when we next came to a stop.

"You'd damn well better not," I replied forcefully.

I was terribly worried about Susan Studd and Bob McLaurin. It was not a good sign that I had seen the rebels sporting the belongings stolen from their tent. I was sure they had been killed in their beds. My mind kept conjuring a detailed image of their clubbed, bloody bodies sprawled in their tent.

We shuffled down the steps that led from the camp to the road. Their guns prodding us into position, our captors again lined us up at the bottom, single file, facing east.

Confronting us now were dozens of rebels — close to fifty, maybe more. They eyed us hard, and soon they swaggered up and down in front of us, smashing bottles at our feet, throwing fake punches at the men, guffawing when someone flinched or cried out. I stood still, alert and frustrated, my hands half-balled into fists, working to tally up the number of captives and captors. There were sixteen of us and, as I looked down the road, I counted between seventy-five and a hundred of them, mostly healthy, muscular men in their twenties. Drinking the camp's sodas, playing singsong African music on the cassette decks they had stolen, they were strutting their stuff, enjoying their moment of power.

One rebel pretended to knee the man to my right in the groin. When the hostage — a stocky New Zealander whose name, I would learn later, was Mark Avis — doubled over defensively, the rebels howled with laughter. The man who pretended to knee Avis was maybe twenty-five and squat, with a pointy, triangular face. He was wearing an unzipped pink windbreaker and his laugh was the kind that digs under your skin. He was not carrying a rifle — just a sidearm — but he was brandishing a short, stocky club and seemed to be one of the leaders.

Still laughing, wielding his club, the rebel turned to me and pretended to smash me in the face. I just stared at him and tried to not even blink. For my trouble, I was rewarded with a smash across the face with the club.

The pain exploded in my cheekbones and my skull. I rocked back but kept my eyes locked on this tormentor, furious that he might mistake the tears in my eyes for crying instead of the automatic response they were.

The rebels moved on to other humiliations. Cavorting to the music on the cassette decks set on the ground before us, they tried to goad us into dancing. I never dance and was not about to make an exception. Our captors overlooked me, but they kept bullying and prodding the others, dancing more themselves to show how it was done. The hostages were mute, dancing numbly. The rebels looked ridiculous — awkward clowns moving gracelessly under their AK-47s.

Suddenly I was smashed again across the back with a club wielded by a different rebel. The blow reverberated all the way around my ribcage and up and down my spine, and I arched my back in reaction. But this time the impact on me was different. *This* made me angry; *this* snapped me out of my haze. I tightened my jaw and made my resolve even more rigid — that I would pull myself out of the tunnel of fear. The sharp pain brought me back to reality. I would concentrate, I would focus, and I would fight these bastards to the end.

The man who had hit me then gestured for us to start marching. We were off again, walking south toward the Impenetrable Forest. After about a hundred yards on the main road, with Rob and Susan buckling as their bare feet hit the road's small stones, we were forced west and herded up a tight, precipitously uphill grass trail toward the Congo border. This confirmed my suspicion that our group had been conscripted to serve as traveling hostages, human armor that would expedite the rebels' retreat. I told Rob and Susan what I thought was happening and they listened dully, so unresponsive that I doubted they were even understanding me.

Huge trees rose around us on the steep valley walls, their tops still patchy with morning mist. I had been up here several times over the years to visit the "K" group of gorillas, the only habituated group living on the western slope of the valley. The other gorillas are on the eastern side, where we had trekked yesterday, going farther into Uganda; today we were being marched westward, up out of the main valley that runs north-south — and we were heading toward the Congo. I knew we had a hard trail ahead. I concentrated on the task of walking — breathing steadily, resting briefly between steps, holding my arms loose and low, consciously conserving my strength.

The path was narrow, only a meter or so wide, and it snaked steeply up the imposing hill. The rebels were spaced between the tourists, and because there were about five feet between each person and the next, the single-file line seemed to stretch endlessly in both directions. Early on, Linda fell behind and I lost sight of her, but I made sure that Rob and Susan stayed close to me, because I was worried about them. If we were indeed headed for the Congo, they would have to negotiate the rough terrain, barefoot, for several grueling hours — enough to exhaust even an experienced trekker.

"Don't talk much," I said to them as we halted briefly. "No need to draw any extra attention." None of us was being hit just for talking, but the horrendous risk wasn't worth it. Susan was having a hard time breathing, thanks to the effect of the exertion, the high elevation, and most of all her huge and understandable fear. She closed her eyes and crumbled onto my left shoulder. I held her. "Hang tough," I whispered forcefully. "Breathe easy, Susan. Just keep going. Be tough for a while." Her slight nod seemed like a breathless effort. I didn't have the heart to tell her that we would probably have to hike at least as far as the Congo border, which was still a good four miles away, and that our usefulness to the rebels would probably end where the two countries meet. I also didn't mention that by now I was all but certain I knew who our captors were — and that they were not known for their decency.

I looked over at Rob. He wasn't able to help his wife; his face was blank, and as we got up to move he seemed almost catatonic. Soon I saw him stumble blindly into Susan. He hadn't even seen, or comprehended, that his wife, whom he loved so dearly, had collapsed right in front of him.

I was able to read one rebel's watch, which said 7:22. Though the whole episode to this point had lasted less than an hour, it seemed like half the day. And it was just beginning. I redoubled my effort to stay conscious and focused. I concentrated on catching times, names, weapon types, even serial numbers. Besides, every little bit of data might help us get out alive or even help deliver justice later.

We continued to walk in the low morning light. In some places, the equatorial sun broke through the trees and we grew briefly hot and sweaty; the rebels had not given us any water. Yet under the canopy of the forest it was still quite cool. A soldier told Rob to take off his fleece. He was already barefoot and without a shirt, and now his only clothing was a pair of pants. It was cold, so I unbuttoned and untucked my shirt. "Rob, come on — we'll take turns wearing it," I urged him. But he shook his head, so I said I would give it to him later on. He only nodded, and we stumbled on into the forest.

I was still aching and angry from the blows I had suffered earlier. Periodically the whole line came to an abrupt halt, sometimes for minutes at a time, which baffled me, especially when the path had become wide open, so it wasn't that steep or overgrown. Susan was bent over at the waist, breathing hard with her eyes shut. A few times she fainted away completely, collapsing to the ground. "What is holding us up?" a rebel asked me. "What is wrong with her? And with her?" he asked, gesturing to another young woman who was lying panting among us. That woman, I would find out later, was Rhonda Avis, the wife of Mark, the New Zealander who had reacted to the rebel's faked kick in the groin.

As we got up and trudged forward, Susan was moving more sluggishly than ever, her eyes shut tight, barely able to stay on her feet. Maybe I could get Susan out of harm's way. In Kiswahili, I asked one of the nearby rebels if he could send her back down, because she had a heart problem. Susan had no such condition, but I insisted that she did.

The rebel looked at me skeptically. "What is wrong with her heart?"

"All I know is that she was a part of my tourist group and that she has this problem," I said evenly.

"I cannot make such a decision," the rebel said to me, his voice perfunctory. "I will ask." He went off to the head of the line. Evidently, there was a chain of command within the rebel group, which was difficult to discern from either their speech or their dress, but the three men giving most of the orders did not carry any rifles or machine guns, only sidearms.

The rebel returned. "She'll be able to return," he said, stone-faced.

"I'm grateful," I replied. "She doesn't

need an escort. She knows her way down." The idea of Susan's walking back alone bothered me, but it troubled me less than the thought of her with one or more of these men, separated from the main force.

This news brought a flood of relief. I was determined to hang in as long as I could, but I didn't believe those of us still hostages at the end of the trek to the border would be set free. Once we had served as cover for the rebels and they reached the border, they would have no reason to keep us as hostages. We would have nothing to offer them; as highly visible white people, we would be nothing but a hindrance. We would go from asset to liability. They would have to free us or kill us, and why would they free us? Why would they take that risk? I thought we would be murdered at the border and shut up for good. I thought the feigned illness would probably save Susan's life.

I had already told her and the others how to get back to camp: simply head downhill to eventually end up in the main valley. Now I took Susan's face in my hands. "Susan," I said quickly, "always go downhill at any fork in the trail." She looked at me. "*Downhill*, Susan — just go downhill at every juncture."

Rob just stood mutely beside us as I spoke to Susan, as if he didn't realize that his wife was about to be released. I truly don't think he did, for he didn't drop back to say good-bye or to touch his wife in any way. He stood by her for a few moments, not touching or talking, and then we were forced on again. Susan remained on the path as we walked away from her. I was shocked, for I knew that Susan was everything to Rob. We were all so scared, so terrified of any action or movement. As we went on, I couldn't see if she was left alone or was accompanied.

After she was gone, Rob remained separated from me by ten or so tourists and a number of rebels, but I tried to maintain eye contact, and I snuck a thumbs-up sign while pretending to scratch my cheek. It seemed vital to somehow stay in touch with one another. Rob was marching along with heavy steps, his head hanging down, arms swinging in useless, shallow arcs. I had to at least try to get him released. During the course of the next long break, I repeatedly said that Rob needed to go with his wife because he had her medicine.

"Is he a doctor?"

"No," I said immediately, not wanting Rob to appear to possess valuable expertise the rebels could exploit. "He is her husband, and he knows her medicine and how to administer it to her."

I had already identified two group rebel leaders — the pointy-faced man who had clubbed me on the road and another with a curly black beard. Now a third leader was brought back down the line to talk to me. He distinctly surprised me. In my early years in Kenya, I had taught in Kenya's central province, the heart of Kikuyuland, home to a prosperous Kenyan tribe. Light-skinned, about thirty-five, this man looked Kikuyu to me, and he spoke a very educated Kiswahili, matching the noun classes and using complicated verb structures, his syntax far different from the jumbled grammatical mixture one so often hears. He was also dressed as if going to work in downtown Nairobi, in a long-sleeved shirt buttoned at the cuffs and collar. Like the others, he was wearing gum boots, but his trouser legs were tucked neatly inside them. He was clean and pressed, energetic. He was also wearing my watch.

Keeping my voice respectful but urgent, I explained to him that Rob needed to go back to take care of his wife. "He has to give her some of her medicine," I lied.

"I cannot make that decision," the Kikuyu told me. He went back up the trail toward the head of the line, disappearing into the forest.

Ten minutes later he came back. "Whom are you referring to?" he demanded. "Why does he have to be sent back?"

I pointed to Rob and explained again.

"No," the Kikuyu said. He turned on his heel and disappeared.

Rob had been watching the whole discussion. He understood that it concerned him, and he must have known what I was requesting. I snuck in another thumbs-up while signaling him to stay put. He kept very much to himself, looking neither sad nor scared, just blank of expression. We continued on.

The trail steepened another notch. The trees up here were shorter, and butterflies the size of small birds fluttered overhead. The morning mist had disappeared, and the sun was almost directly overhead, beating down on us as we walked silently, heads down. I caught sight of someone's watch: 10:30 a.m. We had been climbing for three and a half hours.

About halfway up the incline I heard a woman's voice behind me, speaking to one of the rebels in French, and from what I could understand she wanted to relieve herself. I looked back. It was the Swiss woman, Dani, and she appeared vigorous and alert, all things considered. After a brief discussion, one of the rebels led her about ten feet off the trail into the bush.

I stopped cold. This terrified me. Wet your pants or pee in front of us, I thought — but do not leave the group for any reason, much less to half undress yourself in front of these men. In addition to being proficient with machetes, the Interahamwe are notorious for being savage rapists. I was sure that we were about to witness something horrific, and I felt helpless to prevent it.

I lost sight of Dani, but not of the soldier. A few long minutes passed. My mind raced. I wondered whether I could wrest a rifle away from one of the rebels and take my own hostage, but this would surely have gotten us all killed. The rebel didn't move. The Swiss woman reemerged. I determined to warn her never to leave the group again, no matter what. My relief turned to concern when I heard her and her escort engaged in what sounded like casual conversation. No doubt Dani thought that becoming friendly with our captors would improve our situation, but I feared that nothing could be further from the truth.

Soon we stopped again. As we caught our breath, one of the rebels came toward me carrying Bob's laptop computer. He wanted help starting it. "The battery is low," I told him truthfully, when I couldn't get it going. Another tourist back down the line introduced himself as a computer guy and said he might be able to help. I thought to myself, "How dumb — don't make yourself useful or you may be here a hell of a lot longer than you want."

Next I had to explain that a cell phone is not a radio. "Could it reach Kampala, the United States, Nairobi?" they asked.

"Perhaps," I said, "but it might be password protected."

Other stolen items were brought for my inspection — cassette decks, radios, earphones, cameras. As the only person in our group who spoke Kiswahili, I became the designated technician. I was asked to explain bottles of medicine, perfume, deodorant, lotions, makeup, pills. *"Hii ni, nini, ni dawa, chakula, au mchezo?"* What is this thing — is it medicine, food, or a game? Painfully senseless exercises, and absurd in light of what had already taken place. I wanted our captors to get to the goddamn point already and tell us what was in store.

At the top of a steep rise the trail turned right, or north, and we reentered the woods and descended on a couple of switchbacks into taller timber and heavier growth. Again we stopped and were sternly told to sit down. I continued my inventory of weapons, identifying SAR 50s and either SAR 80s or 20s (I couldn't see the full number), and some automatic weapons with oriental-style script. Two types of hand grenades were in the arsenal. One of the classic pineapple type had its pin held in by a piece of inner tube. Odd and risky. It also struck me as odd that a number of other rebels wanted to see this type of grenade, which led me to believe that perhaps they had stolen it.

We marched on. The rebels didn't seem to have a plan: Sometimes they behaved like thugs, but at other moments they seemed to follow strict rules of conduct. What were they up to? Again we stopped. Several minutes passed. We waited in silence. More time passed. What was going on?

We rose and resumed our forced march. After fifteen minutes of steady climbing, at exactly 11:30 according to a rebel's watch, we turned and headed back in the direction from which we had just come. This U-turn brought me past Rob, who was sitting directly in the path. Determined to keep him with me, I reached down and began to pull him up by his upper arm, but a rebel stepped in front of me, slammed me in the stomach with his rifle butt, knocking me onto Rob, and then immediately pulled me back up and violently propelled me forward.

I fought to rasp out breaths and keep stumbling ahead at the same time. When I recovered enough to look behind me, Rob was fifty feet back, still sitting, surrounded by a group of rebels. Along with two other men, my friend was being separated from the group. But why were they doing this? I couldn't think of a good reason for this separating and backtracking; maybe there had been an argument among the rebels about where to cross the border into the Congo, and these dissidents within the rebel camp were taking their own hostages for their separate escape. I knew that splitting up the group would be disastrous for us.

Rob sat with his legs drawn up, his arms wrapped around his knees. Completely resigned, defeated, and sad beyond words, he was looking right at me — an image that will haunt me for the rest of my life. An inner voice told me I would never see Rob again, and I hated myself for that awareness, and for the powerlessness with which I had to accept it.

On the trail, seeing him like this, I almost cried, almost lost my own resolve, defeated by my sense that this would indeed prove to be a fatal day. As we were marched back across the mountain, I looked across the slope for Rob at every opportunity, hoping he might be following behind, but he and the others were gone.

After backtracking for ten or fifteen minutes, we turned onto a freshly bushwhacked trail across a steep, slippery traverse leading to the west-southwest, toward the distant ridge that I knew was the Congo border. One rebel threw away a pair of shoes, and I marked the spot because I didn't know this new trail. We might need this marker later, as well as the shoes, if we escaped. A party of five great blue turacos landed on a high tree down-slope from us, therefore right at eye level. Out of instinct I watched and pointed them out to the group, who, understandably, took no notice whatsoever.

I had counted 117 rebels but knew there were more, because I could not see the front of the line. Rebels had remained with Rob and the others as well. There were now just six hostages, and I took the chance to introduce myself and get everyone's name in return: The Swiss woman was Danja Walther, or Dani, and she hung close to Gary Tappenden, a slight man with bleached hair and earrings. Michael Baker, a tall Australian, had offered to help with the computer; he was soft-spoken and clearheaded, remarkably agile in bare feet. Mark Avis had been stumbling often on the trail and often fell behind. (I learned much later that the rebels had stolen his glasses.) A Canadian, Mitch Keifer, appeared scholarly and had a quiet, careful manner. He, too, kept falling behind. "We have to stay close together from here on out," I told them. "No matter what. We just have to stay together — and I mean within a meter or so." Some nodded quietly. The others responded as if they had not really heard my words at all.

We stopped often along this traverse, for about ten minutes at a time, presumably because of the man on the stretcher, who had been brought onto the lawn by rebels early in the day. During one of these rests, a rebel started a conversation with Dani, and he continued talking with her on and off in French for a long time. I even saw them swap addresses, which they had written down on little scraps of paper and passed back and forth. Later, as we walked, I saw the man start to keep a close, appraising eye on Dani, staying close to her, which alarmed me greatly. I knew that for more than a decade, the Lord's Resistance Army, a group that operated way north of Bwindi and entirely unrelated to these rebels, had been abducting hundreds and hundreds of Ugandan high school girls, making long-term prisoners and slaves of them. As soon as Dani and I got close enough on the trail to talk, I told her she had better call off these friendly conversations. "It could end very badly if you keep this up," I said in a low voice. "Listen, pretend your French isn't that good. Give short answers."

She seemed to falter as she comprehended what I was driving at. The guy persisted with his advances, so I switched places with Dani during the next break, putting her one place farther down the line, with me between her and the rebel. For some reason, this ploy worked. The rebel didn't move back to be next to her. I was a little relieved, but still wary. Dani wasn't out of danger.

As we stopped again, at approximately one o'clock, water bottles were passed down from the head of the line. We had been hostages for more than six hours and hadn't had a drink the whole time. As I swallowed the warm water, I thought again about Bob and Susan. Most likely, they had been killed in their tent. I recalled a newspaper story I read about a tour group, four New Zealanders I believed, who were captured by rebels in the Congo several months earlier. One of them was released, but the other three hadn't been seen since, dead or alive. Were we in for days, weeks, even months of this nomadic prison life? Or would we simply be killed at the Congo border, which was now no more than a couple of miles away?

The well-dressed Kikuyu rebel broke in on my thoughts. "Do you know what this war is about?" he asked me. Another asked Dani the same question in French.

It was the first political remark I had heard. I played dumb, staying very carefully neutral, but he was on to me. "How could you live in Kenya for so long and not know what we're fighting for?" he demanded. "What would you say about our cause?"

"Tell me what you're fighting for," I replied. I felt desperate pressure to stay impartial — I didn't want them to kill us for picking the wrong side.

They told us about the wars across Africa, especially East Africa, and said they were "hunting Tutsis." Finally, their purpose became clear to me. As I suspected, they were Interahamwe, Hutus who blamed America and Britain — and Uganda — for supporting a Tutsi-led government after the slaughter in 1994. Abducting us was a terrorist bid for publicity that would damage and maybe even destroy the tourism business that is a mainstay of the Ugandan economy.

"Write down your cause," I suggested quietly, "and I will take the letter back to the U.S. ambassador and get it to the press." The Kikuyu said nothing. He probably saw through my ruse and knew I was just trying to get the rebels to believe there was value in allowing us to survive.

At the next break I asked for one rebel's spare set of boots for Dani, who had given her shoes to a hostage having a hard go of it. When we were refused, Dani rested her head on my knee, crying, with Gary right beside her. One of the rebels who had beaten me earlier asked what was wrong.

"What the hell do you think is wrong with her?" I shot back, in maybe too strong a voice. "She's *scared*, goddamn it," I said, in Kiswahili. "We've been stripped, robbed, and beaten, and we're scared, tired, and hungry."

Friends and wives had been taken away in front of our eyes. If we slowed down or got hurt or tried to help someone, we could join the missing or the dead. We had been on this trail, some of us barefoot, all of us exhausted, for seven goddamn hours. What the hell did he expect?

My outburst was unpremeditated, but just moments later, as if it worked a spell, water and sodas were passed to us, along with a round loaf of sweet bread with raisins. I divided it among the group, urging everyone to eat, especially Mark, who looked on the verge of losing his will.

The Kikuyu man reappeared. "You shouldn't be afraid," he said stonily in Kiswahili. "You're going to be all right. What would you say to the world when you returned?"

Now I got my first glimmer of hope in hours — guarded hope. Maybe we *did* have something to offer the rebels, after all. I jumped at the opening, making an effort to keep my voice calm and relaxed, and speaking in Kiswahili the entire time; I didn't want the other hostages to know what I was talking about to the rebels, because they were having a hard enough time staying focused in the present. "We would tell everyone that you hadn't hurt us, that you had actually fed us, given us water and soda."

The Kikuyu pushed, asking what we would say about the cause. I said we could take back any message they wanted, anything at all. It was left at that, but minutes later he returned and again told us not to be scared, that we would be all right. I did not translate for the others. I didn't see the point in getting their hopes up, because I was far from convinced that we would be left alive.

We crossed a small stream, where we weren't allowed to stop and drink, and proceeded up a very steep slope on the other side. From our position across the narrow valley, I watched the litter case, trying to determine if the man was alive or dead. I could see no massive bloodstains on him or on the sleeping bag on which he was lying, yet he seemed unconscious. His head swiveled freely from side to side with the rocking of the litter, but at one point he briefly raised his right arm, so he was still alive, if barely. And he would be alive, wouldn't he? There would be no point in slowing down the whole group for the benefit of a dead rebel, who couldn't provide any information to a pursuing army.

At the next break, the Kikuyu rebel and I had another conversation, in Kiswahili. He repeated his question about what I would say to the outside world. Staying as neutral as possible, I again asked him to write everything down and I would guarantee that it got to the press and into the hands of the U.S. ambassador. The Kikuyu told me not to worry, that we would be released at three o'clock. I looked at his watch: 2:41. I debated with myself whether I should tell the group. I finally did *not*, and at three o'clock I was glad I hadn't, because the hour simply came and went.

I found out the time only after spending two minutes trying to read a watch that didn't have any hands on it. But when I was able to read one that worked and discovered that the hour had passed, I wasn't deflated. We were not at any natural ridgeline, river, valley bottom, or trail crossing — there was no point marking a boundary or border. If they did let us go, that kind of terrain would be the place.

About forty minutes later we broke into a burned-out area some two hundred yards below the ridge crest that marked the border with the Congo. Apparently, local villagers had burned it to make a field, and I made note of one fallen black tree and one fallen and still-burning white tree, which would be our entrance into the forest. From here, it would be easy, even in moonlight, to follow the worn track all the way back to camp.

At the top of the ridge, we all stopped. The sky had turned gray, and a soft rain was falling through the trees. The other five hostages sat down. "We're not going beyond here," I told the group. "One way or the other, this is it." The rebels knew this, too, and surrounded us, pressing in on three sides. The psychological pressure and terror was now crushing, with these hundred-plus practiced murderers with machine guns and machetes towering over us. I made a decision: if the rebels wanted to take someone for further protection once they entered the Congo, I would volunteer. I also told myself that whatever happened I would protect Dani. As the only woman left among us, she was the most attractive target.

The injured man on the litter was set

down about twenty feet away, under a large tree, a group of soldiers staying close. One rebel kicked Gary's feet, motioning him to hand over his shoes. Another asked for mine, and I simply looked away. Gary was wearing no socks underneath, and his toenails were painted green — an incongruous reminder of another world.

The soldier who had talked with Dani off and on approached her. "I'm taking this one on," he announced in Kiswahili. He looked around, his eyes settling on Gary, with his green toenails, earrings, and bleached hair. "And that one, too." I wasn't sure, but I guessed he thought Gary was a woman. The rebel spoke in Kiswahili, not in French, but Dani knew that she had been singled out when he violently yanked her by the hair, grabbed her face, and pulled her toward him.

Some deep compulsion to act grabbed me. It had nothing to do with courage; I was angry and terrified, and even resigned to our eventual fates. I yanked Dani back toward me by both shoulders and pulled as the soldier tried to yank her away. It was a tug-of-war that I won, because Dani suddenly fell at my feet. Her composure collapsed at last; she was crying hard, which was good, because the rebels were puzzled.

I untied her fleece, which was wrapped around her waist, covered her with it, and told her to stay down. The soldiers jeered, pressing in very close, as I held her to me. One asked why Dani was crying. Almost in tears myself, angry and scared to death, I cut loose in about the same terms I had used an hour before. The outburst stopped the stupid laughter, at least.

I confronted the Kikuyu commander standing nearby, almost yelling, reminding him in Kiswahili that he had promised me that we would be safe, but look what was happening now. He ignored me at first; then he and the others asked us what we did, what our jobs were, where we lived — all questions asked in Kiswahili, which I translated in a leading way. "None of you are doctors, *are you?*" I asked. We didn't want to be useful. We didn't want to be radio operators, electronics experts, or medical personnel, not if we didn't want to live in the Congo for the indefinite future. We didn't even know how to cook. I claimed once again to be a teacher in central Kenya. Everyone else was a student, probably the safest thing to be.

"I want my knife back," I declared — asked. That request froze all conversation. The rebels asked what I had said. "I want my knife back! It was stolen earlier. It's a very special knife, and I want it back now."

"Who took it?" the Kikuyu asked. After I described the guy, he actually sent a rebel to ask around, and he returned with a Swiss army knife.

"That's not my knife!" I said, and threw it on the ground. The rebels stood back, stunned, watching their commander. I pressed the issue and described the knife again. The rebels seemed to be backing off a bit, caught off guard, so I pushed forward, trying desperately, I suppose, to gain a little more ground. It felt good to assert myself after feeling such total helplessness for so long, and looking back, I think it may have played a part in helping us gain our freedom. The whole psychological balance had shifted. It was obvious, and the key to our lives.

Just then a black man with a cut above his left eye was brought into the group. I naturally took him to be a rebel and told him that one of the other rebels had a topical medicine he could use.

"I'm a *hostage*," he responded, surprised. He said he was not a rebel but *one of us*, a driver back at the camp, which surprised me. I hadn't noticed him the whole day. His name was Masindi. Brought along as labor, he had been at the front of the line cutting trail. Masindi sat wearily among the other hostages, but I remained standing, surveying them, with their mud-caked arms, badly scraped feet, and torn clothes. They hung their heads, their eyes downcast. But the arduousness of the day's journey had not wiped the look of fear from their faces.

It was just after four o'clock. I knew this because I was reading my own wristwatch, worn by the well-dressed Kikuyu. "Three of our troop will remain with you when I and the others leave," he told me.

What was the point of this? They would murder us, that was what! Why else would they stay? But I passed along the news and urged everyone to be calm. Now the man with my watch had paper and a black pen. He had filled up two pages in French. "Read this and translate it to your group."

"I can't read French," I said. "Besides, it is raining, and the note will become illegible."

"Then translate my spoken words," he told me.

This is how we learned that our captors were one of four groups of rebels in the area, all originally based in Kigali, Rwanda; that to them all of Africa, not just East Africa, was a war zone; and that next time they would kill all hostages immediately, no prisoners, no walking, no distinctions of gender or race or nationality. Did we understand? All would die.

As he spoke I translated, and when the rebel thought my translations were not long enough and therefore incomplete, he prodded me to finish. I noticed his men adjusting their weapons and cargo, as if preparing to move again. When the commander finished speaking, I folded the note into quarters and put it in my shirt pocket. For the sheer hell of it, I asked the commander for my wristwatch.

He looked at me, paused, said, "Buy another," and then he and the others were gone, just like that, striding out of the clearing and fading into the jungle, across the border into the Congo. Before we had time to fear the three rebels left with us, they turned and followed the main group into the forest.

We hostages were all alone, and I, for one, was in a state of disbelief. I could *describe* these men; I even had some *names*. But nevertheless we were free. Free, but far from elated. No one said a word. Tentatively, we rose to our feet. There was no hugging, no shouting, for we were completely numb.

12

The Journey Back

The rebels receded into the forest, then vanished.

The rain had slowed to a light drizzle. "We can take it easy going back," I said to my fellow freed captives, inhaling deeply and steadying myself, working to believe that we had truly been released. "We have time. We're okay. You know, most mountaineering accidents occur on the way down after all energy, emotional and physical, has been spent. We'll just go slowly, help each other, make it back down." The trail in the forest would be easy to follow — after all, more than one hundred people had tramped along it. Then I was reminded of a less assuring prospect. "Did any of you notice if those rebels carried land mines?"

This was a discouraging thought, but our captors would have been smart to lay land mines behind them. A single detonation would have forced any pursuers to abandon the trail and spend valuable time cutting a parallel one instead. But none of us had seen any land mines.

The driver, Masindi, took off in near panic, much too fast. In the lead, I kept the rest of us lagging behind him. I had to physically restrain Mitch from charging ahead, and even then, some of the others told me to slow down, though I was going quite slowly already. We were falling and slipping all the time, although the terrain, while steep, was not that difficult to navigate. Mark Avis took one bad fall, his leg folding up beneath him; since the rebels had swiped his glasses, he had a hard time assessing the ground beneath him. "It won't be too long until we make the main trail!" I said, to muster everyone's strength and keep us all focused. "And if we don't make it down by dark, we can wait for the full moon."

At a stream, when Dani and I filled the water bottles, someone asked if the water was safe to drink. For the first time all day, I smiled. Just drink the water, I wanted to say. I paid attention to the birdcalls: I heard a group of great blue turacos, perhaps the same ones from that morning, followed by the call of a hairy-breasted barbet. I was amazed that they were still there, that the forest was still functioning. I had forgotten about the forest.

"I think we should say a prayer of thanks for our survival," said Michael Baker, the tall Australian. "And a prayer of hope for the others." Okay, I agreed, maybe it would help some of us, and it certainly couldn't hurt. We held hands and Michael began to speak, then invited others to say what they wished.

Someone else spoke briefly, his voice tentative in the vast forest. I failed to come up with anything, which I felt bad about, but there was still so much left to do, so much uncertainty. Prayer would have been hypocritical of me at this juncture. It was too early for prayer, I thought, or too late.

We set out again, and about thirty minutes later we encountered a small group of armed soldiers. The sight of them unnerved us, since by then we were unconditionally leery of any men with guns, but their uniforms gave me confidence. They were Ugandan, it turned out, pursuing the rebels, and us. I stopped and gave them the information I had about the rebels, their numbers and weapons, and I showed them the ridge line across the valley where we had been released. The burned area was still easily visible. The soldiers reacted fiercely, angrily, at what I told them, as if they were itching for a fight. They hoisted their guns and declared they wanted to start shooting up toward the rebels from where we were, which would naturally have invited the rebels to fire back. I wanted out of there. "Remain with us," the commander stated.

"No," I said emphatically, "absolutely not." When they insisted, I pushed Dani down the trail and told everyone else to keep going, that I would catch up. One soldier demanded again that we stay and got right in my face. I pushed him back, and he tripped over some vegetation. When he got up again, I angrily stared him down. "Are you here to fight us or the rebels?" I demanded. I shoved past him and started after my group, which had stopped just ahead, watching the argument. "Go! Go!" I told them. "Go!"

Two soldiers would accompany us back to the camp, their leader said. "Fine," I told them. "Do whatever you want. We're leaving."

We reached the main grass trail that led down to the valley and our camp, and I found the shoes that the rebel had thrown away and gave them to Masindi. Earlier I had told the group that I would split off here to go look for Rob, because I had last seen him on the trail that led to the north. But now that I was here, seeing such fear in the eyes of the others, I wondered if I should stay with them. It was almost dark, we had a distance to go, and whatever had happened to Rob and the two others with him had probably already happened. I couldn't dwell on that thought, but I had to figure out where to expend my efforts most usefully.

As I debated with myself, the two escorting soldiers showed up beside me. "We need to search for my friend," I said to them. "The rebels led him that way." I gestured up the northerly trail.

The soldiers stated that other troops had already been sent up the northern path where I had last seen Rob. That settled it. I would let those soldiers search while I continued down with the group.

After we had walked the grass trail for another twenty minutes, maybe less, we ascended to the top of a steep section, and looking down from my position in front I saw three bodies lying ahead of us, on the right side of the trail.

Some soldiers were just approaching them from the other direction. "Stay put,"

I said to Dani and the others. They saw what I had seen and sat down without a word, stricken. I proceeded on down, terrified, overwhelmed, drowning in the horrible reality of the fate of our companions, which all of us had been trying to avoid for hours. The emotion is inexpressible.

I instantly recognized Susan Miller by her green pants and yellow shirt. Rigor mortis had already set in, leaving her left arm thrust in the air. She was covered with blood; her head had been repeatedly slashed with a machete. I didn't recognize the other two women, hacked and bloodied, one lying on her back, her clothes pulled above her waist. It looked as if she had been raped.

I backed away, dropped to the ground, and retched, crying. I felt as if I had been knocked to the ground by an actual blow. And horrible thoughts flashed through my mind: Who had been murdered first? Who had had to watch and listen? Susan had been murdered. Her life must have ended within fifteen minutes of her brief goodbye with Rob. And I thought of Rob, not sure if he was alive — and if he knew Susan was dead, would he rather not be?

I struggled to surmise what had happened. When Susan had been allowed to start back down, a small group of rebels had apparently accompanied her, but instead of escorting her to the camp, where the Ugandan army must certainly have been by that time, they must have simply waited until we left and then saved themselves hours of walking and the risk of being attacked by killing her and the other women on the spot. But I couldn't really grasp the fact.

I climbed slowly back up the trail and told the group that one of the bodies was certainly Susan, and one of the others was perhaps Linda Adams. Utterly blanked out, we waited uphill, sitting mutely on the trail while the soldiers constructed a makeshift litter, loaded the bodies, the heads now wrapped in cloth, and started back down the trail. We followed at a distance, some falling down, as I worried that they would see the dark red drops of blood that steadily speckled the leaf-covered trail. But no one said anything. It took longer than I imagined to get back to the road, where we finally arrived with the last glimmer of twilight.

We were met at the entrance to the camp by the Ugandan army commander, who took me aside to give me bad news. The park warden had been killed; he had his arms and legs broken and was burned to death alive. Five tourists were confirmed dead: the three women found on the trail and a British couple who had refused to start up the trail at all that morning. I was told the murdered couple had not comprehended what was going on — the attack was so unbelievable that they couldn't take it seriously, and they died because of their disbelief.

I trudged back to my group, which was still huddled together, still ravaged by shock, and passed this news along. Only now did I realize that Mark Avis had gotten separated from his wife, Rhonda, much earlier in the day. The sight of the three bodies on the trail had devastated him, and he had not been able to look to see if either of the other women was Rhonda.

A second commander introduced himself and quite sincerely offered his condolences. "Please tell me immediately when your search party locates my friend Robert Haubner," I told him. "He may still be out there on the trail, along with the two other missing hostages."

The commander blinked at me. "There are people not accounted for?"

I realized with an inner shudder that this

army unit was unaware that Rob and other men, and perhaps more were still out there somewhere. The soldiers on the trail had lied about sending out a search party. There was none.

I had been misled, lied to. And now I was racked by the agonizing realization that Rob could still be lost in the wild, and we'd lost time. I should have stuck to my decision and gone along the other route, I told myself bitterly.

Because I had been lied to once, I didn't believe the commander when he said that Bob McLaurin and Susan Studd were alive after hiding outside their tent that morning. It seemed impossible. "Your friends, they are not here now. They are already in Kampala," he announced.

If what he said was true, there must have been embassy people here at the camp at some point, supervising the rescue. But now, aside from this army contingent, there was no sign of an official presence. At least sixteen people from four or five nations had been taken hostage. But here we were, alone, with no one to give us medical attention or to provide means to get us back to the capital. Concerned, I pressed the army commander, who confirmed that the other tourists had been evacuated that same morning, only a few hours after the attack occurred. It seemed as if the embassies hadn't expected to see any of us alive. But we were alive — if far from fully alive — and slowly becoming aware that we were on our own. How would we get out of here?

Masindi left with some of his friends, and I sent the rest of the group down the road to the Mantana camp, which had not been raided, in the company of someone who would provide tea and blankets. "Soon you're going to feel very cold," I told them. That was how shock worked. "So please drink, wrap up, and stay with one another." That last bit of advice was unnecessary. They parted from me, at once relieved and unnerved to be leaving my company and this place we had so sought to return to.

I stayed to tell the army commander what I knew. I carefully described where Rob and the others had last been seen. I gave him the names of the three junior rebel commanders and described the well-dressed Kikuyu tribesman, the one possibly Kenyan soldier in the group. When the army commander asked how we had gotten away, I mentioned the note I had agreed to bring down the mountain. When he asked for it, I refused. I said I would give it to the American embassy.

Finally, in total darkness, I ventured into the Abercrombie & Kent camp, moving from tent to tent. The camp looked as if it had been abandoned for years, with broken tents, bits of trash, and shattered glass scattered randomly about. Even the branches that overhung the path were now broken and dying. The ghostly silence that hung over the camp made my solitary exploration all the more frightening. I half-expected to see a rebel soldier, armed with a machete, jump out and come after me. When I reached Rob and Susan's tent I pulled back the unzipped tent flaps and forced myself to go in. I was petrified. Their bedding was torn apart, pillows thrown aside, and toothpaste, razors, and a hairbrush lay haphazardly between the broken beds. I paused for a moment, shaking, and then had to leave. At the camp gate, I saw a bicycle and I mounted up and started pedaling down the road toward Mantana.

At the camp, my group was huddled in blankets and drinking sodas. I asked for tea. I also asked for showers for everyone, sending them off in pairs, one person to stand guard by the shower tent as the other showered.

We had a dinner of chicken and rice, which was soothing. The others decided that instead of sleeping two to a tent, as I had arranged, we would put mattresses on the floor of one tent and all six of us would pile in there together. This arrangement found Mitch on one side of me and Dani on the other.

We lay wide awake, not surprisingly. I had my arm around Dani, who cried quietly off and on for the entire night. At least twice Mitch sat up, and I could see the tears on his face, reflected by the moonlight coming through the open tent. I sat up and put an arm around him, saying nothing. I felt helpless, desolate, incredibly sad.

Later, as I sat there sleepless, vigilant, keeping guard, Mark Avis asked me to try to identify his wife among the bodies that we knew were lying on the gravel parking lot, uncovered in the moonlight.

I went out with him. Still handicapped by having lost his glasses, Mark tried to describe Rhonda's clothes, and I peered at the bodies, all of them splattered with blood that glowed black in the moonlight, seeking to confirm, one way or the other, if his wife was one of the dead. I wasn't able to. Mark reeled back to the tent and I followed.

A couple of hours later he asked me to try again, and again the two of us left the tent and walked out to the moonlit parking lot. Once more, I tried to identify Rhonda by her clothes, as Mark quaveringly described them to me, and still I failed to recognize the body. As our voices reverberated in the night air, I was surprised by how deathly silent and peaceful the forest was. There is always some sound rolling across the grasses of the African plains, usually some predator, but here all was very still; even the air held its breath.

Later, I rose from among my sleepless survivors and went back outside, to tell the patrolling soldiers to stop walking by our tent: the sound of their footfalls was panicking all of us. Like fading shadows they disappeared up the path.

Toward dawn someone outside, a man, called my name, calmly and evenly. I sat up and answered, but got no response. Perhaps twenty minutes later, just as I was finally fading off, the voice called again. Who could this be? Again I sat up and answered quietly, but there was no response. I went outside, where I found only the perversely peaceful night. Suddenly overwhelmed, I sat on the dirt path and wept. "Where are you, where are you?" I cried out. "Please, please keep talking to me. Explain, explain!"

There was only the silent and unresponsive night. Knowing that some were dead, others missing, that we were still out here, absolutely vulnerable, that we had no means of communication, that no one had been waiting for us, that they thought we were dead: this night was the longest, blackest ordeal of my life, certainly, and I imagine it had to be for the others as well, especially Mark Avis. We listened for gunfire and hoped that its absence meant that the missing had not been killed. All it meant was that they had not been shot.

The first robin-chat calls were a blessed relief. Light, so long in finding us, was on the way, and the normal sounds of a stirring camp were more than welcome. We quickly consumed the tea and coffee and biscuits delivered by the apprehensive, soft-spoken camp staff. Once more, Mark Avis asked me to try to find out if his wife was one of the five bodies still lying uncovered on the parking lot, which in the daylight were blackened, bloodied, crusted, violated. But based on his description, I still couldn't be sure if Rhonda was one of them.

We stayed huddled on the tent floor, unwilling or unable to go out and confront the morning. A small vehicle drove up to the tent. The driver turned out to be a white man named John who owned a camp in Kampala for overlanders, the kind of place that was more or less an overnight truckstop, with tents and other basic facilities. He had heard of the raid at Bwindi and had driven the 250 miles from Kampala during the night to help. He was charged up, talking fast, moving quickly, determined to get things done as rapidly as possible. Seeing him was a tremendous relief. We six survivors would have to get ourselves out, and with John there it seemed that we could. I still could not comprehend that we had been abandoned the way we were.

John said that we probably wouldn't be able to talk to Kampala until 8:30, but then he did get through by radio to the tourist office in Kampala that ran the Mantana camp. Whoever was there wanted to know the names of the survivors and their nationalities. It took some running back and forth to the tent and repeated transmissions to provide all the information. When I asked if there was any plan to airlift us out, the office man in Kampala said he didn't know but would call the embassies and find out. I told him I would call back at nine o'clock. There remained no word from any official representatives of the American, Australian, Swiss, or Ugandan governments.

Meanwhile, our group decided they wanted to walk up to our old camp, now ransacked, burned, and destroyed, to see what had occurred there. I asked them to wait until we knew what the plan was to get us out. I then went to confront the army commander, asking him if there was any news of Rob and the others who were still missing. No news. "They haven't radioed in?" I asked.

"We do not have radio contact with our soldiers on patrol," the commander admitted. I was dumbstruck. "But our troops are still searching for your missing tourists," he went on to assure me. I wanted to believe it.

Where *was* Rob Haubner? I knew him as a calm, methodical thinker, and if the rebels had indeed released him, he would have been able to shake off his shock and make it back to camp by now. I could only conclude that he was either dead or had been taken across the border into the Congo as a long-term hostage. Either prospect revolted me.

Memories of our safaris together flooded my mind, unbidden. I saw Rob with Susan Miller on their honeymoon in the Maasai Mara, by the fire after dinner. Rob, with Susan curled within an outstretched arm, had lain on the ground with his back against a log. The conversation had wound down, and Susan had finally given a wicked smile and wink, saying they had better get off to bed early, since they would be getting up early the next day. "We need the extra rest, don't you think, Rob?" And they smiled at me, said good night, and walked hand in hand to their tent. I saw them on the cliffs over Lake Elementaita, watching from high above the water as the sun sank into a cluster of orange and purple clouds. I heard again Susan's playful laugh as she took another Thomson's gazelle brochette off the fire and gleefully bit into it. I remembered how the next morning we flew low around the lake with the doors off the airplane, filming the thousands and thousands of pink flamingos congregated there. Every night of that safari had been a perfect reminder of how unusual the two were, how much joy we had all gotten from traveling together. And finally I visualized Susan as I had seen her two nights before, dancing around the blazing fire with the local village women, beckoning Rob and Susan Studd to join in, as Bob took digital photographs and later showed them to the women on the computer the rebels had stolen ten hours later. Rob's face was lit with the joy of sharing. Susan had both her arms around him as he crouched by the screen. I remember thinking at that exact moment how they dovetailed, so naturally happy in each other's company.

At nine o'clock, I got on the radio to the tourist office, only to discover that there was no official plan to get us to Kampala. I was furious, unbelieving that no effort at all was being made to evacuate us. Stunned, I realized that we were still very much on our own. There was no choice in the matter. I would be forced to fly us out myself.

Getting out on our own was better than waiting for a vehicle or airplane that might never arrive. My plane was at the Kayonza airstrip, about ten miles away, and it was just large enough to fit everyone. I was uneasy at the thought of flying, desperately afraid that in my distress I would somehow miscalculate. From everyone at Mantana, we gathered up all the keys that we could find, in the hope that one would open the door of the plane and another one could get it started. The group followed me around mutely, urgently, up and down through the camp as if we were in a funeral procession.

We trudged back up the road toward the truck burned out by the marauders that had brought in Dani's group and the ruined A&K camp, to gather any small mementos that might be there. All the local folks stood along the roadside, naturally, for they knew what had happened. They stared silently, group after group of them quietly pulling together, as if for safety, when we walked past. Before we reached the camp, I got delayed talking to some parks people, and when I walked into the parking area I saw Gary Tappenden sitting by himself on the sidewalk slightly above the camp, his elbows on his knees, just looking down on the destroyed mess below. He was sad and dejected, unable to speak. Dani Walther and Michael Baker, along with Mark Avis, were checking the burned hulk of the truck and sifting through the trashed possessions from the camp that had been dumped there, gathering up the occasional letter or scrap of cloth, discussing whose it had been, what to do with it.

The camp caretaker was loading up an old, rundown minibus. John's vehicle was too small to transport all of us together, so I asked the caretaker if he could run us to the Kayonza airstrip. He replied that he was going to Kampala and, if we paid him, we could ride as far as Kayonza. Though I had no money, I agreed. He ever so slowly finished his loading as I stood there bouncing on the balls of my feet, my nerves aching to get going, to get out. Finally, we piled in with the remaining camp equipment. We had no luggage. We lacked everything, from passports to shoes. Since I had no belt, I had to hold my pants up.

On the way to the strip, we passed two contingents of the Ugandan army. When one of the vehicles halted, we stopped too, and I got out, to be greeted by a commander who hugged me so tightly it hurt my back. He apologized with real sympathy for everything that had happened. I laid out our plan and he gave me 100,000 Ugandan shillings, about $100, in case we needed it. I gave half the money to our driver and off we went to Kayonza.

Not surprisingly, a large crowd was gathered at the airstrip. The rebels had killed a man near here. From a distance, my blue-and-green Cessna looked untouched, and after a "walk around" I decided it still seemed fine; even though some of the rebels would have strode right past it, they must not have thought there was anything in it of immediate portable value to them. The crowd pushed it onto the strip and I started trying various keys in the door. Almost right away one opened it. We were in!

"That's the easy part," I muttered. "Ignition's going to be more difficult." I was right. John and I spent some time trying to file down one key, and then I tried a fish knife that someone had found on the floor of the minibus. It did turn halfway, so I decided to load everyone in and did a thorough preflight just in case the knife turned all the way the next time. If it did, we probably wouldn't get a second chance, so we had to be ready.

I held my breath, turned the knife over and worked it gingerly in, grasping it right at the ignition. Amazingly, it turned all the way through, and after a brief pause the prop turned, caught, and the engine was running and vibrating, which caused the knife to fall out. But that shouldn't matter now that it was running, I decided. John said good-bye through the open window, and we waved to him and Mitch Keifer, who had decided to stay with him. "We'll make a low pass if everything looks okay!" I shouted to John over the engine's roar. If it wasn't — well, we would land.

We took off and everything appeared to be fine; I felt so damned proud of my little airplane. I made a low pass. We were free of this place, we would live. But almost instantly we slipped back into total quiet, each of us in his or her own space in the crowded little plane. I pulled up and set course through the rain for distant Entebbe. Keeping focused on the various calculations a pilot must make was very difficult for me. I had been monitoring frequency 118.2, the general traffic frequency, and finally picked up another aircraft, and I asked this crew to relay to Entebbe that a planeload of survivors of the Bwindi raid was inbound and would be arriving in 1.4 hours and would like to be met by staff from the U.S. embassy, but we did not require an ambulance. Not long after this communication, I was able to contact the Entebbe center directly and apprise them of the length of time until we arrived, and they wanted to know the time of arrival itself. None of us in the plane had a watch; mine was now in the possession of the Kikuyu commander. "Look at your own clock!" I retorted. "We'll be there in about an hour and twenty-four minutes."

Entebbe center persisted. What time would we arrive? This was maddening, and went on and on and on until another pilot listening in on the farcical exchange computed the time of our destination himself and gave it to Entebbe center.

Throughout the flight, I kept worrying that I would adjust the variable mixture too lean, possibly causing the engine to cut out, or maybe run it too rich and get a "rich cut" that would flood the engine until it stopped, or maybe run one of the fuel tanks dry just by not paying attention. I had never done any of these things in my life, but given my state of mind they suddenly loomed like real, even imminent, possibilities. No restart was likely, since I didn't have the key, so I kept the knife on my lap, in the off-chance I needed to try it again, but mostly I kept a tight eye on the EGT gauge and the fuel quantity in each tank.

The rain diminished about ten miles from Entebbe. I ducked under the clouds and saw the runway in the distance. I struggled to land the plane, floating it a bit, but we were here — free and alive.

Still, all of us were worried — what kind of reactions would we receive here?

As we taxied toward the buildings, I saw a man waving us over to two cars and a small group of men in coats and ties. This had to be the U.S. embassy contingent, I thought. My group slowly got out of the plane and now, for the first time, we hugged and held one another.

Among those meeting us was Mike Mc-Kinley, the U.S. deputy ambassador. They had the keys to my plane, which had been found in a pack that had not been stolen from my tent and which the others had taken with them on the morning of our kidnapping, so I was able to turn off the engine.

Once we were all on the ground, Mark asked about his wife. Mike McKinley's face said it all even before his voice did. Mark broke down in tears and slumped onto the tarmac. I had no words for him, so I simply crouched beside him, put an arm around his shoulder, and placed my head next to his.

Rhonda Avis had been murdered. She had been pulled out of the line with Susan and one other woman. Her body had been there on the trail as we passed.

As we loaded ourselves into the automobiles for the trip to the U.S. embassy, Mike told me that word was going around that the Ugandan army had rescued us and that those murdered had died in the crossfire between the army and the rebels. This massive piece of misinformation incensed me. But I was more concerned about finding out the fates of my friends. I took Mike aside. "Any news about Rob Haubner or the other two?" I asked.

"No news," Mike said simply. That sickened me.

Probably because of finding out about Mark's wife, I was very afraid to ask about Bob and Susan. The Ugandan commander had told me the night before that they were safe, but I had thought he was simply placating me or had not wanted to be the bearer of bad news. And the two of them had not, after all, met us at the airport, which I would have expected.

On the ride into town from Entebbe, as the road ribboned beneath our car, I stared straight ahead. "Tell me the truth about Bob McLaurin and Susan Studd," I said to Mike. Maybe Mike wouldn't know, since he and Joel and the others didn't know anything about Rob, and certainly had so many details of our escape wrong.

"They're safe," Mike said, in a voice that

I did not doubt. "They're here in Kampala." Mike explained that Bob and Sue had heard the shot fired at me, which had happened right outside their tent. They had heard other shooting earlier, but this shot was the one that spurred them to hide. It seemed surprising, under such incredible pressure, but there it was; and they were definitely alive. He related in detail how they had lain concealed while the rebels came past them on three occasions, walking right by without seeing them. Then, after hours, they emerged to find us all gone, the camp destroyed, the trucks burning, and three dead bodies lying on the ground. I would get to see Bob and Sue, Mike assured me.

I was overjoyed, but it still did not raise my hopes the slightest about Rob.

Linda Adams was also safe. To my great surprise, she had not been one of the other women whose bodies we had found on the trail. She had collapsed on the trail and the rebels simply ignored her and passed her by as she lay on the ground. Fiona Marley, the leader of another tour called the Acacia group, told her to stay down. After hiding in the trees, the two women eventually made their way back to the camp by themselves.

It was early afternoon by the time we reached the U.S. embassy, which shared a compound with the British High Commission. The hikers from the other safari group who had not been kidnapped were already there, and they rushed to greet Mark, Michael, Gary, and Dani, hugging and crying. They did not know me, so I just sat in the corner and watched.

Soon the officials debriefed me, asking clear, terse questions about what had happened and who the rebels were. I turned over the rebels' two-page note to the world that had probably saved our lives. They glanced at the note, saw it was in French, and said they would give it to the ambassador. I was neither thanked nor blamed for my efforts.

The American officials were extremely good to all of us. They were gentle, thorough, understanding of what we had been through, and very efficient at restoring to us items like passports, plane tickets, and photos. The embassy and the British High Commission had set up a phone that we could use to call our families and relatives around the world, to let them know we were alive. I realized that I had no one to call. I had no family I was still in contact with, and the entire experience seemed too weird for me to feel I could simply call up even a good friend to discuss it. I waited until late in the afternoon, and then, on the spur of the moment, decided to telephone Joe, a close friend in Colorado who puts me up when I make my trips to the United States; I would let him know that we had been kidnapped, that there had been at least six murders, but that I had survived. Joe was startled to hear from me, because at the very moment the telephone rang, the FBI was in his house telling him I was dead. I still have no idea how the bureau found out about him or how they decided I was dead. I understood for the first time that the world was aware of what had happened to us in this small corner of Africa. I kept the call short, probably perfunctory, and rang off. It seemed that telling him I still existed was enough.

Bob McLaurin and Susan Studd had still not appeared at the embassy. I found myself quite afraid to see them, although I wasn't sure why. I was even shaking. I knew that they already had been informed of Susan's death, and neither they nor I were certain of Rob's situation. How would they react to the terror and the killing?

Our group selected me as the spokesman

for a news conference that evening at a hall nearby. The only former hostage present, I stood blinking in the lights at the front of a room crammed with about fifty reporters and photographers, which didn't surprise me. I had worked with news bureaus; I knew the news of kidnapping and murder would continue to make headlines. I had never had a press conference before and wasn't sure how it would or should work, so I just asked the crowd how they wanted to do it. A reporter I already knew, Martin Dawes of the BBC, suggested that I just give a narration first, covering the whole event, and then they could ask questions afterward. I agreed.

For about half an hour I told of our ordeal, relating it as evenly and factually as I could, like a returning soldier giving a battle report. As I spoke, the press stayed hushed, in a way that the embassy press attaché, Virgil Bodeen, said later he had never witnessed before. I was interrupted with questions only a few times.

When I said that we survivors had met up with only a small group of Ugandan army soldiers as we made our way back to the camp, the reporters were all extremely surprised. The press had been told that the army had rescued us and that those that were killed died because they were caught in crossfire.

This misinformed or deliberately distorted version of events infuriated me, as it had when I heard it earlier. I set the record straight, in no uncertain terms. No one rescued us, no one died in crossfire, and no one that did die was even shot. All of them were hacked to death.

I went on to answer more questions, all of which were fair and considerate, with the exception of a query from one woman who asked me to describe what the bodies looked like. I declined.

After the press conference I was taken, exhausted and spent, to the home of Wayne Hanning, the counsel general at the embassy. He and his wife had a very nice American home with children and good books and an art collection. Finally, finally, I felt safe. Wayne offered to have me spend the night, but the group of five who walked down from the Congo had asked that I spend the night with them at their hostel, John's overlander camp, and I was driven there. In the pitch black of that night, we walked out into a quiet, open space on the lawn, sat in a large circle, and quietly lit candles for our murdered friends. No one spoke; some held hands and cried, rocking slowly back and forth. Both of the candles in front of me fell over and their flames went out before I could stand them up again. I just cried and felt crushed again. Even the damned candles wouldn't work for me now.

The following morning, after failing to sleep, I was given a second medical exam (the first had been the night before), and I guess I passed, despite the huge lump in my stomach from being hit with the rifle when Rob and I were separated on the trail, and the blood in my urine, because I never heard anything.

At the embassy, after I was further debriefed by the FBI and got a new passport, Sue and Bob walked in, looking exhausted but beautifully alive. I rose and hugged them both, which was a first, and we all sat down with Mike McKinley and talked very calmly, very softly. Mike took a deep breath and made it clear he had something to tell us. "I'm afraid that Rob has just been found, dead, inside the Congo, along with the other two missing men," he said. The rebels marched Rob and two hostages from the Acacia group into the Congo and murdered them there.

Susan broke into tears, and Bob held her. I sat there alone with my feelings. I had been the last of us to see Rob alive, and had failed to keep him alive. I could not be comforted.

We talked, searching for some way to cope with the horror of the murder of our friends. Bob in particular was very steady, businesslike, and professional. Susan spoke quietly, gently. It became clear that neither Bob nor Susan blamed me in the slightest, which was not what I had expected. I just felt ruined. I could not then share with them — or anyone — the final image of Rob that was seared in my mind: my friend sitting on the trail, arms around his knees, his sad little-boy eyes looking straight at me. I would feel even worse later, but I never felt more alone than I did at that moment. My friend and my responsibility, Rob Haubner, was dead, murdered in the Congo.

The FBI debriefing focused on the facts of the crimes and on the evidence involved, and as I recounted the events it seemed to me that Rob and Susan had been murdered only for their clothes — a dreadful thought. I was haunted by the awful notion of the rebels' wearing the couple's clothes. In spite of the strain of answering their questions, I would find the FBI agents were by far the most sensitive and efficient of the officials I would meet over the next several weeks. Billy Corbett, an FBI agent based in Nairobi investigating the U.S. embassy bombing from the previous fall, was wonderful. During his inquiry, unlike everyone else, he would do a lot of things he didn't have to, including returning my phone calls and repeatedly checking on me in person. This impressive pattern with the FBI would be continued when I returned to the United States and met with special agents Butch Luker and Jennifer Snell.

The BBC asked for a press conference with another source, and Dani was their chosen candidate, maybe because she was a woman, maybe because she was a Swissair flight attendant who had been a stand-by for flight #111 that had gone down in the sea off Nova Scotia the previous September, which provided a macabre counterpoint to her ordeal in the Impenetrable Forest. Dani had not gotten on that flight, but several of her close friends had. She had been on *this* trip in order to get away for awhile. She agreed to do the interview, but only if I was present, and she didn't want to meet at the embassy or with a large group. Martin Dawes from the BBC, an extremely warm and sympathetic journalist, said he would get a woman reporter, tape the interview in a private hotel room, and then share it with the press pool. As I listened and provided what support I could, Dani began speaking. She had a hard time getting started, but finally she unloaded and they couldn't stop her for an hour and a half. She cried a great deal, and at one point Martin reached out and pushed the camera to one side. I'll always remember that Martin put his consideration for the victim above getting his exclusive tape.

That afternoon we finally went to the hospital, where Fiona Marley would identify the bodies from her group, and I would identify Susan and Rob. Both of us had been told we would have to do this and had been dreading the moment. Billy Corbett came along, which I greatly appreciated. As we stood before the morgue, he sought to prepare us for the horror ahead: The bodies were behind those closed doors, he told us, on the floor, covered up. Even though the bodies had been cleaned up, a lot of discoloration and deformities would be visible and their heads had been crushed in by machete blows. We would walk down the line and the hospital officials would uncover just the faces, one at a time, and Fiona or I would say the name if we recognized the person.

Fiona was crying and I was shaking wildly as we were led into the room. They uncovered the first face, and Fiona identified that person. Then the second. Then the third. One was so damaged Fiona couldn't look, and they said we'd come back to that one, but she waited and then made the identification. And then when they were ready to pull down the sheet covering the next face I was entirely terrified. It was Susan. Rob was the last one.

The following day, Bob McLaurin and Susan Studd accompanied the bodies of their friends, Rob Haubner and Susan Miller, to the United States. Everyone was eager to depart Uganda for home as soon as possible. We had all been herded around a lot by the embassy; our farewells were scattered. I never got to say good-bye to Bob and Susan.

I arranged for my pilot friend Dennis Naylen to fly commercially from Nairobi to Kampala and then fly us back in my plane. I had been instructed, twice, by Mike McKinley, that when we landed at Wilson Airport in Nairobi, we should go straight to my hangar, because the American embassies in Kampala and Nairobi had jointly arranged for us to bypass Kenyan customs and immigration.

From the moment we landed in Nairobi, the media hounded Dani and me. Right on the tarmac, we were trapped by the dozens of reporters who mobbed the plane. They dogged us as we made our way into the airport and then they cornered Dani in the men's toilet. We finally escaped in a car and holed up at my house. From the moment we were back down out of the Congo, Dani had not wanted me to leave her alone, and she had insisted on staying at my house instead of at the Swiss embassy. All that was fine with me and proved to be not the slightest problem. It was probably better for me to stay busy taking care of others than being alone with my feelings.

We arrived back in Nairobi on a Thursday, and spent the night at my house, but Friday evening we were told that Kenyan immigrations was "after us" — that in bypassing customs we had entered the country illegally. It was only now that I realized the U.S. embassy in Kampala had not contacted the U.S. embassy in Nairobi, which meant we had not been cleared by Kenyan customs or immigrations. We had, truly, entered Kenya illegally, and under very high-profile circumstances. The Kenyan government could lock us up on Friday and keep us there until Monday morning. And my pilot friend Dennis Naylen had been arrested by Kenyan immigrations, his pilot's license threatened. He was, understandably, furious, since all he had done was to fly out to assist us.

All hell was about to break loose over the issue of our entrance, and rightly so, in a way. Following the embassy bombing, the Kenyans had been under pressure from the United States to tighten their security, but now the United States had played fast and loose with the rules without informing them, so the Kenyans were justifiably upset. I talked with immigrations on Saturday morning and they said we all had to turn ourselves in. Obviously none of us were in any condition to be harassed, interrogated, or locked up. To safeguard our independence and privacy — and to escape the unceasing telephone calls at my house from press people demanding interviews that in all but one case I would decline — I moved myself and Dani to a friend's house, where we would be safe until Monday morning. Dani left the country on Sunday, using her Swissair flight attendant ID, which was flown down to Nairobi on a Swissair flight.

On Monday morning, I went down with the FBI agent, Billy Corbett, to straighten everything out with the Kenyan immigrations — no thanks to the American embassy staff, who were almost uniformly unhelpful at best, actively obstructionist at worst. Wednesday, however, the airport authorities chained up my plane without telling me. Until they got a letter from the U.S. embassy, that plane was not moving, whether I had cleared immigrations or not. I spoke with the head of the Kenya airport authorities, who was kind and helpful, but who needed this letter. Again, the American embassy staffer I dealt with was downright hostile. Only through the intervention of Billy Corbett was I able to get the embassy to write a vague letter, admitting no mistake in handling our entrance into Kenya, that the airport authorities accepted nonetheless. Thanks to American bureaucratic intransigence, my plane was chained up for twenty-two days. It was an unnecessarily grueling postscript to a devastating experience.

Still in Kenya a few weeks later, I could

not attend the memorial service in Portland for Rob Haubner and Susan Miller, but in April I flew to the States and visited with their families and with Bob McLaurin and Susan Studd.

I was afraid to return to America. I knew I had lost a lot of weight, about twenty pounds, and was not sleeping at all yet. I was not looking forward to how people would react to the physical toll the kidnapping and murders had taken on me, or even to the very fact of my presence. Many of those fears proved to be well founded.

I was met at the airport in Denver by a number of friends, but I could tell by looking in their nervous eyes that they were unsure of what to do, what to ask, how to act around me. Even as people sympathized in a general way about what I had endured, physically they would keep their distance, as if I had been tarred by a tribulation that could somehow rub off on them. I was clearly not the person I was before, a fact that unnerved not only me but those who used to know me.

Even my good friend Michael, who had flown down from Vancouver to provide some succor, didn't know how to respond to me, and I certainly didn't know what to do with myself. Resisting sleeping pills, sleep continued to elude me. I tried getting out a little bit but any noise or sudden motion — a car passing by, the telephone ringing, a door shutting hard — would terrify me, so I had no choice but to stay in a great deal. I was too weak to exercise very much, and the idea of running, out in public, was impossible. Desperate not to be alone, I was unable to reach out. My stay in Colorado, which was supposed to be a time of recuperation and renewed security, was instead awkward and unsettling.

Driving from the Seattle airport to meet Bob McLaurin and Susan Studd, I felt the same sort of fear I had experienced while waiting for them to arrive at the U.S. embassy in Nairobi. I was not especially worried about meeting Susan Miller's and Rob Haubner's family members; I was more resigned than apprehensive about those encounters. And I was actually looking forward to meeting Rob's son, a man in his twenties whom I had heard about for years. However, reuniting with Bob and Susan frightened me because I didn't know how they would treat me, how they would react.

To my surprise, our visit went well. We spent a lot of time at their house in Portland, sitting around the kitchen table drinking coffee. Bob, in typical fashion, didn't really want to talk about Bwindi at all. This was a fairly normal reaction, as I was finding out, among those of us who had survived March 1, 1999. Most survivors find themselves silent in the face of their memories or otherwise avoid reentering the tunnel of trauma. We survivors also know that others will never be able to fully grasp our horror and sadness, so we can't talk about it because it becomes diminished in their eyes. Living in their lovely house, resuming their routines, Bob and Susan had their old lives back, a notion that seemed as alien to me as a weekend excursion to the Garden of Eden.

That night, the families of Rob Haubner and Susan Miller visited. Rob's son would not come; he was, perhaps, just unable to accept the enormity of his loss. That disappointed me and left me sorrowful.

As we talked over drinks and hors d'oeuvres, it was Susan Miller's sister, I think, who asked me why, knowing the dangers of Bwindi, I had still gone there. I gently told her that I had believed the gorilla camp to be absolutely safe; I would never have ventured there otherwise. From her neutral face and her subdued response

I couldn't tell if she believed me or not, but that was where we left it. Among us all, the conversation was understated; for all of us, it tread painful territory.

The following morning Bob left to go to work and Susan stayed behind with me. After breakfast we went out in the front yard and talked and drank coffee. I found myself crying once more; that last image of Rob's boyish and lost face loomed before me. My tears confounded Susan. She asked if discussing the ordeal at Bwindi always stirred such emotions for me. Coming from a trained psychologist, the question struck me as quite surprising, and I told her so. She reminded me that her and Bob's last views of Rob and Susan were at the dance and by the fire afterward, the night before the rebel raid. Susan and Bob had not been kidnapped or witnessed brutally murdered bodies. They lived a different reality than mine, I realized. As Susan and I sat there sipping coffee, it dawned on me that no outsider would ever quite comprehend or embrace the truth of the shattering experience that day in the Impenetrable Forest.

I returned to Africa that spring knowing that I would leave someday. Or at least begin living here only part time. Yet the continent has been my home for my entire adult life, and I've gained so much from it. It has provided me with everything I have: a job, money, friends, recognition, a sense of belonging where I never had one before. When I do depart, I hope it will be my own choosing, a result of my own timing. Leaving at this point would have seemed too much like running, and I'm not keen on defeat.

In Nairobi, I found it as hard as it had been in the United States to see my friends once again; everyone was afraid to talk to me, and still I ached to be back with those I knew in the places I loved. I knew I had to face my fears of Bwindi, or else be forever beaten.

As expected, it wasn't a frightening experience to be back in the bush. By May I was back at work in Kenya, flying a family of Californians to Samburu, Mount Kenya, and the Maasai Mara. It was good and proper to be back in the fields of Africa where I belonged, even though the African wilds could never be the same for me. All the sounds, smells, and sights I encountered were familiar. The gentleness and predictability of the bush had not altered; only I had changed, and that had occurred through the hand of man, not "beast." How ironic, the word "beast."

Dani and her mother came out on safari that summer, an endeavor intended simply to get Dani back in Africa, and to give her mother a chance to meet the man she said had saved her daughter's life. We went to a private wildlife refuge and to the open grasslands of the Maasai Mara Reserve, encountering lions, leopards, cheetahs, and the wildebeest migration. The trip went well, except for the fact that Dani could not be left alone at any point. We had one bad experience when we were stalking into thick cover, after a leopard that had a kill, and all of a sudden Dani just turned and bolted, crying. The whole experience, the thick bush, danger ahead, the blood and the killing, brought all of Uganda rushing back up for her, she told me later. Curiously, I felt the opposite: here on safari was the only comfortable and happy ground I knew.

Gorilla-trekking in the Impenetrable Forest may have ended forever on March 1, 1999. All tourism to Uganda was suspended for a month. Now, travelers are again allowed to visit, but few are choosing to do so. Most Western countries maintain strongly worded advisories against traveling there. Two companies in the region are having bookings canceled left and right. If the violence persists and the visitors stop coming, the landowners may raze the forests and plant over the places where the gorillas and other wild things live. The rebels will have successfully robbed revenue from the government they hate. Thus the natural economy of flora and fauna may die, too.

For weeks after that day in the Impenetrable Forest, I bled inside from the rifle jab I received. Africa still bleeds. I know no cure for the horror and grief we all feel, for the wars that split and ravage our land, for what has happened in Africa. The continent remains the love of my life, but now there is trouble between us.

13

"Sobat!"

In spite of the brutal horrors and "forever" scars of the violent crimes at Bwindi, I still live in Kenya and still love being out on safari. I grasp the good from every day and night and hold it as close as I hold Susan and Rob. I will never allow myself to forget. When the dawn chorus of birds wakes me from my slumber on the ground in the Maasai Mara, or when the chiffon winds of the Serengeti brush my face at the close of an exhausting day with my clients, a part of me is sad but the rest of me is happy I am there. When I remember the day I met Ole Ndutu and Pakwo, I am thankful. I will not allow myself to forget these moments either.

The Ewaso Ngiiro River was surprisingly dry in July of 1995, a wide swath of orange-brown sand "flowing" east toward the Indian Ocean, but there was hidden water within, as the elephants well knew. They came on a daily basis to dig their wells in the river bed. Oryx, impalas, and zebras came too, drinking from the holes tusked out and encircled with the massive droppings scattered like loaves of dark bread around each damp hole. The bush crackled and popped in the shimmering heat and dry wind. Much of the day my clients and I were confined to the shade of the trees or the verandas of our tents, but the two children and their adoptive parents seemed not to care.

On this morning, we had come back relatively early from our game drive, retreating from an unrelenting sun that had already driven every living thing under cover for the duration of the day. By nine o'clock we were sitting at our breakfast table, which was covered with tropical fruit, fresh bread, and coffee. Nancy and Jim Johnson kept a casual eye on their little girls, Nicole and Daniella, who trotted back and forth between their tent, the kitchen, and the river bank, playing with and poking at whatever caught the attention of their seven- and nine-year-old eyes. I sat slouched in my canvas-and-wood camp chair and picked up where I had left off in my book by the fire the night before. Out of the pulsing heat, from across the river, came the distant tinkling of a

Samburu cow bell, soon followed by a second and third bell. Reading, I occasionally ran an eye across the river to see if the Samburu were approaching. This river stretches a long, long way from the Laikipia plateau in the south to the eastern swamp, Lorien, but given a chance the Samburu will come to the spot by *your* camp to water or wash. They evidently find it entertaining to accomplish their duties while surveying the oddities of the *wazungu*, or white, campers.

Indeed, the first cattle soon arrived, a mosaic of red, white, black, and brown, trudging head low and single file down the trail toward the narrow band of rock that bordered the far river bank. Three warriors tailed their herds. Dressed in their deep-red *shukas*, their lithe bodies shining red with a painted mixture of ochre and cow fat, the colorful trio provided a splash of contrast to the desert made anemic by the strong sun. Even at this distance, we could hear their confident voices as they drew nearer with each springing stride.

Nicole and Daniella watched the approach of these strange men and their cattle and retreated from the river bank to their parents' tent, where Nancy and Jim sat watching the procession with curiosity.

The Samburu studiously paid not the slightest attention to us as they drove their hump-shouldered livestock into the shade of three spreading tortillis trees thirty yards back from the dry river bed. The collection of animals broke of their own accord into smaller herds, perfectly filling the shaded sand below each of the three trees. Impressive discipline, and without a command the cattle stayed in the shade, heads at their knees, while the warriors walked straight onto the open river bed and slammed their spears, butt first, into the sand. The ostrich feather sheaths covering the spear points shimmered shiny black in the intensity of the light.

Flipping my book facedown onto the canvas table top, I walked over to Nancy and Jim's tent as they were putting longer lenses on their cameras. They asked if it was okay to photograph the warriors. Yes, I said, we were here first, and these *morani*, or warriors, had most likely chosen this particular site because it offered them a chance to study us while they watered their cattle. Nancy and Jim could fire away without being culturally rude or intrusive. If we had approached them, wanting to take their pictures, they would have had the right to decline or to ask for nominal payment. But I also told my clients that they should expect to be challenged anyway.

One of the *morani* got down on his knees and began scooping away the hot sand with a calabash gourd, rapidly building a mound of discarded sand beside him. Considering the heat and sunlight, direct and reflected off the sand, he seemed to be working at an incredible rate, and almost immediately we could see, even at our distance, his black skin and red body paint take on the brighter sheen of sweat. His red braids of shoulder-length hair swayed left and right with each plunging scoop. The two other warriors stood beside him, their legs crossed casually as they leaned on their spears, propping themselves with one arm bent, a hand firmly grasping the shaft in the classic profile of the African warrior, photographed and reproduced a million times.

When Jim repositioned to a vantage point unobstructed by the acacia branches, the warriors called out loudly and waved their free arms. We didn't have to know their Maa language to understand that they were challenging our right to take their pictures. They well knew this situation would arise.

"Tulikuwa hapa kwanza," I called out in

Kiswahili, which many Samburu also speak. We were here first.

"Haithruru," the warrior replied. *"Hapa yote ni ya Samburu."* It doesn't matter. All here is the Samburus'.

"Laikini Ewaso Ngiiro ni mto mrefu, na mmechagua kushimba hapa hapa, mbele ya kampi yetu, tu." But the Ewaso Ngiiro river is long, and you've decided to dig right here, in front of our camp.

The warrior now standing in the broad pit he had scooped out continued his labors. After a brief pause, one of the other two repeated the warning that we couldn't take pictures. The well-traveled Johnsons chuckled as I translated the exchange, and I told them to go ahead and take all the pictures they wanted, that this was just casual banter despite how it might sound. The two little girls sat meekly and uncomfortably on the sand beside their parents, unnaturally quiet.

The digging warrior now vaulted out of the hole and one of his associates took his place. The first digger wrapped his *shuka* around him with the sweep of an arm and a tucking twist that must be centuries-old, if not millennia-old, and he instantly duplicated the classic pose of the resting warrior. The sand tossed from the hole began

534

turning from pale orange to a dark red-brown, and it was getting wetter. In another ten minutes, water was flying out of the earth along with each calabash full of sand. One of the *morani* unrolled an ancient and crinkled leather skin and stretched it across a worn wooden frame that his age-mate had rigged by the well. The third Samburu now took his turn in the well and slowly filled the skin trough from the dipping gourd. The pace of work slowed as noon neared. The mourning doves and the emerald-spotted wood doves had fallen silent, but a pair of slate-colored boubous searching for insects around the base of a salvadora bush occasionally broke the silence: *klook-klook — kweek, klook-klook — kweek*. The *moran* in the well suddenly began to sing; his melody of flutelike clarity and yodeling words matched the motions of his work. On our side of the river, the five of us watched spellbound and listened intently as the beautiful tones reverberated the length of the broad river valley and faded into the simmering bush. The warriors' cattle also responded to his song, though instead of growing still with wonder as we had, they ambled forward toward the river bed. But not all of the cattle, just one of the three groups standing beneath the three trees. Our cameras came up again as we realized that we were witnessing an amazing symbiosis between man and beast. The cattle did not stampede to the water, which they surely must have smelled. Instead, they lined up in a nearly flawless double row and patiently waited their turn before the well. I had been in Africa many years, but I had never seen or known about such disciplined behavior in domestic stock. We were enthralled, enchanted by the peace, the order, and the partnership of it all, and by the haunting tones of the warrior's voice as he sang.

The Samburu had glanced at us as we moved about to get an unobstructed view, and instead of yelling at us again, they told me if we were going to take pictures we should at least come down closer so we could truly see what was happening and properly admire their cattle. When I translated, the family looked at me with questioning faces. I shrugged and said, "Well, we might as well go down." I took one girl's small hand in each of mine, and with their parents following, we negotiated the little embankment and walked up the packed sand of the river bed to the parched watering hole.

The Johnsons took a number of photographs from a distance but soon joined me and their children beside the shining Samburu warriors. I translated as we discussed cattle and the possible coming rains with the two resting *morani,* as the one in the well continued filling the leather trough for the animals. After ten minutes the first group of cattle, their thirst apparently quenched, turned and filed back to the shade of the tree from which they had come. Their drink would keep them alive for another three days, perhaps longer. A new *moran* took over at the well and filled the heat-dried air with Gregorian-like chanting as he dipped and poured, dipped and poured, and now the second group of cattle left the shade of their tree and in orderly fashion filed down, heads low, to the life-giving water. With the patience borne of years, they too queued up and waited their turn. When this second group of cattle was sated, they returned to their shade tree and the third warrior dropped into the well and began singing and the final group of cattle came down to the sandy water.

I'd ridden in rodeos and been to many stock shows and auctions from North Dakota to eastern Washington and down to

West Texas, and never had I seen herds move in such a peaceful, knowing, and organized system. Nor have I seen it since. Even Nicole and Daniella sensed that they were observing something quite remarkable, asking how the cattle knew when to come to the water and why they didn't run to the well like the girls' two dogs ran for their food bowls every evening. I interpreted, and one of the warriors replied that the cattle recognized the voice singing to them, telling them it was their turn. But the songs, he went on, were not about cattle or water, but rather about this Samburu tribe, its history, some great warrior or event, some wonderful and successful cattle raid or death-final lion hunt. I asked the man if each herd truly knew the sound of its owner's voice. "Of course they do. They always have, ever since they were small calves and were in the *boma*s with us, sleeping with us at night."

What was obvious to him was almost beyond the belief of five Westerners. "I would need to see them in the *boma*s at night to understand that," I said.

"Come tonight," came the disarming response, "just at sunset, when we bring them in, and you will come to understand for yourself how we know each cow, and how they know us."

Surprised, I paused and then translated for the Johnsons. It seemed that we were being invited to their village to stand with the men and watch as the cattle were brought into the thorn enclosure, milked, and settled in for the night. The Johnsons, as I had come to expect of them, jumped at the opportunity and carefully explained to their daughters that we were being offered a rare chance to visit a Samburu *manyatta*. Nicole and Daniella were a little less than thrilled, but I told the three warriors we would be there, and that I would like to pay them a fair price for a goat if they were willing to slaughter and roast it for us, and make us tea as well. We agreed, and the men bounced off to their waiting herds. They whistled loudly through their teeth and otherwise encouraged the reluctant animals to leave the shade, re-form into one herd, and head back up onto the plateau. Within minutes we could hear only a few echoing bells before the midday silence regained its oppressive hold.

At four o'clock I made the rounds, rousing everyone from their siestas, which was a slow process in this heat. The girls were so drowsy I had to help dress them and then lead them down to the table for afternoon tea, or, in their case, Coca-Cola. It was still too stifling for even them to eat the chocolate cake. I was halfway through my second mug of *chai* when two of the three warriors we had met earlier came striding across the baking sand, calling out a loud *"Sobat!,"* the traditional, casual Samburu greeting, not the "proper" salutation used between those of equal age or rank. We whites rated only this greeting because of our ignorance of the Maa language and the more appropriate greetings that would normally apply.

"Enta sopa boge," I called in return, turning my head to see them. *"Karibu chai."* Welcome to a cup of tea. I poured two more cups as they pulled up chairs so nonchalantly you would have thought it was their daily routine, while in fact the Samburu seldom engage tourists and their guides in this way. These two warriors, Ole Ndutu and Pakwo, shook strong hands all around as I introduced them to my people. Nicole's and Daniella's thin fingers and small hands were engulfed by the long sinewy grips of the warriors, who sensed their temerity and leaned forward, saying softly, "Hello." In English.

Ole Ndutu and Pakwo had come, they proudly said, to escort us to their *manyatta*, and we needed to get going, either in the truck or on foot. We opted to walk, and everyone scurried off to change into better shoes as I reminded them to grab a sweater as well. The moment the sun dropped below the distant Laikipia Plateau, the temperature would plummet.

"Màbe!" they exclaimed when we had regrouped. Let's go! And of course their long limbs and springing stride had them well ahead of us within minutes. The Samburu (and their kinsmen, the Maasai) can eat up the ground, as I had learned on my very first visit to Kenya, when Mike Rainy dispatched his students to spend the night with the Samburu and I had struggled to keep up with my two hosts. I had to call out to Ole Ndutu and Pakwo and remind them of the two girls, and they pulled up to wait for the shorter legs. Pakwo then fell in beside Nicole and Ndutu matched steps with Daniella, while Nancy and Jim and I brought up the rear of our marching expedition.

I have strolled through and spent so many nights in the *manyatta*s of the Maasai and Samburu that I hadn't thought to really prepare the Johnsons for the experience. It was only when I saw the faces of Nicole and Daniella as we came through the gap in the tight thorn fence that surrounded the collection of dung huts that I realized this scene could be a shocking eye-opener for anyone unaccustomed to the more primitive living conditions of the Third World, if not the Fourth, out here in the Samburu Reserve.

The other members of the settlement paid us surprisingly scant attention when we arrived. A few children couldn't help but look at us, obviously intrigued by their counterparts with fair skin, light eyes, straight hair, and strange clothing. But even the children were far too polite to say anything, much less run up and touch us, though I greeted them all and encouraged the sisters to shake hands and say hello. This they did, while keeping a bear-trap grip with their other hand on one of their parents. Even though the cattle and goats had not been brought inside the safe confines of the thornbranch fence, the *manyatta* was fairly seething with flies, forcing all of us, black and white, to continually sweep a hand across nose, mouth, and eyes as the flies sought every drop of moisture they could procure. A few bag-of-bones dogs, lots of trash, and neatly stacked faggots of wood tied with leather strips rounded out the Johnsons' initial impression of the *manyatta*. And smoke, always the smoke. Smoky clothing and bodies, smoky huts, smoky air, even tattered dogs that smelled of smoke.

Our two hosts formally introduced us to the elder, Ole Tinga, a man whose face was so weathered, and his eyes such narrow slits, that he looked freeze-dried. Yet he was incredibly alert and strong of grip. When Nicole and Daniella were produced for him, he casually rested his hand on the top of each of their heads in turn, as is the custom of Samburu elders when greeting ones so young. The girls stood quietly beneath his touch while I explained this action and continued with an explanation of the overall social setup. The fact that a Samburu man may have more than one wife, if he can afford it, was lost on the children, but Nancy and Jim raised their eyebrows at a description of such polygamy as a way to guarantee, among other things, a labor force for the extended family. The wives are almost always soon best of friends, if they weren't already, each with her own hut within the *manyatta*. The first wife's hut is to the right of the entrance in the thorny wall. The second wife's hut and all subsequent wives and their huts are on the left side. The wealthiest warriors or elders could have four or five wives.

We ducked low and followed Ole Tinga through the dark and curving entrance of his dung hut. Inside it was almost pitch-black, and we stood hunched far over in the tunnel-like entrance while our eyes slowly adjusted. One of the two girls backed into me, and I reached down and gently rested my hands on her tiny shoulders, telling her it was all right. She stayed pressed back against my knees until I slowly guided her forward in the near dark, steering her by the shoulders. After a few feet, the arched entrance opened up into a single round room some fifteen feet in diameter. In the center was an idling fire, just three pieces of wood and three rocks, one stone between each gently glowing branch. The smoke reached gradually upward, forming a sharply edged gray cylinder where it passed through the beam of light thrown from a hole in the wall. The confined home smelled pleasantly of acacia smoke, old leather, and young goats and calves.

An old woman with a smooth-shaved, ancient head and narrow-eyed face, leather straps embroidered with rows of glass beads hanging from stretched earlobes, indicated to us the flat rocks that formed a ring around the tiny flames. I sat on one rock and gently pulled Daniella onto my lap. Nancy and Jim found worn sandstone perches as well, and Nicole sat on the ground between Jim's feet. The weathered woman said nothing but leaned forward and blew slowly and evenly into a long hollow reed, directing the small charge of air at the apex of the three pieces of wood. The fire rose slightly and the woman balanced a battered and blackened *sufuria*, a round, tin cooking pot, full of milk and water between the three stones.

This woman was Pakwo's grandmother, whose name we were never told. Pakwo sat next to her and glanced around, as if noticing the inside of the hut for the first time himself, and proceeded to point out the features we could make out in the dim and smoky light. To his left, behind his grandmother, was the sleeping pallet, some eight inches higher than the packed dirt floor of the hut. Worn cowhides covered that area; against the gently curving wall at the back were seven wooden pillows, which also doubled as stools when needed. Nine people would share that area, Pakwo told us, sleeping with a *shuka* over them or with nothing at all, because the wavering flame, the young goats and calves, and the heat from the cramped humanity were enough to keep the hut warm. The gourds beside his grandmother were cleaned and sterilized daily with burning olive sticks before they were filled with fresh milk and cow's blood. Corked, these gourds would keep the mixture for several days. Together with tea and the occasional bit of meat, this is the only food the Samburu eat. This staple of blood mixed with milk is what makes a Samburu warrior so strong and enduring. No fruit or vegetables are grown or harvested, and meat is eaten only on special occasions. On behalf of my group, I declined Pakwo's generous offer of a sample of the milk-and-blood drink. I have drunk it, but this time I said we could hold out until the roast meat was ready. He shrugged, puzzled that I would decline such a staple, and translated our response for his grandmother, whose eyes and mouth creased at the corners in obvious amusement and understanding.

We talked with Pakwo about the rains and the grass, the cattle's health, and what he expected for the next season of rain. He discussed possibly moving soon to a better grazing area, depending on when the rains came and how heavy they were. I tried to explain to the children that the future here never really extends beyond the next rainy season. Life is so precarious, it is even impolite to ask about the children, because there is always the very real likelihood that one has died during the last dry season.

As the milk rose up in a boiling foam, a leathery hand reached out and tossed in a carefully measured handful of loose tea and repositioned the *sufuria* on the hard-packed ground between two of the fire rocks. The woman spoke and Pakwo rose, saying he was going to get the goat meat, as the tea would soon be ready. We grew silent in his absence, because I was unable to converse in Maa and Pakwo's grandmother did not speak Kiswahili. Nancy casually asked her daughters what they thought of it all. Nicole ventured the observation that even though the floor was dirt and the walls were cow dung it didn't seem dirty or smelly within the living space. Daniella looked at Nicole in surprise agreement. So did the old woman, smiling almost imperceptibly in her direction.

Pakwo returned with three men of his age carrying two trays of woven dry grasses. Spread haphazardly across the trays were irregular strips of blackened meat. These they put down before us, and then sat themselves on the remaining sandstone blocks. One of Pakwo's friends reached behind him to a small hidden shelf and withdrew a number of enameled tin cups, which he placed on the ground next to the *sufuria*. Pakwo's grandmother used no cloth or leather as a hot mitt to hold the *sufuria* as she carefully poured each cup three quarters of the way full with the milky tea. The warriors distributed the cups to us, the children last. We sat quietly, waiting for a clue regarding etiquette. In the Samburu homes I've been in, you always wait for the elders, so when the woman raised her cup to her mouth, I felt free to wrap my fingers through the handle of my cup, which I almost immediately dropped, it was so hot. The Samburu laughed at my tenderness. Grandmom couldn't contain herself and rocked back and forth with giggle after giggle, covering her mouth with the back of her hand like a shy schoolgirl. The warriors also took great delight in her amusement.

The warriors passed the meat. Pakwo said his grandmother could no longer chew the meat herself, so someone chewed it for her first, quietly spitting it out onto a mat for her to then ingest. Nancy told us that various Indian groups of North America often did the same for their elderly. Daniella looked inquisitively at the selection of blackened meat and then carefully picked out a piece and started slowly chewing on it. All eyes were on her, including her sister's. Way to go, Daniella! The old woman spoke and Pakwo translated. Does the girl like the meat? I translated next, and Daniella gently nodded her head in the affirmative. This so pleased the woman that she clapped her hands and rocked forward to touch Daniella on the arm, her gap-toothed smile reflecting the firelight, her girlish laughter completely filling the small hut.

Eventually the tea was cool enough to sip, and in spite of the fact that we white folks were dewy with glistening sweat, we drank the incredibly sweet and steaming mixture. Nicole and Daniella truly seemed to enjoy it. Children and sweets are universal, I mused. The conversation slowly went around, usually with me translating questions and answers; at other times the three warriors were lost in a staccato of rolling "r"s and guttural tones. Soon the only sounds were our gentle chewing, the light sucking as tea went over lips, and the erratic soft popping of the narrow flame. The column of blue smoke faded away as the darkness swept slowly over the land beyond the dung walls encircling us.

The warriors definitely ate the most meat. Any excuse to dance and any excuse to eat roast meat seems to be the Samburu way. No time to be shy. So the two trays were soon empty and the *sufuria*'s contents were reduced to a thin layer of foam at the bottom of the battered tin pot. The girls were almost asleep on their seats, and camp was still over an hour's walk away, so I told Pakwo that we had to be heading back, and that we greatly thanked his grandmother for both her hospitality and her generosity with her food. As he translated, she stared at the three glowing sticks and said nothing. When I stood up to take her hand, both of her arms came out of her lap and enclosed my hand in a grip much stronger than the wrinkled skin implied. *"Ole Sera,"* she intoned. *"Siera nage."* Thank you. Go well. Nancy and Jim shook her hand in turn and reminded their daughters to say good-bye. Nicole and Daniella did so, and we followed the warriors out into the now-dark bush.

Pakwo said they would walk us back to camp. I knew the way and told them so, but they insisted and I did not contradict them, as it would have been impolite. On the spot, without asking permission, without even thinking about it, I'm sure, one warrior scooped up Nicole, and Pakwo raised Daniella off the ground. They looked briefly at Nancy, who made not a face or a sound of protest, but simply fell into line behind Pakwo, who was already weaving his way out between the tightly packed herd of cattle now standing in, and completely filling, the *manyatta*. The third warrior removed the small thorn tree that served as the gate, and we padded through the dung and out into the inky, star-dappled dark.

An African night is seldom black but rather pulses with an immensely deep indigo blue. Shadowy acacia trees and sandstone ribs suddenly appeared quite close by as we threaded our way toward our camp. My sandals and the Johnsons' shoes crunched on the hard sand and gravelly rock, though the Samburu sandals landed noiselessly. It was entrancing to watch the thin bands of lightness that were the girls' arms and legs, floating like apparitions, undulating up and down in time with each long stride of the warriors holding them. No voices broke the reigning silence.

Our camp was small, only three sleeping tents and one dining tent, yet it seemed imposing and garish, dotted as it was with candles and lanterns. We could see it from hundreds of yards away, its fire burning a bit too brightly. I greeted my own worried staff and reassured them that everything was not only all right, but couldn't be better.

I softly thanked Ndutu and Pakwo for the wonderful evening. Pakwo held my hand, stating that the sisters would sleep well tonight after such a healthy meal, that they would wake stronger tomorrow. By the time Nancy and Jim were back from putting the children to sleep, the three warriors had already stepped back into the night. My staff had prepared roast beef and Yorkshire pudding and a lemon meringue pie, but we only drank tea and couldn't be budged from our places before the fire.

The next day, after a morning game drive and breakfast, we loaded up for the Great Rift Valley. As we drove out of camp for the airstrip, a clear call broke through the chorus of morning bird calls. *"Sobat!"* was the salutation, and on the track ahead of us waited Pakwo, Ndutu, and Ole Tinga. The three tall men walked purposefully up to the side of the truck. Nicole stretched her arm far from the roof to shake hands with each of them in turn, and Daniella did likewise, saying a bold *"Good morning,"* which needed no translation.

"Tumekuja kusema kwaheri tu," Ole Tinga intoned. We came only to say good-bye.

"Na tunashukuru kwa hii, kwa jana usiku pia," I replied. We are grateful for that, and for last night, too. *"Kaa salama, na chunga nanya yako na ngombe yenu vizuri."* Stay well, and take good care of both your grandmother and your cattle.

"Bila shaka." Without a doubt. *"Na safari salama, na chunga hawa wadogo."* Travel well, and take care of the little ones.

I told them I would see them again next month, and that then the roast meat and tea would be served in my camp, and that Pakwo's grandmother would have to come as well. With that we wound our way slowly out of the acacia grove onto the open high ground of the bleached desert. Before we reached the airplane the radio crackled. My friend Michael, camped west of us, was calling to ask if we had seen the female leopard with the split ear yesterday. No, I said. Then he asked if we had joined that flotilla of minivans that had more or less surrounded the two cheetahs. I said that we hadn't even seen the vehicles. A silence followed, after which Michael said that at least all the elephants at the wells in the river bed must have been good entertainment, but I had to tell him we hadn't seen those either, not in the afternoon. There was another long silence before Michael finally asked what we *had* seen during yesterday evening's game drive.

"Nothing in particular."

Pause. "There are days like that sometimes. Sometimes, no matter how you work it, you just get nothing."

I agreed, rang off, returned the microphone to its hook on the dashboard, and turned to look at Nancy and Jim. They were grinning slightly, and so were the kids, smugly. They had been following the conversation. Daniella gently fingered the beaded bracelet Pakwo's grandmother had given her.

Acknowledgments

Without clients willing to follow me into the fields of Africa I would never have been able to live the life I've grown to love. In particular, I thank David and Diane Reesor, and Bob and Birgit Bateman, who always had the patience to wait out the possibilities.

I have been blessed to colead with a number of guides who have taught me just by being who they are. David Wolf, especially, broadened my horizons and shaped the way I guide. I also gained much in the presence of Susan Scott, Ed Harper, and Leon Varley.

Thanks go to Will and Emma Craig, who gave me such freedom at Lewa Downs, and also to Judy and Mike Rainy, whose combination of humor, knowledge, and patience are still with me on every single safari. I am also in debt to James Waweru for his wisdom and advice, and to my drivers Patrick Nganga, Mungai, and Mike Ndiema.

Around planes Geoff Price, Will Wood, and Phil Mathews were generous with their time and taught me well. Similarly, the high standards of my flight and aerobatics instructors, Tad and Gad, and Drew Chitiea, forced me to be better.

In Tanzania, thanks to Willy Chambulo and Emanuel Zelothe for hours of patience and their ability to hang tough when being charged.

In the face of the kidnappings and murders in Uganda several people never lost sight of the personal element of the loss and horror. My thanks to FBI agents Billy Corbett, Jennifer Snell, and Butch Luker, and also to Mike McKinley, Joel Reifman, and Wayne Hanning for their care and grace while dealing with the tragedy.

Martin Dawes, John Larson, and Christian Martin all became supportive friends during the course of our work together.

Many friends bore with me patiently during my recovery after Uganda. None cared more than Omar and Seher Khan. Will Marshall, Mark Lynch, and Michael Gustavson helped keep me alive. I am also indebted to Joe Bozzuto, whose tireless support was invaluable.

And in New York I would like to thank Virginia Heffernan, Jonathan Burnham,

Mike Bryan, and David Groff. A very special thanks to a patient and tireless Farley Chase, who listened and directed so well.